Palgrave Studies in Gender and Education

Series Editor
Yvette Taylor
School of Education
University of Strathclyde
Glasgow, UK

This Series aims to provide a comprehensive space for an increasingly diverse and complex area of interdisciplinary social science research: gender and education. Because the field of women and gender studies is developing rapidly and becoming 'internationalised' – as are traditional social science disciplines such as sociology, educational studies, social geography, and so on – there is a greater need for this dynamic, global Series that plots emerging definitions and debates and monitors critical complexities of gender and education. This Series has an explicitly feminist approach and orientation and attends to key theoretical and methodological debates, ensuring a continued conversation and relevance within the well-established, inter-disciplinary field of gender and education.

The Series combines renewed and revitalised feminist research methods and theories with emergent and salient public policy issues. These include pre-compulsory and post-compulsory education; 'early years' and 'lifelong' education; educational (dis)engagements of pupils, students and staff; trajectories and intersectional inequalities including race, class, sexuality, age and disability; policy and practice across educational landscapes; diversity and difference, including institutional (schools, colleges, universities), locational and embodied (in 'teacher'–'learner' positions); varied global activism in and beyond the classroom and the 'public university'; educational technologies and transitions and the (ir) relevance of (in)formal educational settings; and emergent educational mainstreams and margins. In using a critical approach to gender and education, the Series recognises the importance of probing beyond the boundaries of specific territorial-legislative domains in order to develop a more international, intersectional focus. In addressing varied conceptual and methodological questions, the Series combines an intersectional focus on competing – and sometimes colliding – strands of educational provisioning and equality and 'diversity', and provides insightful reflections on the continuing critical shift of gender and feminism within (and beyond) the academy.

More information about this series at
http://www.palgrave.com/gp/series/14626

Rowena Murray · Denise Mifsud
Editors

The Positioning and Making of Female Professors

Pushing Career Advancement Open

palgrave
macmillan

Editors
Rowena Murray
School of Education
University of the West of Scotland
Ayr, UK

Denise Mifsud
Euro-Mediterranean Centre for Educational Research
University of Malta
Msida, Malta

ISSN 2524-6445   ISSN 2524-6453 (electronic)
Palgrave Studies in Gender and Education
ISBN 978-3-030-26186-3   ISBN 978-3-030-26187-0 (eBook)
https://doi.org/10.1007/978-3-030-26187-0

© The Editor(s) (if applicable) and The Author(s) 2019
This work is subject to copyright. All rights are solely and exclusively licensed by the Publisher, whether the whole or part of the material is concerned, specifically the rights of translation, reprinting, reuse of illustrations, recitation, broadcasting, reproduction on microfilms or in any other physical way, and transmission or information storage and retrieval, electronic adaptation, computer software, or by similar or dissimilar methodology now known or hereafter developed.
The use of general descriptive names, registered names, trademarks, service marks, etc. in this publication does not imply, even in the absence of a specific statement, that such names are exempt from the relevant protective laws and regulations and therefore free for general use.
The publishers, the authors, and the editors are safe to assume that the advice and information in this book are believed to be true and accurate at the date of publication. Neither the publishers nor the authors or the editors give a warranty, express or implied, with respect to the material contained herein or for any errors or omissions that may have been made. The publishers remain neutral with regard to jurisdictional claims in published maps and institutional affiliations.

Cover image: © Richard Sharrocks/Getty

This Palgrave Macmillan imprint is published by the registered company Springer Nature Switzerland AG
The registered company address is: Gewerbestrasse 11, 6330 Cham, Switzerland

Contents

1 Introduction: The Positioning and Making of Female Academics—A Review of the Literature   1
  Denise Mifsud

2 Being Tough, Being Humorous and Being Explicitly Feminist—The "Intrinsically Disordered Nature" of My Ways Around Academia   27
  Isabel Menezes

3 'You Must Wait to Be Asked': Career Advancement and the Maternal Body   49
  Caroline Gatrell

4 Babies Taught Me How to "Do" Academia: Crafting a Career in an Institution That Was Not Built for Mothers   75
  Catherine M. Mazak

5 Writing Myself into an Academic Career   89
  Rowena Murray

6	Academic Fluidity? An Unconventional Route to the Professoriate *Jackie Potter*	113
7	My Personal Journey on the Pathway of Resilience *Sarah Skerratt*	133
8	Actively Constructing Yourself as a Professor: After Appointment *Beverley Anne Yamamoto*	155
9	Mis-Making an Academic Career: Power, Discipline, Structures, and Practices *Devorah Kalekin-Fishman*	177
10	A Personal Journey of a Long and Winding Road to Professorial Status: An Alternative Pathway and the Challenges, Trials and Tribulations *Moira Lafferty*	201
11	How to Fall into a Career Trap (Without Even Realising) *Inger Mewburn*	217
12	Conclusion: The Process of *Becoming* a Woman Professor and *Unbecoming* Gender Equality: A Female Drama of Resistance *Denise Mifsud*	221

Index   235

Notes on Contributors

Caroline Gatrell is Professor of Organization Studies, University of Liverpool Management School, where she holds the position of Associate Dean, Research. Caroline's research centres on work, family and health. From a sociocultural perspective, she examines how working parents (both fathers and mothers) manage boundaries between paid work and their everyday lives. In so doing, she explores interconnections between gender, bodies and employment, including the development of the concepts 'Pregnant Presenteeism' and 'Maternal Body Work'.

Caroline is Co-Editor in Chief, *International Journal of Management Reviews* and Past Chair of the Northern Advanced Research Training Initiative (NARTI).

She is a Fellow of the Academy of Social Sciences and a Fellow of the British Academy of Management.

Devorah Kalekin-Fishman is a Senior Researcher in the Faculty of Education, the University of Haifa. She has published widely on alienation, the sociology of everyday life, the sociology of knowledge, sociology of the senses, and problems in education. Authored and edited books include: *Ideology, Policy and Practice* (Kalekin-Fishman, Kluwer, 2003),

Radicals in Spite of Themselves (Kalekin-Fishman and Schneider, Sense, 2007), *From the Margins to New Ground* (Hagoel and Kalekin-Fishman, Sense, 2016), *Practicing Social Science* (Kalekin-Fishman, Routledge, 2017), *Alienation and the Millennium* (Langman, L. and Kalekin-Fishman, D., eds., Krieger, 1996), *Multiple Citizenship in Europe* (Kalekin-Fishman, D. and Pitkanen, P., eds., Peter Lang, 2007), *The ISA Handbook in Contemporary Sociology* (Denis, A. and Kalekin-Fishman, D., eds., Sage, 2009), *Everyday Life in Asia* (Kalekin-Fishman, D. and Low, K. eds., Routledge, 2010), *The Shape of Sociology for the 21st Century* (Kalekin-Fishman, D. and Denis, A. eds., Sage, 2012), *Approaches to Educational and Social Inclusion: An International Perspective* (Verma, G. K. and Kalekin-Fishman, D., eds., Routledge, 2016). Currently, she is involved in a study of the implementation of her model for 'Acquiring Literacy in Participatory Citizenship' (Kalekin-Fishman, D., Hagoel, L., et al., in progress).

She serves on the editorial boards of several international journals, is associate editor of *Sociopedia*, and was Vice-President for Publications in the International Sociological Association (2006–2010).

Moira Lafferty is Professor of Applied Sport Psychology and Deputy Head in the Department of Psychology at the University of Chester. She is a Health and Care Professions Council registered sport and exercise psychologist and Chief Supervisor for the Qualification in Sport and Exercise Psychology for the British Psychological Society. With a career in higher education spanning 25 years, she has held numerous roles and positions at department and faculty level.

With a diverse portfolio of activity, she has expertise in applied practice, teaching and learning and academic management. Moira has been in receipt of external grants to explore teaching and learning in higher education and has written journal and book chapters exploring this. As an applied sport psychologist, Moira has worked with numerous teams and individuals at national and international level and has a wealth of experience helping athletes maximise their potential. Currently, she is part of a UK-wide research group exploring the supervision of neophyte practitioners and has a strong interest in supervision within both research and practice. Her research exemplifies her desire to help and support others and she is the principal investigator and leads on the CHANGES programme, working in partnership with British Universities and Colleges Sport.

Catherine M. Mazak is a tenured Full Professor at the University of Puerto Rico, Mayagüez, where she specialises in translanguaging and bilingual education. She blogs about academic writing at https://www.cathymazak.com.

Isabel Menezes has a degree and a Ph.D. in Psychology and a habilitation in Educational Sciences from the University of Porto, where she is a Full Professor in the Department of Educational Sciences. She is a member of CIIE, a research centre in educational research and intervention, and teaches in the fields of educational research, educational and community intervention, political education and political psychology. Her research deals with the civic and political participation of children, young people and adults, with a special interest in groups at risk of exclusion on the basis of gender, sexual orientation, ethnicity, disability and migrant status, and the ways formal and non-formal education (including artistic) experiences can generate more complex ways of relationship with the political. She coordinated several funded research projects comprising the Portuguese participation in international projects such as IEA Civic Education Study, FP7 PIDOP and H2020 Catch-EyoU. More recent interests relate to doctoral education and university social responsibility as a way to explore how universities can creatively and proactively respond to societal challenges. Some recent projects include Erasmus+ EU-USR, HE4U2, ESSA, ENGAGE and SOLVINC. She is since 2017 the president of the SPCE (Portuguese Educational Research Association).

Inger Mewburn has been working with Ph.D. students and early career researchers to develop their professional skills since 2006. Aside from editing and contributing to the Thesis Whisperer blog, she writes scholarly papers, books and book chapters about research student experiences, with a special interest in employability and social media use.

Dr. Denise Mifsud is the Gozo College Principal, besides being an independent education researcher and consultant, and a Fellow

Associate of the Euro-Mediterranean Centre of Educational Research. She previously held a full-time lecturing post at the University of the West of Scotland as well as being a part-time lecturer at the University of Malta. She was awarded her Ph.D. by the University of Stirling in 2015. Research areas of interest include educational policy analysis, generation, reception and enactment; leadership theories, with a particular interest in educational leadership, especially distributed forms; school networks and educational reform; power relations; Foucauldian theory; Actor-Network theory, as well as qualitative research methods, with a particular focus on narrative, as well as creative and unconventional modes of data representation. Of late, she has also been researching initial teacher education, with a particular focus on the construction and performance of professional identities in pre-service teachers. She has presented her research at various international conferences, besides winning the following academic awards: the 2014 American Education Research Association (AERA) Emerging Scholar Award; SAGE 2014 Early Research Bursary for EERA Annual International Conference 2014; and the SERA 2015 Estelle Brisard Memorial Prize.

Rowena Murray has an M.A. from Glasgow University, Ph.D. from the Pennsylvania State University and was International Fellow of the American Association of University Women. She is Professor in the School of Education at the University of the West of Scotland and a Principal Fellow of the UK's Advance Higher Education. She has held visiting academic appointments in Australia, Ireland, Japan and South Africa. Her teaching and research focus on academic writing. Her research has been funded by the British Academy, Carnegie Trust, Nuffield Foundation and Strathclyde University.

Jackie Potter is Professor of Learning and Development in Higher Education at Oxford Brookes University where she leads the Oxford Centre for Staff and Learning Development. Jackie is an experienced academic and organisational developer, as well as a qualified coach. She develops people, practices and policies that improve student learning and engagement as well as the staff experience of higher education. Her recent funded research has focused on leadership in higher education, the scholarship of teaching and learning and on flexible learning.

Current projects also reflect her diverse interests. They include working with Cristina Devecchi to produce an edited book on delivering educational change in higher education for leaders and practitioners, team-based academic development and exploring students' conceptions of teaching excellence. Jackie is a Principal Fellow of the Higher Education Academy and a Senior Fellow of the Staff and Educational Development Association. You can read more about her background and work at https://www.brookes.ac.uk/ocsld/about-ocsld/staff-profiles/jackie-potter/. You can follow her on Twitter @Jac_Potter and connect through LinkedIn at Jackie Potter.

Sarah Skerratt is Professor of Rural Society and Policy. She is Director of Policy Engagement at Scotland's Rural College (SRUC) and sits on SRUC's executive team. Sarah is driven by evidence for social justice, with a specific focus on rural, lived-experience data. For 30+ years, Sarah has researched rural community resilience, empowerment and disempowerment; poverty; leadership; and broadband. She has recently focused on rural mental health, working with the national charity Support in Mind Scotland. Through her research, Sarah aims to enhance rural and national policy, *and* make a difference in rural communities. She works with the Scottish Government on numerous task forces, Scottish Parliament, universities, private, public and third sectors, communities and development agencies in Scotland as well as internationally. Sarah recently completed a two-year secondment with Audit Scotland, bringing a 'rural lens' to their work, and is now retained as their rural adviser, having established their Islands Forum in 2017. In 2018, she completed the 'Recharging Rural' research for the Prince's Countryside Fund, gathering evidence across rural UK as to what makes rural communities sustainable to 2030 and beyond. In 2017, Sarah was appointed as a Fellow of the Royal Society of Arts (RSA) in recognition of her work in rural poverty and rural policy. In 2018, she was appointed as the new Scientific Director of the Scottish Consortium of Rural Research (SCRR).

Beverley Anne Yamamoto is a Professor of Critical Studies in Education for Transformation in the Graduate School of Human Sciences, Osaka University. She is Deputy Director of the International College and

Chair holder for the Osaka University UNESCO Chair in Global Health and Education.

Originally from the UK, after studying sociology at undergraduate level and education and Japanese language and society at postgraduate levels, she gained a Ph.D. in East Asian Studies from the University of Sheffield in the UK in 2000. Employing a gender studies approach, she analysed the construction of public and policy discourse around the 'problems' of teenage pregnancy, abortion and motherhood in Japan. Since then, her research has continued to focus on issues around sexuality, gender, sexuality education and health promotion in schools. Beverley is also interested in gender equity, inclusion and diversity issues in and through education. More recently, she has been involved in a number of innovative research projects focusing on patient engagement in medical research and dissemination.

Beverley has combined an active academic life with raising two kids with her husband and passion for singing.

List of Figures

Fig. 2.1 Number of students and of female students in higher education in Portugal (1960–2018) (*Source* DGEEC/MEd—MCTES—RENATES, PORDATA) 30

Fig. 5.1 The Social Writing Framework (*Source* Adapted from Murray 2015) 96

Fig. 7.1 40 years of resilience research (1978–2018) (Adapted from Skerratt [2013]) 135

1
Introduction: The Positioning and Making of Female Academics—A Review of the Literature

Denise Mifsud

Female Academics Within the Neoliberal Higher Education Arena: Problematizing Gender Im/Balance

> The notions of quality and excellence so prevalent in higher education do not sit easily with those of equality and diversity … managerialism has not demolished the masculine hegemony, and may even re-emphasize it, while inequality practices still persist, although in a less obvious way than in earlier decades. (Teelken and Deem 2013, pp. 531–532)

The present-day pace of change in higher education is unprecedented, rife with an acceleration and intensification of neoliberal praxis, spurred on by the marketization of education, a model that has now become the norm in the UK and beyond (Thwaites and Pressland 2017). As a result, several changes have taken place at both meta- and micro-levels,

---

D. Mifsud (✉)
Euro-Mediterranean Centre for Educational Research,
University of Malta, Msida, Malta

© The Author(s) 2019
R. Murray and D. Mifsud (Eds.), *The Positioning and Making of Female Professors*, Palgrave Studies in Gender and Education,
https://doi.org/10.1007/978-3-030-26187-0_1

an example of which is a more diverse student body harbouring higher expectations of higher education due to their newly established rights as '*product purchasers*' (author's emphasis). Academic staff, therefore, meet burgeoning pressures to meet these student expectations while producing 'world-class, ground-breaking research', where higher education existence shifts its focus to 'playing the game' (ibid., p. 4), that is, surviving, rather than progressing along a 'successful' academic career. Pressures on exceptional performance across all levels of teaching, research and administration have grown, with research remaining the most prestigious area, thus leading to the 'casualization' of higher education (Lopes and Dewan 2014, p. 29) through short-term, hourly paid and zero-hours contracts handed out to early career academics who are expected to cover teaching and administrative duties within an unsecure and unstable status. Thus, this precariousness unfolds at the early career stage, with early career academics constituting what Standing (2014) labels as 'the precariat' (p. 13).

Within this precarious context, gaining entry to the higher education field as an early career academic presents insurmountable ordeals for these Ph.D. graduates who have to be constantly looking out for their next role. Data reveals that a negligible percentage of female Ph.D. candidates (12%) desire staying on in academia to work as lecturers and researchers by their final year of study (Rice 2012), an indication that they are being dissuaded by a tough job market or 'the precariat' situation within and even beyond the initial stages in the present academic world. Given the situation, how more difficult must it be for female, feminist early career academics?

Universities are aptly described as 'gendered organizations nested within a gendered hierarchy' (Britton 2017, p. 5) due to the prevalence of male dominance within the highest prestige institutions, the highest paying disciplines and the most influential positions. Despite women's and feminist involvements in academe over the last five decades, hegemonic masculinity in higher education is still rampant. The gender gap has reversed for undergraduate students, whereas for women as academics it remains resistant to change as male power dominates (David 2015). Men still wield more powerful positions within and beyond higher education. Congruently, in the past four decades there has been a steady increase in the number of women attending higher education as undergraduate students, so much so that they have outnumbered their male counterparts (UNESCO 2012). Notwithstanding, the feminization of the campus has not translated into many women breaking through the ivory ceiling (Macfarlane 2018). The situation worsens the higher up the university management ladder one climbs (Savigny 2014). This predicament is expressed as the 'pyramid problem' (Mason 2011) due to the evident disparity in gender equity as manifested in representation on the faculty, pay and family formation. There are far fewer women than men at the top of the academic hierarchy; they are paid less and are much less likely to have had children. The situation is somewhat reversed at the bottom of the academic hierarchy.

She Figures (European Commission 2016) illustrates how limited women's penetration into the senior ranks of university research and administration in European higher education institutions has been—the higher up the academic ladder, the wider the gender gap. Women are a minority among senior academics in many European countries and hold few positions in academic leadership. In Canada, men professors earn more than women professors on average (Canadian Association of University Teachers [CAUT] 2016), while in the United States, men out-earn women at all faculty levels (American Association of University Professors 2017). The same can be said for women on academic contracts in the UK (University and College Union 2017). Slightly more than a quarter of professors in Indian academia are women (Government of India 2017), while Japanese universities lag behind at all ranks from university teachers up to the professoriate (Government of Japan 2017). In the United States, women are less likely than men to achieve tenure (Finkelstein et al. 2016), with the under-representation of women of colour in academia (National Centre for Education Statistics 2016) while mothers in academia often face a 'baby penalty'. It is clear that gender equality is nowhere near being achieved in academe today anywhere in the world (UNESCO 2012). According to Bekhradnia (2009), women's academic careers are characterized by 'strong vertical segregation', with the situation appearing more favourable for the youngest generations of female academics (due to the highest proportion of women full professors being in the humanities and social sciences), but the gender gap still persists. The increase in the number of female students does not signify a more than formal equality in terms of 'the numbers game'—this merely serves as a 'mask for continuing power plays whereby the "rules of the game" remain misogynistic' (David 2015, p. 23). The corporatization of higher education institutions has put gender equity under threat again, with the junior female academic facing an uphill battle in terms of career aspirations. According to Thwaites and Pressland (2017), these early career female academics provide support to universities as the foot soldiers of higher education institutions akin to the 1960s and 1970s frustrated housewives supporting the economy by providing a happy and healthy home and hearth for their salaried husbands.

One of the most notable explanations for these disparities in gender is the metaphor of the 'chilly climate', originally coined by Hall and Sandler (1982) to describe patterns of inequitable treatment that inhibit women's confidence, self-esteem and accomplishment as they accrue within organizational contexts. Gender thus becomes salient in interactions, structures and culture. According to Ridgeway (2011), work environments are perceived as gender-neutral by women (and men), whereby gender exists as a background identity 'that is rarely the ostensible focus of what is going on in the situation' (Ridgeway and Correll 2004, p. 516). Gender becomes visible to actors momentarily when it emerges from the background into the foreground, as interference into a seemingly gender-neutral context.

The under-representation of women in the professoriate internationally is a widely acknowledged phenomenon representing 'both cultural misrecognition and material and intellectual oppression' (Morley 2005, p. 109). This 'endemic gender gap' (Harford 2018, p. 2) can be attributed to multiple systemic barriers that exist within the organization and culture of universities. Changes to gender equality in academia across the globe reflect wider societal changes, in addition to being directly affected by other influences including government legislation, regulatory frameworks, cross-institutional action plans, university strategies and committed individuals (Winchester and Browning 2015). Several initiatives have been taken to address the imbalance in leadership roles in academia. The Athena Scientific Women's Academic Network (SWAN) Charter, launched in 2005, in order to recognize the commitment made by higher education institutions to the advancement and promotion of women's careers in science, technology, engineering, maths and medicine (STEMM), was expanded to recognize work undertaken in arts, humanities, social sciences, business and law (AHSSBL). The charter now recognizes work undertaken to address gender equality more broadly, rather than just barriers to progression that affect women. Athena SWAN bestows UK universities with bronze, silver or gold awards accordingly.

Despite these policy efforts and initiatives, inequality remains, which Teelken and Deem (2013) attribute to three main factors, namely the lack of knowledge that determines further career steps for women; the power relations underpinning such relationships; and a failure to understand the interaction between governance, and the daily activities of academics and other university employees. The fluid power relations constituting the 'gender question' in the academy render women both subjects and objects (Midkiff 2015). Notwithstanding, Pyke (2013) draws our attention to the ongoing increases in women's representation in leadership positions and the corresponding increasing size of the recruitment pool, reminding us that women 'are not "squashed ants" under the weight of a patriarchal structure that conspires to exclude women. Nor is there a rigid glass ceiling that halts progression' (p. 446).

Barriers to Career Advancement in Academia: A Matter of Choice or Fait-Accompli?

Literature is replete with studies that have attempted to identify obstacles to women's career progression in academia (Bagilhole and White 2011; Morley 2013a; O'Connor 2015). Authors have identified a range of factors located at several levels including the individual (in terms of gendered constructions of the self); the interactional (in terms of 'Othering' and gendered expectations); the organizational (in terms of career paths, leadership and organizational culture); and the institutional (in terms of cultural stereotypes, state policies and priorities) (O'Connor 2014).

The progression of students to eventual professorships is called 'the pipeline', and reductions of women in academe at successive stages are referred to as 'leaks' (Jackson 2008). This collusion of circumstances that lead women to leave academic employment at greater rates than men at each key stage of career progression serves to progressively diminish the potential recruitment pool of women for senior academic appointments (Allen and Castleman 2001; Bell and Bentley 2006). Problems appear to begin from the recruitment process (Grove 2013). Van den Brink (2011) argues how recruitment through a closed appointment procedure where candidates are 'scouted' via formal or informal networks leaves out candidates in possession of the appropriate qualifications and experience. Scouts thus 'function as gatekeepers to professorial positions' (ibid., p. 2035), while playing an important role in the composition of the shortlist. A substantial amount of women applicants are systematically overlooked by scouts via three gender practices, namely exclusive network methods; viewing women as different with regard to their level of commitment; and perceptions on leadership style. Female candidates are also less likely to be hired as they are viewed by both male and female assessors as less competent than male candidates (Moss-Racusin et al. 2012). Female professors regard universities as operating according to male definitions of merit, thereby making a strategic choice not to engage in senior management roles (occupying the role of dean level or above) while admitting that there is no room for caring responsibilities in universities, with the female professoriate lacking access to nurturing in terms of validation, selection and networks of support (Harford 2018). One of the major components that account for the 'leaky pipeline' is a combination of the values of the academy and personal familial responsibility (Currie et al. 2002). Another contributor is the long work hours expected of full-time employees (Jacobs and Winslow 2004), with the classic profile of an academic career more aligned to that of the traditional man, thus positioning men's lives as normative, marginalizing women's lives and reducing opportunities in the process (Currie et al. 2002). Women are concentrated in a relatively narrow range of disciplines (Stevens-Kalceff et al. 2007); they commence academic employment at an older age (Diezmann and Grieshaber 2010) and at lower salary levels (Probert

2005). The lack of women in senior positions in itself acts as a barrier to more women reaching higher levels within institutions, with the absence of 'top tier' women perpetuating the dominant male culture in academia (Howe-Walsh and Turnbull 2016). Female professors may undergo extra burdens in their careers simply as a result of their gender, with students having higher expectations of them than their male counterparts, expecting them to 'function like academic mothers' (El-Alayli et al. 2018, p. 137). Female professors must 'walk a line between warmth and agency' (ibid., p. 137), having to work harder in order to demonstrate both warmth and competence simply to be rated equally to their male peers. Besides shouldering a disproportionately large workload at home in ways that might disadvantage them professionally, female professors are also 'taking care of the academic family' via disproportionate service loads (Flaherty 2017). This is likely to have an impact on productivity in other areas of faculty effort such as research and teaching, with the latter activities leading directly to salary differentials and overall success in academia (Guarino and Borden 2017).

'Younger women entering academe are virtually as likely as their predecessors to encounter the ideology that one must sacrifice a personal life in order to have a professional life' (Armenti 2004, p. 80). Childbearing and subsequently childrearing serve as an impediment to the career progression of women academics presenting a dilemma to combining the roles of professor and mother. Academic motherhood may be regarded as a 'silent experience', in that women's lives as mothers remain invisible in the academic milieu (Leonard and Malina 1994). Childrearing further limits the careers of women academics in that they are less mobile for job-seeking purposes (Caplan 1993), with the male partner's job being more likely to determine the family's place of residence. Women with children in academe are subject to the contradictory discourses of 'good mother' and 'successful academic' (Raddon 2002). Moreover, women, who on average receive a Ph.D. in their early thirties, must contend with the clashing of biological and tenure clocks, in addition to ensuing family commitments (Armenti 2000; Wolf-Wendel and Ward 2003). Research has determined the strong presence of a gender regime within universities as they 'remain structured largely on the male lifestyle and scholarship course' (Armenti 2004, p. 77), in addition to the time frame for career development based on the prototypical male opportunity to steer his efforts to a lifetime of work in pursuit of knowledge. Women have been assimilated into a pre-existing structure that has not done much adaptation to accommodate their lifestyle (ibid.).

Research exploring the 'chilly climate' (The Chilly Collective 1995) has identified four main barriers that are 'hidden', namely stereotyping; devaluation of women's successes; gendered isolation; and revictimization. Academia encourages a 'double standard' whereby treatment of women differs compared to men of the same status and occupying the same roles of either student or faculty (Muscarella 2004). Women often find their credibility and the value of their work questioned more readily than a male faculty member (Wylie 1995). Women academics are often isolated through standard mixed-gender conversation and interactional patterns with colleagues through sexist humour, for example. When women challenge these practices of exclusion, stereotyping and the like, they become victimized through the very practices they challenge (Monture-Okanee 1995). Research has also identified a 'bias against care-giving' (Drago et al. 2005, p. 22), whereas despite the introduction of family leave policies in higher education institutions, faculty rarely use them due to their fear of a negative reaction during the tenure process if they take them. They often return to work sooner than required after the birth of a child or another family leave. Moreover, more women are delaying marriage or families for the pursuit of academic promotion. A very sizable proportion opt to avoid the dual challenge of work and family by deciding not to have children (Gappa et al. 2007), in addition to fearing the notion that bearing children makes them seem less serious about their careers.

Pyke (2013) challenges human capital theories that relegate women's under-representation in higher education leadership to women themselves choosing not to make the investment, but with the aspiration made 'within a set of conditions that shape the feasibility and desirability of pursuing promotion … [while] conditions of academic employment remain powerful in positioning women and men differently and unequally within structures' (p. 445).

Higher Education Leadership and Hegemonic Masculinity: The 'Othering' and 'Domestication' of the Female Academic?

The global academy is contradictorily constructed in terms of innovation and hypermodernization underpinned by the archaism of male-dominated leadership (Morley 2011, 2013a, b). Consequently, 'Gender equality in academic leadership has escaped organizational logic and rationalities in most national locations and the pattern of male dominance of senior leadership positions is visible in countries with diverse cultures, policies and legislation for gender equality' (Morley 2014, p. 118). A key question, therefore, is 'whether women are *desiring, dismissing* or *being disqualified* from senior leadership positions in the global academy' (ibid., p. 114, added emphasis).

Research evidence shows a gradual increase in the numbers of women in leadership positions in higher education, despite their under-representation at senior levels (Fitzgerald 2014). Notwithstanding, major stumbling blocks still exist for accomplished female academics who aspire to and manage to engage in these key leadership positions (Bagilhole and White 2011). Women leaders are therefore located in 'an ambiguous and paradoxical position' (Fitzgerald 2018, p. 1), due to the masculinity of power inherent within higher education leadership where men are the institutional (and institutionalized) norm and their presence and numerical dominance a taken-for-granted, unquestionable assumption (Meyerson and Tompkins 2007). Women are thus positioned as 'interlopers' in a predominantly male world (Atewologun and Sealy 2014), as the institutional 'Other' (Gherardi and Poggio 2007) in an environment where it is imperative to demonstrate knowledge and comprehension of the 'rules of the game' (Bryans and Mavins 2003). Their feminine and 'out of place' bodies have to simultaneously 'look' and 'be' good in a masculine environment (Fitzgerald 2018) while they play out their expected parts in an emasculated game.

'The architecture of transnational higher education is through its performative culture, producing an entrepreneurial masculinist leadership habitus that emerges from the dominance of men in normative science, in new management technologies, and as celebrity academics who are mobile, flexible, adaptable, not place-bound and unhindered by domestic connections' (Blackmore 2014, p. 95). The conditions of academic work following the corporatization of the university have created a scenario comprised of intensification, diversification, de-professionalization, specialization and casualization based on a gender division of labour, factors that restrain women's leadership opportunities and aspirations (Bexley et al. 2011). The leaderist turn in academia is value-laden in its setting out of 'cultural scripts for leaders coalescing or colliding with normative gender performances' (Morley 2013a, p. 117) outlining how leaders 'should' be, with an emphasis on qualities that are normatively attributed to males. The academy has been described as a place that 'actively constitutes gender' (Leonard 2001, p. 7, original emphasis) where women are absent from upper-hierarchical positions due to their lack of knowledge of the 'rules of the game', demonstrating a reluctance to be 'involved in the competitive, self-promotional behaviour traditionally associated with dominant masculinities' (ibid., p. 4). These corporate-approved leadership identities and narratives may serve as an identity cage that put off women from higher education leadership.

Morley (2014) examines women's relationship with leadership in HE internationally, consequently identifying a number of gender-related issues in HE, namely enablers and obstacles to women's progression, policies and initiatives that make a difference, as well as networks in the region that support women's career progression. A major barrier to women's leadership identity development is the strongly felt gendered division of labour inside and outside the academy (Bagilhole and White 2011). Leadership is a hierarchicalized affair with an evident 'sex role spillover' (Morley 2014, p. 115) where women are assigned with teaching and student support, while the male academics are steered towards international networks and research. Women's capital is thus devalued and misrecognised, with their opportunity structures being impeded by organizational housework. Women are therefore not strategically positioned on leadership pathways. There is also the presence of a 'gendered research economy' (ibid., p. 116) with a catalogue of female absences and exclusions which undeniably presents a stumbling block due to the consideration of research performance as a pathway to academic seniority and an indicator for promotion. Morley (2014) problematizes this under-representation: Is it simply a case of discrimination or the women themselves making effective and material calculations regarding the costliness of attachment to leadership aspirations? Leadership is often perceived as loss both in the case of unsuccessful and successful applications, with the former situation resulting in loss of status and self-esteem, and the latter leading to loss of independence, research time, health and well-being. A hidden curriculum in the academic setting gives rise to organizational and cultural norms that act as a setback to women's aspirations and career orientations due to gender bias, with the positioning of women leaders as organizational 'others' in the global knowledge economy (Walby 2011). Other issues that deter women from applying for promotion stem from traumatic experiences, timing and leadership perceptions. Aspiring women professors are negatively influenced by bullying, bad management and hostile cultures in the workplace, in addition to shouldering the combined effects of workloads, care responsibilities as well as changing criteria for promotion. Others rationalize in terms of a 'cost-benefit' analysis where they decide that they are happy at their current level and do not want to bother going through the promotion experience itself. Notwithstanding these deterrents, women do make conscious decisions to apply for promotion when they benefit from relatively early entrance into academe and early completion of a Ph.D., coupled with the relative absence of care responsibilities. Support in the form of mentors, colleagues and cohesive work environments is a major source of encouragement (Pyke 2013).

'Women *are* entering HE leadership, albeit in low numbers ... Representational space cannot be the only goal for gender equality' (Morley 2013a, p. 126, added emphasis).

Identity Perceptions of Female Professors

Women's entry into academia transforms identity possibilities for themselves and potential others. Their sense of self as academics in the highly patriarchal domain of the academy as an institution is shaped by discourses of gender, institutional power and other social and cultural influences. In other words,

> coming to an academic identity is a process that is never complete, flawed, contingent, and always open to change ... *Who am I?* ... I am a scholar. I am an agent of change ... I recognize that my identity is partial and flawed, but my success is measured by my work to create openings for others to carry this scholarship forward [a scholarship of equity and social justice]. (Wallace and Wallin 2015, pp. 427–428, added emphasis)

Many discursively constructed conceptions of 'appropriate' leadership performance are culturally ascribed as masculine, a fact that highlights the 'otherness' of the woman leader and the added adversity in 'passing' as a leader and gaining legitimacy in the academy (Read and Kehm 2016). Besides the discomfort experienced by some women in adopting this stance, there is jarring with the expectations of appropriate 'feminine' dress and behaviour (Walkerdine 1990; Walker 1998), which can in turn lead to negative perceptions of women who exhibit masculinized attributes (Ridgeway 2001). This is embedded within a scenario whereby 'the social dominance of the masculine (like *whiteness*) is discursively legitimized to such a degree that it seems *natural* or inevitable, to the extent that it cannot be perceived as dominance as such but as a neutral *natural* order of things' (Read and Kehm 2016, p. 817, original emphasis). The conception of the university academic is culturally gendered like the conception of leadership, with the dominant construction of the academic as male, middle or upper class, and generally white (Leathwood and Read 2013; David 2014). Notwithstanding, female academics are getting engaged in senior leadership positions, although a change in numerical composition does not necessarily signify a transformation in culture.

The prevalence of a highly gendered culture serves as a backdrop for the other distinct factors that constitute a female professor's academic identity, as experiences differ according to where they stand at the crossroads of differing marginalized identities. Migrant female professors 'occupy the unique position of being subjects of *double discrimination* and also occupying the status of *double outsiders*' (Sang et al. 2013,

p. 160, emphasis added), as they are women professors, in addition to being migrants, thus occupying the status as 'subjects of double disadvantage' (ibid., p. 158). They are assigned the positionality of the 'outsider-within', a clear indication of the interdependence of racism and sexism in academia (Patton 2004). Multiple social identities may shape one's opportunities in higher education, with implications for women of colour more specifically. Turner (2002) explores the experience of multiple marginality and being defined due to gender and race/ethnicity. The lives of faculty women are marked by lived contradictions and ambiguous empowerment, as they are often confronted with situations that limit their authority, despite having obtained tenured positions. The interlocking effects of gender and race compound the pressures of the workplace environment for these ethnically diverse women professors who are a minority, thus under-represented. They face challenges from academic old boy networks, which may lead to feelings of isolation. Faculty women of colour perceive that their authority is more likely to be challenged by students than are white male professors. On the other hand, they are in high demand by students with minority issues, due to their scarcity, often called upon to serve as 'mentor, mother, and counsellor in addition to educator' (Andrews 1993, p. 190), which is emotionally draining, besides leaving little time for research and publication.

Macfarlane and Burg (2018), who investigate the ways in which full female professors define their identity and role as intellectual leaders, claim that the micro-politics of the academy may represent a clue to understanding the embedded nature of disadvantage, an academy where one can still detect a 'subtle homosocial culture' (Ledwith and Manfredi 2000, p. 7). Are women professors still regarded as the Other, as strangers in academia? 'As women professors ourselves, we feel as if we are on the thick end of the wedge: there are nowadays many of us, and although it is still uncertain whether our presence will split or solidify the world of academia, our number is also our protection' (Czarniawska and Sevon 2008, p. 236).

Global Narratives and Autoethnography

The female academics whose narratives are presented in this edited volume hail from varying countries across the globe, namely Australia, Japan, Israel, Malta, Portugal, Puerto Rico and the UK. This geographical diversity adds value to this collection of 'making it' career trajectories by revealing international differences in women's career progression, thus providing the context for comparing the experience of a woman professor across different countries. These narratives thus provide examples of overcoming gendered career inequalities in alternative contexts.

Progression to professor generally involves the recognition of excellence in research, together with the ability to demonstrate competence in academic administration and teaching. The main duties of the post revolve around a substantial contribution to the faculty's international research output; supporting the Faculty's research strategy; national and international networking; promotion and dissemination of research and knowledge transfer activities; generation of external funding for research; the supervision of Ph.D. students; in addition to participation in other administration processes and teaching obligations as deemed necessary by the university, in addition to external commitments that enhance the reputation of the faculty and/or university. More recently, routes to the professoriate have allowed for excellence in other categories, thus allowing for the recognition of diverse pathways. The pathways to professorial promotion acknowledge achievement of the highest distinction and are based on an expectation of a continuing contribution in the area for which the title is awarded. Among the various recognized pathways are research; teaching, learning and assessment; enterprise and knowledge exchange; professional achievement; and academic leadership.

Applications are submitted according to the deadlines set by that particular higher education institution, after which they are assessed and reviewed by a committee appointed to assess promotions, with the candidates being informed of the progress of their application in due course. The most common career trajectory in the UK is to progress from lecturer to senior lecturer to reader to professor, with a Ph.D. being the minimum requirement to enter academia. While the route is basically the same across the globe, divergences do exist in terms of the promotion process and academic nomenclatures. In Portugal, the entry level for an academic career is assistant professor (with a Ph.D.), moving on to tenure, associate professor and subsequently full professor. The process from one stage to the next occurs via public tender, and to become professor, one must undertake a two-day exam with a jury of mostly external professors, discussing your curriculum vitae, teaching and research. In Puerto Rico, the same nomenclatures as in Portuguese universities are used. However, promotion is not tied to publications and grants as they are at most US institutions. Candidates are evaluated on what they use their credits to do, depending on whether it's solely teaching, or a combination of research and teaching. In Israel, the academic trajectory is from lecturer to senior lecturer (with tenure) to associate professor, and finally to full professor. In Malta, the nomenclatures used are the same as in Israel, with the difference that tenure, that is permanency, is given from the position of assistant lecturer (for those who enter without a Ph.D.). In Japan, there are two paths to academia—you come in on tenure and you move up seamlessly, or else you come in on a contract with no real career path. The Japanese terms of reference for academic positions are obviously different. The application is put forward to the promotions committee, reviewed and then recommended at the Faculty Senate meeting, where the decision-making for the faculty goes on. The promotion is gradually voted on, following a very strict review process. A two-thirds majority is required. In Australia, the nomenclatures and academic stages are the same as in Malta, with the actual process involving two interviews—one with the promotions panel, followed by another one with the dean after their deliberation.

These female professors represent diverse fields of study, which is very relevant to the scope of the edited manuscript, since disciplinary cultures may vary from one context to another and have different career effects. Among the fields present in this manuscript are architecture; linguistics; psychology; business and management; academic development; social anthropology; sociology; and sports psychology.

Autoethnographic Accounts of 'Making It': A Methodological Bridging of Writing Inquiry and Critique

The female academics who contribute to this edited volume use tenets of autobiography and ethnography in order to '*do* and *write* autoethnography' (Ellis et al. 2011, p. 1, original emphasis), thus presenting narratives divulging their career trajectory, autoethnography serving the methodological purpose of both 'process and product' (ibid.).

As an approach, autoethnography acknowledges and accommodates subjectivity, emotionality and the researcher's influence on research, thus making it a very apt methodology for this particular exposition of women professor stories. It is an approach which draws upon these women's own personal lived experiences, in specific relation to the culture and subcultures of which they are members, as they situate and write themselves in as key players within their research account. They use personal experience in order to illustrate cultural experience (Allen-Collinson 2012), thus making features of the academic culture, in this particular case, familiar for both insiders and outsiders. These female professors 'connect the autobiographical and personal to the cultural and social' by highlighting 'concrete action, emotion, embodiment, self-consciousness, and introspection' (Ellis 2004, p. xix). In these ten narratives, 'autoethnography is setting a scene, telling a story, weaving intricate connections among life and art, experience and theory, evocation and explanation … and then letting go, hoping for readers who will bring the same careful attention to your words in the context of their own lives' (Holman Jones 2005, p. 765). They thus treat their autobiographical data with 'critical, analytical, and interpretive eyes' (Chang 2007, p. 209), with autoethnography serving as an exceptional medium through which to gain a better comprehension of themselves and others. Ellis and Bochner (2006) synthesize it in this way: 'Autoethnography shows struggle, passion, embodied life, and the collaborative creation of sense-making in situations in which people have to cope with dire circumstances and loss of meaning. Autoethnography wants the reader to care, to feel, to empathize, and to do something, to act. It needs the researcher to be vulnerable and intimate' (p. 433). In the ten narratives presented in this volume, the voices and selves of others, significant others, intertwine with the ten female selves and their stories (Wall 2008).

Outline of Monograph

In the *Introduction*, Mifsud explores the positioning of females in higher education as presented in the literature, with a specific focus on gender equity and obstacles along the path to professorial level. The prevalent gender imbalance at professorial level creates a discursive space in which to problematize the gender question in the academy through an exploration of the multiple status differentials and hierarchies. Thus, this critical literature narrative provides a backdrop for the subsequent experiences of 'successful' women professors in the book.

In Chapter 2, *Being Tough, Being Humourous and Being Explicitly Feminist—The Intrinsically Disordered Nature of My Ways Around the Academia*, Menezes projects her professorial career trajectory as a product of her particular social context. She discusses how the severe gender inequality of the dictatorship, her family history of women working outside the home, as well as the social climate of the time paved her way into academia.

Chapter 3, *You Must Wait to Be Asked: Career Advancement and the Maternal Body*, by Gatrell, focuses on the gendered route to the professoriate, with structural inequalities within academic systems making it hard for women to achieve the status of chair. Women academics are at times judged on their maternal bodies, rather than on their performance. Notwithstanding these barriers, some women do make it to the top. Gatrell shares advice from colleagues, in addition to personal experiences that helped her advance in her research career.

Chapter 4 delves deeper into the issue of maternal bodies, carrying on the motherhood and maternity leave theme as experienced in academia. In *How Babies Taught Me How to "Do" Academia: Crafting a Career in an Institution That Was Not Built for Mothers*, Mazak shares her experience of the university's attitude towards a 'mother' professor in

Puerto Rico. She presents a matrifocal academic narrative, while simultaneously revealing how deeply ingrained patriarchal narratives are in the world of academia, anchoring this within her three pregnancies and her success at weaving her maternal narrative into academic work.

In the subsequent chapter, *Writing Myself into an Academic Career*, Murray explores her progress in her academic career by creating 'social writing' for herself and others. Using the Social Writing Framework, Murray analyses her career, explaining how social writing involved developing agency through the active creation of space for her writing, thus producing the outputs necessary for promotion. This approach indirectly provides alternative spaces where women academics can write and do the work needed for career progression.

Chapter 6, *Academic Fluidity? An Unconventional Route to the Professoriate*, charts an alternative pathway into the professoriate, involving a move from one discipline to another while undertaking a range of job roles and work categorized as non-academic activities by the academy. Potter uses storytelling and reflection to present three 'moments' of personal, professional change arising from intentional agency when making career-changing decisions. She explores the notion of academic fluidity that aided her to make sense of her identity.

In Chapter 7, *My Personal Journey on the Pathway of Resilience*, Skerratt explains how the very private goal of becoming a professor by her fiftieth birthday, aged twenty-two, was achieved via resilience and her own decisions regarding 'desirable' and 'undesirable' outcomes. Resilience encompasses proactive human agency; dreaming and imagining futures; as well as reaching out. Skerratt explains how she deployed these resilience characteristics on her professorship trajectory, while having now embarked on the journey 'beyond' becoming a professor.

In Chapter 8, *Actively Constructing Yourself as Professor: After Appointment*, Yamamoto shows how getting the professorship is not an end point but a beginning. As a British woman professor in a Japanese research university, she delineates how she sought to create a space for herself in a highly male-dominated environment with few foreigners in leadership positions.

Chapter 9, *Mis-Making an Academic Career: Power, Discipline, Structures, and Practices* by Kalekin-Fishman, briefly demonstrates how sideways career moves are one way to deal with academia's contingencies. One adjacent possible career in the academy is learning and teaching development, a field dominated by women and often positioned as caring work.

Chapter 10, *A Personal Journey of a Long and Winding Road to Professorial Status: An Alternative Pathway and the Challenges, Trials and Tribulations*, is set in Israel. Lafferty argues that despite the presence of women leaders in academia, discovering what kind of knowledge supplies the means for realizing the promise of a climb to professorial heights can be a challenge. She frames her failure to become professor to an interweaving of the socio-economic realities of the university, the omnipresence of power and the subjective adoption of roles and rules from inappropriate repertoires.

In Chapter 11, *How to Fall into a Career Trap (Without Even Realising)*, Mewburn reflects on her personal journey to professorship and her numerous experiences and diverse portfolio of activity finally came together to have personal and professional meaning. This is done within the changing landscape in higher education and a drive within the UK for universities to show more social responsibility and engagement.

The Conclusion, *The Process of Becoming a Woman Professor and Unbecoming Gender Inequality: A Female Drama of Resistance*, presents a synthesis of these female career progression narratives. Mifsud presents the themes via a semi-fictionalized narrative dramatization crafted from the voices of the female academics, while she adopts the multiple roles of narrator, observer, interpreter, analyst, playwright and researcher. This unconventional mode of data representation mirrors the exceptional path followed by the female academics in a higher education environment pervaded by the hegemonic male discourses. This chapter provides cohesion to the book, suggesting methods for regaining control while providing options for the future.

References

Allen-Collinson, J. (2012). Chapter 9 autoethnography: Situating personal sporting narratives in socio-cultural contexts. *Qualitative Research on Sport and Physical Culture, 6,* 191–212.

Allen, M., & Castleman, T. (2001). Fighting the pipeline fallacy. In A. Brooks & A. Mackinnon (Eds.), *Gender and the restructured university* (pp. 151–165). Buckingham: Open University Press.

American Association of University Professors. (2017). *Visualizing change: The annual report on the economic status of the profession, 2016–17.* Washington, DC, USA.

Andrews, A. R. (1993). Balancing personal and professional. In J. James & R. Farmer (Eds.), *Spirit, space and survival: African American women in (white) academe* (pp. 239–261). New York: Routledge.

Armenti, C. (2000). *Women academics blending private and public lives.* Unpublished doctoral dissertation, Institute for Studies in Education, University of Toronto, Toronto.

Armenti, C. (2004). Women faculty seeking tenure and parenthood: Lessons from previous generations. *Cambridge Journal of Education, 34*(1), 65–83.

Atewologun, D., & Sealy, R. (2014). Experiencing privilege at ethnic, gender and senior intersections. *Journal of Managerial Psychology, 29*(4), 423–439.

Bagilhole, B., & White, K. (Eds.). (2011). *Gender, power and management: A cross cultural analysis of higher education.* Basingstoke: Palgrave Macmillan.

Bekhradnia, B. (2009). *Male and female participation and progression in higher education.* Oxford, UK: Higher Education Policy Unit.

Bell, S., & Bentley, R. (2006, April 11–13). *Women in research.* Paper presented at the Proceedings of the ATN WEXDEV Conference 2006: Change in Climate? Prospects for Gender Equity in Universities, Adelaide, SA.

Bexley, E., James, R., & Arkoudis, S. (2011). *The Australian academic profession in transition: Addressing the challenge of reconceptualising academic work and regenerating the academic workforce.* Canberra: Department of Employment, Education and Workplace Relations.

Blackmore, J. (2014). 'Wasting talent'? Gender and the problematics of academic disenchantment and disengagement with leadership. *Higher Education Research and Development, 33*(1), 86–99.

Britton, D. M. (2017). Beyond the chilly climate: The salience of gender in women's academic careers. *Gender and Society, 31*(1), 5–27.

Bryans, P., & Mavins, S. (2003). Women learning to be managers: Learning to fit in or play a different game? *Management Learning, 34*(1), 111–134.
Canadian Association of University Teachers. (2016). *CAUT almanac of post-secondary education in Canada*. Canada.
Caplan, P. J. (1993). *Lifting a ton of feathers: A woman's guide for surviving in the academic world: A project of the Council of Ontario Universities Committee on the status of women*. Toronto: University of Toronto Press.
Chang, H. (2007). Autoethnography: Raising cultural consciousness of self and others. *Methodological Developments in Ethnography, 12*, 207–221.
Currie, J., Thiele, B., & Harris, P. (2002). *Gendered universities in globalized economies*. New York: Lexington Books.
Czarniawska, B., & Sevon, G. (2008). The thin end of the wedge: Foreign women professors as double strangers in academia. *Gender, Work and Organization, 15*(3), 235–287.
David, M. (2014). *Feminism, gender and universities*. Farnham: Ashgate.
David, M. E. (2015). Women and gender equality in higher education? *Education Sciences, 5*, 10–25.
Diezmann, C., & Grieshaber, S. (2010, July 6–9). *Gender equity in the professoriate: A cohort study of new women professors in Australia*. Paper presented at Research and Development in Higher Education: Reshaping Higher Education, at the 33rd HERDSA Annual International Conference, Melbourne, Australia.
Drago, R., Colbeck, C., Stauffer, K. D., Pirretti, A., Burkum, K., Fazioli, J., et al. (2005). Bias against caregiving. *Academe, 91*(5), 22–25.
El-Alayli, A., Hansen-Brown, A. A., & Ceynar, M. (2018). Dancing backwards in high heels: Female professors experience more work demands and special favor requests, particularly from academically entitled students. *Sex Roles, 79*, 136–150.
Ellis, C. (2004). *The ethnographic I: A methodological novel about autoethnography*. Walnut Creek, CA: AltaMira Press.
Ellis, C., Adams, T. E., & Bochner, A. P. (2011). Autoethnography: An overview. *Forum: Qualitative Social Research, 12*(1), 1–12.
Ellis, C. S., & Bochner, A. P. (2006). Analyzing analytic autoethnography. *Journal of Contemporary Ethnography, 35*(4), 429–449.
European Commission. (2009). *She figures 2009: Statistics and indicators on gender equality in science*. Luxembourg: Publications Office of the European Union.

European Commission. (2016). *She figures 2015*. Luxembourg: Publications Office of the European Union.
Finkelstein, M. J., Conley, V. M., & Schuster, J. H. (2016). *Taking the measure of faculty diversity*. Advancing Higher Education, TIAA Institute, p. 4.
Fitzgerald, T. (2014). *Women leaders in higher education: Shattering the myths*. Abingdon: Routledge.
Fitzgerald, T. (2018). Looking good and being good: Women leaders in Australian universities. *Education Sciences, 8*(54), 1–12.
Flaherty, C. (2017, April 12). Study finds female professors outperform men in service—To their possible professional detriment. *Inside Higher Ed*. Available online at https://www.insidehighered.com/news/2017/04/12/study-finds-female-professors-outperform-men-service-their-possible-professional?width=775&height=500&iframe=true. Accessed on 15 Oct 2018.
Gappa, J. M., Austin, A. E., & Trice, A. G. (2007). *Rethinking faculty work: Higher education's strategic imperative*. San Francisco: Jossey-Bass.
Gherardi, S., & Poggio, B. (2007). *Gendertelling in organisations: Narratives from male-dominated environments*. Copenhagen, Denmark: Liber (Copenhagen Business School Press).
Government of India, Ministry of Human Resource Development. (2017). *All India survey on higher education (2015–16)*. India.
Government of Japan, Gender Equality Cabinet Office. (2017). Education and research fields. *Women and men in Japan 2017*. Japan.
Grove, J. (2013). Glass ceiling remains in place for female academics: Global gender index. *Times Higher Education*. Available online at http://www.timeshighereducation.co.uk/features/global-gender-index-2013/2003517.fullarticle. Accessed on 26 Nov 2018.
Guarino, C. M., & Borden, V. M. H. (2017). Faculty service loads and gender: Are women taking care of the academic family? *Research in Higher Education, 58*(6), 672–694.
Hall, R. M., & Sandler, B. R. (1982). *The classroom climate: A chilly one for women?* Washington, DC: Project on the Status and Education of Women.
Harford, J. (2018). The perspectives of women professors on the professoriate: A missing piece in the narrative on gender equality in the university. *Education Sciences, 8*(50), 1–17.
Holman Jones, S. (2005). Autoethnography: Making the personal political. In N. K. Denzin & Y. S. Lincoln (Eds.), *Handbook of qualitative research* (3rd ed., pp. 763–791). Thousand Oaks, CA: Sage.

Howe-Walsh, L., & Turnbull, S. (2016). Barriers to women leaders in academia: Tales from science and technology. *Studies in Higher Education, 41*(3), 415–428.

Jackson, L. D. (2008). Reflections on obstacles and opportunities: Suggestions for improving the retention of female faculty. *Women's Studies in Communication, 31*(2), 226–232.

Jacobs, J., & Winslow, S. (2004). The faculty time divide. *Sociological Forum, 19*, 3–27.

Leathwood, C., & Read, B. (2013). Research policy and academic performativity: Compliance, contestation and complicity. *Studies in Higher Education, 38*(8), 1162–1174.

Ledwith, S., & Manfredi, S. (2000). A study of the experience of senior women in a 'new' UK university. *European Journal of Women's Studies, 7*, 7–33.

Leonard, D. (2001). *A woman's guide to doctoral studies*. Buckingham: Open University Press.

Leonard, P., & Malina, D. (1994). Caught between two worlds: Mothers as academics. In S. Davies, C. Lubelska, & J. Quinn (Eds.), *Changing the subject: Women in higher education* (pp. 29–41). London: Taylor & Francis.

Lopes, A., & Dewan, I. (2014). Precarious pedagogies? The impact of casual and zero-hour contracts in higher education. *Journal of Feminist Scholarship, 7*(8), 28–42.

MacFarlane, B. (2012). *Intellectual leadership in higher education: Renewing the role of the university professor*. London: Routledge.

MacFarlane, B. (2018, June 4). *Women professors, pay, promotion, and academic housekeeping*. Retrieved from https://wonkhe.com/blogs/women-professors-pay-promotion-and-academic-housekeeping/ Accessed on 25 Oct 2018.

Macfarlane, B., & Burg, D. (2018). *Women professors as intellectual leaders*. London: Leadership Foundation for Higher Education.

Mason, M. A. (2011, March 9). The pyramid problem. *The Chronicle of Higher Education*, pp. 1–3.

Meyerson, D. E., & Tompkins, M. (2007). Tempered radicals as institutional change agents: The case of advancing gender equity at the University of Michigan. *Harvard Journal of Law and Gender, 30*, 303–322.

Midkiff, B. (2015). Exploring women faculty's experiences and perceptions in higher education: The effects of feminism? *Gender and Education, 27*(4), 376–392.

Monture-O'Kanee, P. (1995). Surviving contradictions: Personal notes on academia. In The Chilly Collective (Ed.), *Breaking anonymity: The chilly climate for women faculty* (pp. 11–28). Waterloo: Wilfrid Laurier University Press.

Morley, L. (2005). Sounds, silences and contradictions: Gender equity in British Commonwealth higher education. *Australian Feminist Studies, 20*, 109–119.

Morley, L. (2011). Imagining the university of the future. In R. Barnett (Ed.), *The future university: Ideas and possibilities* (pp. 26–35). London: Taylor and Francis.

Morley, L. (2013a). The rules of the game: Women and the leaderist turn in higher education. *Gender and Education, 25*(1), 116–131.

Morley, L. (2013b). International trends in women's leadership in higher education. In T. Gore & M. Stiasny (Eds.), *Going global* (pp. 279–298). London: Emerald.

Morley, L. (2014). Lost leaders: Women in the global academy. *Higher Education Research and Development, 33*(1), 114–128.

Moss-Racusin, C. A., Dovidio, J. F., Brescoll, V. L., Graham, M. J., & Handelsman, J. (2012). Science faculty's subtle gender biases favour male students. *Proceedings of the National Academy of Sciences, 109*(41), 16474–16479.

Muscarella, T. S. (2004). *A qualitative and quantitative investigation of barriers for women attaining leadership positions: The effects of role expectations, gender stereotyping and role incongruity of being female and a leader.* Dissertation Abstracts International. Section B: The Sciences and Engineering, 470.

National Center for Education Statistics. (2016). Full-time instructional staff, by faculty and tenure status, academic rank, race/ethnicity, and gender (degree-granting institutions): Fall 2015. *Fall staff 2015 survey*, IPEDS Data Center, USA.

O'Connor, P. (2014). Understanding success: A case study of gendered change in the professoriate. *Journal of Higher Education Policy and Management, 36*(2), 212–224.

O'Connor, P. (2015). Good jobs—But places for women? *Gender and Education, 27*, 304–319.

Patton, T. O. (2004). Reflections of a black woman professor: Racism and sexism in academia. *Howard Journal of Communications, 15*(3), 185–200.

Probert, B. (2005). 'I just couldn't fit in': Gender and unequal outcomes in academic careers. *Gender, Work and Organisation, 21*(1), 50–72.

Pyke, J. (2013). Women, choice and promotion or why women are still a minority in the professoriate. *Journal of Higher Education Policy and Management, 35*(4), 444–454.
Raddon, A. (2002). Mothers in the academy. *Studies in Higher Education, 27*(4), 387–403.
Read, B., & Kehm, B. M. (2016). Women as leaders of higher education institutions: A British–German comparison. *Studies in Higher Education, 41*(5), 815–827.
Rice, C. (2012, May 24). Why women leave academia and why universities should be worried. *The Guardian*. Accessible online at http://www.theguardian.com/higher-education-network/blog/2012/may/24/why-women-leave-academia. Accessed on 25 Oct 2018.
Ridgeway, C. L. (2001). Gender, status and leadership. *Journal of Social Issues, 57*(4), 637–655.
Ridgeway, C. L. (2011). *Framed by gender: How gender inequality persists in the modern world*. New York: Oxford University Press.
Ridgeway, C. L., & Correll, S. J. (2004). Unpacking the gender system: A theoretical perspective on gender beliefs and social relations. *Gender and Society, 18*(4), 510–531.
Sang, K., Al-Dajani, H., & Ozbilgin, M. (2013). Frayed careers of migrant female professors in British academia: An intersectional perspective. *Gender, Work and Organization, 20*(2), 158–171.
Savigny, H. (2014). Women, know your limits: Cultural sexism in academia. *Gender and Education, 26*(7), 794–809.
Standing, G. (2014). *The precariat: The new dangerous class*. London: Bloomsbury.
Stevens-Kalceff, M., Hagon, S., Cunningham, M., & Woo, A. (2007). *Maximising potential in physics: Investigation of the academic profile of the school of physics at the University of New South Wales*. Sydney: University of New South Wales.
Teelken, C., & Deem, R. (2013). All are equal, but some are more equal than others: Managerialism and gender equality in higher education in comparative perspective. *Comparative Education, 49*(4), 520–535.
The Chilly Collective. (Ed.). (1995). *Breaking anonymity: The chilly climate for women faculty*. Waterloo: Wilfrid Laurier University Press.
Thwaites, R., & Pressland, A. (2017). Introduction: Being an early career feminist academic in a changing academy. In R. Thwaites & A. Pressland (Eds.), *Being an early career feminist academic: Global perspectives, experiences, and challenges* (pp. 1–28). London, UK: Palgrave Macmillan.

Turner, C. S. V. (2002). Women of colour in academe. *The Journal of Higher Education, 73*(1), 74–93.

UNESCO. (2012). *World atlas on gender equality in education*. Available online http://www.unesco.org/new/typo3temp/pics/d7af2fe604.jpg. Accessed on 15 Oct 2018.

University and College Union. (2017). *The gender pay gap in higher education 2015/16 data report*. UK.

Van den Brink, M. (2011). Scouting for talent: Appointment practices of women professors in academic medicine. *Social Science and Medicine, 72*, 2033–2040.

Walby, S. (2011). Is the knowledge society gendered? *Gender, Work and Organisation, 18*(1), 1–29.

Walker, M. (1998). Academic identities: Women on a South African landscape. *British Journal of Sociology of Education, 19*(3), 335–354.

Walkerdine, V. (1990). *Schoolgirl fictions*. London: Verso.

Wall, S. (2008). Easier said than done: Writing an autoethnography. *International Journal of Qualitative Methods, 7*(1), 38–53.

Wallace, J., & Wallin, D. (2015). 'The voice inside herself': Transforming gendered academic identities in educational administration. *Gender and Education, 27*(4), 412–429.

Winchester, H. P. M., & Browning, L. (2015). Gender equality in academia: A critical reflection. *Journal of Higher Education Policy and Management, 37*(3), 269–281.

Wolf-Wendel, L., & Ward, K. (2003). Future prospects for women faculty: Negotiating work and family. In B. Ropers-Huilman (Ed.), *Gendered futures in higher education: Critical perspectives for change* (pp. 111–134). Albany: State University of New York Press.

Wylie, A. (1995). The contexts of activism on 'climate' issues. In The Chilly Collective (Ed.), *Breaking anonymity: The chilly climate for women faculty* (pp. 29–60). Waterloo: Wilfrid Laurier University Press.

2

Being Tough, Being Humorous and Being Explicitly Feminist—The "Intrinsically Disordered Nature" of My Ways Around Academia

Isabel Menezes

I am 9. I am bored. I am sitting on 'my father's couch' in the living room and the TV is on but there is nothing happening with the exception of some military marches playing again and again. My mother is excited and apparently happy. I am upset. I want to see the TV. My mother turns the radio on and she and my grandmother look like they know a secret – there are some songs playing, and her eyes are bright. She is really excited. I am really upset. They don't tell me or my older sister what is happening: "maybe tomorrow, they say, when your father comes back from work". He is working the night shift, as my mother also does – telephones and telegrams never stop, so they have to work shifts. The next day is not better. I go to school and our teacher tells us to go back home – the school is off. I am very disappointed – no TV, no school. I like school. I come back home. When my father arrives he finally explains what is happening – it's a revolution. He is also very happy. It seems that the president and the prime minister were bad people. In my classroom, there are photos of both of them on the wall. It seems that they were dictators. This is a new word. – In a couple of months, I will be fluent in this new language:

I. Menezes (✉)
University of Porto, Porto, Portugal
e-mail: imenezes@fpce.up.pt

© The Author(s) 2019
R. Murray and D. Mifsud (eds.), *The Positioning and Making of Female Professors*, Palgrave Studies in Gender and Education,
https://doi.org/10.1007/978-3-030-26187-0_2

dictators, fascists, communists, socialists, social-fascists, politics, revolution, comrades, constitution, elections, democracy, counter-revolution, colonialism, decolonization. But not just yet. – My father tells me that the government did not let people think differently or speak out. I feel this is very stupid. They send people to prison because of their ideas. This is very mean. It is also unfair. Even being 9, I don't like things to be unfair. And I like to speak out. Sometimes people complain – I speak my mind too often, too openly. I am quite lucky that I can grow up during a revolution when speaking what you think is a good thing. When you can discuss openly all the time, and say that you disagree. I like it and I am not bored anymore.

The Portuguese revolution that restored democracy—a distinctive and "historically unusual social revolutionary pathway to democracy" (Fishman 2018, p. 22)—in 1974, when I was 9, is the major reason why a girl from a middle-class background like myself got to the university. Women in my family have been working for, at least, four generations. In this sense, mine is a non-traditional story. This results from the fact that both my great-grandmother and my grandmother worked in factories, as women on the late 1890s to the mid-1900s mostly worked in agriculture or domestic service, frequently as unpaid work (Nunes 1991). But the unconventionality was reinforced by my mother's continuous commitment to her job, after childbearing. In fact, the percentage of women in the labour force declined during the first decades of the twentieth century up to a minimum of 18% in the 1960s and only restarted to grow close to the revolution, probably due to the combined effects of the colonial wars and high levels of emigration (Baptista 2014). It was only after the revolution that social rights were granted: maternity leave, day-care centres for small children and women's rights. For the women in my mother's generation, continuing to work, even when their husbands could "support them", was their (non-normative) way of staying independent. Paid work clearly was—as before, in the history of citizenship (Marshall 1950; Bosniak 2002)—a precondition to equality,[1] even if women in those days were by law subordinate to man. During the Portuguese dictatorship (1926–1974), work was a strategy to resist "women's subordination" (Pateman 1992, p. 28) that limited their access to the public sphere and chances for equality. The other strategy, like my mother, my father and other women and men in their generation knew too well, even if not from personal experience, was (school) education.

The first woman who voted in Portugal was Carolina Beatriz Ângelo, a medical doctor and a widow who, in 1911, used the fact that the law granted voting rights to "people" with more than 21 years, who could read and were "the head of the household". This was, unfortunately, a "mistake" corrected by the 1913 law that explicitly restricted voting rights to "men" older than 21 years, who could read and were "the head of the household". From 1931 onwards, women's voting rights were granted for some elections, but always dependant on being (i) "the head of the household", or (ii) single but paying taxes, or (iii) with secondary or higher education degrees (Vieira 2018). Only after 1974, gender equality was included in the Constitution as a basic principle for non-discrimination and universal voting rights were granted after the age of 18. Nonetheless, education was not only a symbolic instrument towards equality of rights but also a way to guarantee social mobility—and, therefore, it is not surprising that women from my generation onward were encouraged, by their mothers and fathers, to attend university: in a 1993 study with a sample of secondary and higher education students, ensuring economic independence still was, for female students, the most significant motivation for attending university (Morais and Carvalho 1993). The increased presence of women in higher education is remarkable (Fig. 2.1): while in 1960, less than 1/3 were female students, by 1986 they were half of the student population. Since then, women are the majority (around 53% since 2007, after a peak of 58% from 1993 to 1996), even if the distribution is unbalanced across areas: not so much in Mathematics, Sciences and Informatics

---

[1]A precondition that generates its own inequalities: until today, when women are almost half of the workforce, they earn significantly less (16.7%) than their male colleagues (http://cite.gov.pt/pt/destaques/complementosDestqs2/Desigualdade_salarial.pdf).

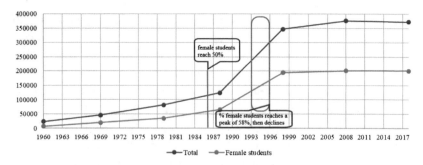

Fig. 2.1 Number of students and of female students in higher education in Portugal (1960–2018) (*Source* DGEEC/MEd—MCTES—RENATES, PORDATA)

(43%), but clearly in Engineering (28%). Women are also the majority of graduates, including Ph.D.: in 1970, only 7% of doctorates were concluded by women, a percentage raised to more than 50% since 2006 (Ribeiro et al. 2012).

Hence, revolution, democracy and, later, inclusion in the European economic/political community had a tremendous effect on policy and practice in terms of women's citizenship. Still, policy changes tend to be much more intense than practical changes. In an analysis of gender policies in Portugal, Ribeiro et al. (2015) conclude that

> access to rights, work and education has not been sufficient to guarantee (…) de facto inclusion, recognition or voice, as illustrated by women's lower access to elected positions, lower access to income and higher risk of poverty and of gender-based violence. (…) To promote the efficacy of the policies and to challenge economic and political inequality between women and men, issues of power and distribution would have to be brought to the table and maybe in a manner that is more inclusive, informed by everyday life, and focused on bringing to the hands of everyday women the economic and political power which is necessary for them to change their lives and our societies in ways that do not make things different so that some things can stay the same. (p. 416)

Nevertheless, as Fishman argues, "Portugal's post-25 April road to democracy (…) [had] much greater consequences for society, the economy and culture than more common pathways to democracy"

(Fishman 2018, p. 21) with an intensity of "the *cultural legacies* of social revolution and their ongoing impact on socio-political life" (p. 24, italics in the original), such as "the cultural or civic sophistication of young people" (p. 30) born after the revolution. But for my generation, for those who were young/old enough to witness and to remember what Fishman describes as the four components of 25 April—"political revolution, democratic transition, social revolution and socialist transformation" (p. 23)—the intensity and vitality of the political and civic climate of that period is also a long-lasting individual legacy that coexists with its socio-historical significance.

In those days, political discussions happened everywhere and involved almost everybody, and demonstrations, rallies and protests were frequent. Children were not excluded from these activities, and I probably participated in more demonstrations and political rallies from 1974 to 1976, than since then. But if I could trace the most significant everyday life implication of those days, it would be the possibility to discuss everything in political terms—meaning that no issue was out of the possibility of being questioned, reconsidered, debated and transformed through interaction, in an environment where pluralism was, not only expected but normalized. These are truly, to quote as Hannah Arendt says, "the activities of freedom" (1990|1963, p. 235), typical in revolutions as political events that embody the "hope for the emancipation" (p. 11). I am more than ready to admit that this might be a benevolent reading of the intense conflictual nature of the revolutionary period—as there were also episodes of political violence—but I am not trying to give a historical account of the period; instead I am focusing on my personal (and surely biased) recollection. In my family, my parents, and especially my father, were actively involved in politics; by those days and since then, politics was always on the table. I remember ordering alphabetically, with my sister, the registration forms for the first free elections in my village, back in 1975; both me and my sister frequently went campaigning with my father; the whole family went to demonstrations or political gatherings, and I asked several times (with no success, I am afraid, as this was generally a night-time activity) to go glueing political posters on the streets. This intrinsically democratic climate was something very new, both in private and in public spaces, strongly contrasting with the fear to speak out and the respect for authority that was dominant during the dictatorship—and that, I must regretfully admit, still persists, in private and public spaces, until today. Although it might seem a little prosaic to overemphasise this open democratic climate given the amount of social and political transformation in the country—democratization, civil and political rights, decolonization, universal access to education, social security and health care, etc.—I still feel this is one of the most important legacies of the revolution.

Being Tough, Being Humorous

Freedom of speech is, of course, a very important and distinctive trait of democratic public spaces. But it also has significant, though less recognized, implications in private spheres. In the context of a democracy, it is certainly easier for families to openly share stories of previous oppression and discrimination, a phenomenon of transgenerational transmission that has been detailed in relation to extreme cases of political violence, in various contexts (e.g. Faúndez and Goecke 2015).

My grandmother came from a poor working family—they were eight children, all working since a young age. She herself started working outside the house at the age of eight, and after some time, she went to a stocking factory; she stayed there for the rest of her working life until I was born and she quit so that she would look after me and my mother could keep her job.[2] The factory had many women and therefore many stories: of being discriminated against, of being abused, of being harassed, of being exploited, of being forced to abortion, of being in love, of being pregnant, of having babies, of crying and of laughter. It was a feminine reign, even if the rulers were men. This was also the case in my mother's workplace, a telephone company where women were the majority, with men as technicians and engineers in the back, and, obviously, in the top management. Even if these women would probably not label

---

[2] A tradition of "welfare family" that, in Portugal and surely in other South European countries, has compensated for the rudimentary status of a "welfare state".

themselves as feminists—which implied a cultural capital they did not possess—they knew from experience what subordination, discrimination and exclusion meant. These stories marked our life in the path to democracy, where women's rights were granted by law but questioned every day by practice—there were clearly huge changes, but also persistence of discrimination in both public and private spheres. And these were stories of how women were (alas!) many times defeated, but also of how they resisted, confronted and dealt with oppression, sometimes by being tough and sometimes by being humorous.

Deborah Nelson (2017) describes toughness as an intentional strategy of avoiding sentimentality by women authors such as Hannah Arendt, Mary McCarthy or Susan Sontag. Of course, she is using the concept to describe an intellectual endeavour that, I argue, can also be recognizable in the private discourses and actions of women confronted with discrimination and oppression. The intentional emotional containment that was used to talk about these stories was also an important lesson in women's resistance. Being tough was nothing much, it was really nothing one should brag about and especially not to confront all the popular clichés regarding the weak and strong sexes. The message was: being tough is part of being a woman. Many times people misunderstand this as being "aggressive". Nelson describes exactly the same type of reactions to the work of Arendt, accusations of being "heartless" from reading the intentional emotional detachment—the "unsentimentalism"—she uses to address unspeakable emotional events. (Mis)Interpreting women's emotional detachment as a moral fault is really not a new phenomenon, as there is "a mythological tradition rich in terrible, ruthless, and powerful females" (Vasillopulos 2014, p. 41) that generates an association between lack of emotionality in women with evilness and malignity.

Curiously enough, the uses of humour by women are also a topic of controversy (Billingsley 2019; Crawford 2003; Sauzon 2012). I am not addressing here the many situations where humour is used in gendered work contexts to bond or generate solidarity, to defuse conflicts, to exclude or mock the "other" or even as a self-defeating strategy (Cahill and Densham 2014; Crawford 2003; Watts 2007), but rather the situations where humour has an "emancipatory potential"

(Crawford 2003, p. 1424). As in other political situations of oppression (Hart 2007), humour can become "a promising method of feminist resistance, allowing women to shift oppressive scripts of discourse that discourage women from speaking to a context where women can speak on their own terms" (Billingsley 2017, p. 1). I want therefore to refer to "the uses of humour as a feminist political practice" (Billingsley 2019, p. 10), especially by exposing incongruity (Watson 2015) between rhetoric and practice in relation to gender. Cate Watson[3] discusses how humour can be used against "hegemonic discourse" (p. 417) and demonstrates the role of irony and sarcasm as significant critical analytical tools in relation to contemporary life in academia (2011).

In this melting pot of revolution and oppression, becoming a feminist was, therefore, nothing exceptional. Many times, in and out of classes, the discussions when I was growing up revolved along gender differences and equality—a discussion that, I admit, I later decided to stop having. But, whether you wanted or not, gender was always an issue and the discussions about what was "proper" behaviour for a man or a woman were particularly vivid.[4] Nevertheless, topics that were related to women were a consistent part of my academic pathway as a psychology undergraduate. Now that I think of it, my self-selected assignments always included women: a socio-historical account of women's participation in the labour market, a critical vision of the emergence of motherhood, a review of feminist identity for women (Downing and Roush 1985), the study of witch hunting in the modern ages as a model to conceptualize deviance, and a senior undergraduate internship in the Commission for Feminine Condition (CCF),[5] on a cabinet where interdisciplinary teams of lawyers and psychologists consulted women with a variety of needs, but mainly victims of domestic violence. Even with all

---

[3] I thank Denise Mifsud for pointing me in the direction of Cate Watson.

[4] As a witness of my two daughters' pathways to young adulthood, I am happy to say that some of these discussions are miles away from today's reality, but unfortunately, some of the problems do persist, as the statistics in relation to gender discrimination and dating violence confirm even for the younger generations (UMAR 2019; UNI+ 2019).

[5] That still exists under the designation of Commission for Citizenship and Gender Equality (https://www.cig.gov.pt/).

the stories of exclusion, discrimination and oppression that my grandmother and my mother shared, from before and after the revolution, it was brutal to see how these stories persisted in real life.

> *I am 22 and it's my first day in the CCF, where I will be doing my internship for the whole academic year. Rosa, a psychologist who completed her degree a couple of years ago, is there so that I can learn how a psychologist intervenes in this specific context. She will be there with me for a month and then I will be on my own, although there are lawyers around whom I can turn to. Rosa is really the nicest person, calm and supportive. We talk a bit about what we are supposed to do. The first lady who enters the rooms wears sun glasses. She comes with her daughter, who is a few years older than me, though she is already married. When the lady takes her glasses off, I see the marks: purple to black, around the eyes. She has been beaten up by her husband. Apparently, he does this frequently, and also to their children when they lived home – not surprisingly, they left as soon as they could. They come from an upper class background. She never worked outside the house, and therefore has no money for a lawyer – but she cannot take it anymore. She is afraid. But she speaks out: her tears roll down as she tells us the story of her marriage, of the violence with which she copes forever. She is really frightened; she thinks he might kill her. Never in my life, I saw someone so frightened. Then I look at the daughter, and I see that she too is terrified. Rosa does a wonderful job in supporting both of them, helps the mother find a place to go and tells her how she can get free legal help and psychological support. When they leave, she also does a wonderful job in helping me cope with this – with the sorrow and the rage that comes from listening to these stories. I complete my internship and stay in the CCF for several years, as a part-time extension of my job at the university. This implies doing with other students what Rosa did with me. I really like doing this – but for sure I cannot supplant the nice and supportive ways of Rosa. And, no matter how many years I stayed there, I never, ever, managed to listen without feeling that same kind of sorrow and that same kind of rage. Unfortunately, I saw people frightened and terrified many more times. Unfortunately, I explained (too) many times how these women could find a place to go, free legal help, psychological support. Unfortunately, only very rarely I witnessed their abusers going to jail.*

'Doing Gender' in the Academia[6]

In a relatively recent report by the European Commission, *She Figures 2015*, Portugal stands out, as expected from the data presented above, in terms of the percentage of women graduates, including at the Ph.D. level, and also regarding women working as researchers in higher education, government-based agencies and business sector. But when it comes to women's presence at top levels of academic careers, the picture is clearly different:

> (…) comparing the proportion of women grade A staff within all women academic staff with the proportion of men grade A staff within all men academic staff. In 2013, the concentration of women was lower than the concentration of men in all but two countries (the former Yugoslav Republic of Macedonia and Malta). The highest proportions of women were found in Iceland (27.5%), Malta (25.2%) and Croatia (19.2%), whilst the lowest proportions were found in the former Yugoslav Republic of Macedonia (0.8%), Portugal (1.9%), Lithuania (2.0%), and Germany and Belgium (2.9%). (European Commission 2016, p. 130)

The report includes a "Glass Ceiling Index (GCI)" that compares "the proportion of women in academia (grades A, B, and C) with the proportion of women in top academic positions (grade A positions; equivalent to full professors in most countries)" (p. 137). In 2013, for the 27 EU countries, this index ranges from 0.7 to 3.2, and Portugal is in the EU-27 medium with 1.75, showing that it is more difficult for women to achieve a higher position. This is also evident in a report from the Portuguese Directorate General for Statistics on Education and Science for 2016/17: while the percentage of women working in public universities was 41.7%, at the top positions of the career the asymmetry was much higher for the minority (4.8%) of full professors (23.4%) (Direção-Geral de Estatísticas de Educação e Ciência 2018).

---

[6]Although the concept of "doing Gender" is a classic proposed by Candace West and Don Zimmerman (1987), this subtitle was inspired by the translated title of a book by Maria do Mar Pereira (2012).

When I finished my degree in psychology, I applied for a position as a teaching aide at my faculty. This was not something I had anticipated during my student path and resulted, for the major part, of my internship at the CCF—I admit that I loved the work and found the possibility to apply for this position very exciting. This means that I started working at the university at age 23, with only an initial degree—in my case, a 5-year degree ("licenciatura") in psychology—as was typical in those days when the entrance in the career was pre-doctorate; I signed my first contract on 26 April 1989, and, in December, I got a more stable position as a trainee assistant teacher, again after an open public competition. This was a four-year contract and progression to the next level (assistant teacher) depended on the conclusion of the master degree or (as master courses were rare at the time) an equivalent academic/professional public examination after at least two years. On those days, the presence of women was even lower—a report published in 1991, for my university, shows that women were approximately 30% of the total full-time academic staff, but only 9.5% of full professors (Santos 1991).

However, universities were still governed by a collegial structure that involved people in management since the early years of their academic career—so I got involved in my faculty management bodies early on. This is obviously the advantage of working in a relatively "new" faculty—the faculties of Psychology and Educational Sciences were created in 1979 in the major public universities, after the revolution, as the dictatorship was always suspicious of social sciences and prevented their development in academia (Fernandes-Jesus et al. 2012; Madureira Pinto 1998). Mine was also a predominantly female faculty, with women being the majority of the students and the teaching staff, while men were the minority—nevertheless, both the vast majority of professors and presidents of the students' association were men.

My interest for gender issues continued as an academic: my lecturing included a systematic inclusion of gender as a relevant issue, and the advocacy of non-discrimination, be it in relation to the condition of women, but also of the gay and lesbian community. I wrote what I later learned was the first paper in Portugal advocating affirmative psychotherapy[7] with homosexuals (Menezes and Costa 1992), and in my classes of adolescent and adult development psychology and community psychology, these topics were always included and openly discussed, including gender violence and LGB sexuality. I owe to my supervisor abandoning my initial idea of exploring gender differences in identity construction processes—that I was approaching under a very unsophisticated comparative perspective—and moving towards education for democracy, citizenship and politics, a topic whose personal interest my biography surely helps to understand.

As for my personal experience as an academic, in those early years, I really did not recognize it as exceptionally gendered—well, of course, we "do gender" in our everyday interactions at all time (West and Zimmerman 1987), but the university environment did not appear to me as more misogynous than other life contexts, and, as a public institution, it was surely more regulated by gender equality (in terms of equal career path, equal pay) than private companies. There were plenty of opportunities to explore and develop your research interests, including international collaborations, even if many of those feel a little bit awkward in comparison with the resources we have today, the Internet included. I completed the equivalent to master academic/professional public examination in late 1991, as soon as my contract allowed,[8] and moved to the next step of the academic career as an assistant teacher—a six-year contract during which you were supposed to prepare and present your Ph.D., eventually asking for a three years leave from teaching,[9] which I did not.

---

[7]Affirmative psychotherapy refers to recognizing and advocating homosexuality as a valid identity/sexual orientation, as opposed to currents that use to view homosexuality as a mental health problem or a deviation (Carneiro 2009).

[8]In case you did not have a master degree, the law previewed this alternative academic/professional public examination, but demanded that you had at least a two-year experience teaching at the university.

[9]In my university, almost everyone asked for this three years leave to complete their Ph.D., and I can't remember anyone being denied this time off teaching. I convinced myself I could do the Ph.D. while continuing to teach, and so I did. Of course, it took me five and a half years to complete the Ph.D., but one does silly decisions all the time in real life.

I dare to say that it was only a little later, in relation to mothering, that you were confronted with how being a woman really was a central issue. In those days, having and not having children was always discussed in relation to concluding your Ph.D. My colleagues, who had children, frequently expressed how difficult it was balancing their careers and their responsibilities as mothers and how they felt distressed trying to cope with both roles. One time, I was commenting I wanted to conclude my Ph.D. as soon as I could, and one of my female colleagues immediately stated: "then, you are not going to have children!". To be honest, the whole process of being guilty about the time you spend with your kids *vs.* about the time you spend with your Ph.D. seemed a little too complicated for me, and the idea to postpone motherhood looked smart. It is relatively sad to recognize how the difficulties that my colleagues were living on those days went silenced and unsupported, even when there were women in leadership positions at the faculty. In any case, I/we ended up deciding that having a baby was too important a project to be postponed, and I got pregnant in 1996.

It is "when biology gets you" that you really understand how being a woman is at the centre of your career. Everyone is giving you advice on how to deal with everything from now on. Colleagues from other countries, namely the UK, asked how many years I was going to stop working—and were shocked to discover my maternity leave was only three months. Some female colleagues recommended I should never accept the "medicalization" of pregnancy, and use any kind of anaesthetics during childbirth, that was a "natural" phenomenon—while my mother did not need to remind me how she had two stillborn children for lack of proper medical assistance back in the 1950s. But one is naively convinced that one can transcend structural oppression in one's life: I ended up suggesting to "compensate" for my maternity leave by doubling my course load in the second semester, a suggestion that still shames me until today—but that no women professor, including the dean of the faculty or the president of the scientific council, both women at the time, thought was (as it was) stupid. It was only five years later, when I had my second child, after my Ph.D., that I left the "problem" of my maternity leave to be solved by those whose job was to solve it, *i.e.* the faculty's management boards, not me.

This is not to say that I had a particularly complicated time during my early motherhood years, which I did not—we had paid help, and my family close by. So, I completed my Ph.D. one and a half years after my first daughter was born and became an Assistant Professor; four years later, I applied for a position as an Associate Professor in the Department of Educational Sciences. But the whole process was revealing of how there is a "gendered organisational culture in higher education" (Neale and White 2016, p. 18), and women's academic career paths involve particular challenges that go unrecognized, undiscussed and unsupported—even in departments where we openly label ourselves as feminists. The dominant culture in universities takes men (literally) "as the measure of all things" (Protágoras, 153 BC cit. in Pinto 1995), creating a situation where woman risk inadequacy and disempowerment. As there are no institutional devices, either formal or non-formal, to generate a "strong reflexivity" (Harding 1992), this dominant culture is internalized and, as with other situations of oppression, any personal deviation is interpreted as the individual's fault or wrongdoing, generating a situation where the "victims" are blamed for their own "inadequacy" (Ryan 1971), with potentially severe consequences on their power to promote wellness and resist oppression (Prilleltensky 2008).[10]

During the years after my Ph.D., my emphasis on citizenship and politics became more and more central to my work—and so did my approach to Political Psychology and Citizenship Education, even if strongly flavoured with strong connections with other disciplines such as Educational Sciences, Political Science, Political Sociology, and Political Philosophy. My tendency to find crossing (disciplinary) borders more interesting than staying inside your "own discipline" (Rappaport 2005) did not start here, but the topic of my research clearly reinforced this. The fact that I got a position in the Department of Educational Sciences is both a recognition and a reinforcement of this tendency, as Educational Sciences are founded on disciplinary and methodological

---

[10]This patriarchal culture was probably more pervasive for students, as gender issues—especially LGB topics—were frequently approached in a very unsophisticated way, when not overly conservative and discriminatory. This coexisted with feminist approaches, but also with openly affirmative and anti-discrimination discourses.

hybridism (Charlot 2006; Hofsteter 2012). In this sense, my academic path, although agentic, is not really an example of directionality, of that kind of "entrepreneurship" that one might recognize in academics who always make the "right" choices in terms of issues to research and people to connect to. On the contrary: my appreciation of pluralism and diversity, my strong conviction that we can learn even in the most unpredicted places and my love for intervention (and, I admit, the fact that I sometimes get bored) make my career having an "intrinsically disordered nature" where connections with multiple others, people, topics and disciplines, is the *motto*. And, of course, this was only possible because several people in my faculty and beyond provided the care, the support, the encouragement and the trust without which we do not exist as someone who is free to act and free to think—these many others who were there for me, seeing and hearing (Arendt 1958).

Anyway, it was only when I started to interact more broadly at the university level, beyond my own faculty, that the gendered culture of the organization definitely revealed itself, including some expression of open sexism. And it is then that you need all your toughness and your humour to resist and confront oppression.

Confronting Power by Being Explicitly Feminist

In the last decades, a neoliberal agenda transformed European universities (Veiga et al. 2015): from "primarily government by academics" with the protection of the state that controlled "non-academic matters", into "corporate-like models of government (…) [with] increased institutional autonomy" (p. 398). However, the rise in managerialism resulted in an evident loss of autonomy, with a "shift from a republic of scholars to a stakeholder organization (Bleiklie and Kogan 2007) and empowered boards in university governance as key structures in defining the organization's strategies" (p. 399). In Portugal, this was materialized in 2007 by a new legal framework that resulted in significant changes on governance, with lower levels of collegiality, the involvement of "civil society" external stakeholders, and the creation of smaller governance structures with the argument of effectiveness.

The revision of the statuses of my university was marked by some intense public discussions, where concerns for what some of us felt as a diminishing of participation and democratic legitimacy were voiced. For instance, the rector was now to be elected by a board of 23 people, including 15 internal representatives (12 academics, 4 students and 1 staff) and 6 external stakeholders, instead of an assembly of more than 200 representatives, who were elected by the university but also within each faculty. The first elections after the revision were particularly marked by these concerns, and several organized lists of candidates appeared, with also very diverse visions of what the university should be. The electoral process involves a combination of list and uninominal voting: each voter selects an individual candidate inside a list. Even if this raises problems, particularly for smaller faculties, it also creates opportunities for higher control by voters. In my particular case, it was my reputation for being tough that got me into becoming a candidate—and, although I never asked, my impression is that it was my faculty colleagues' trust in my toughness that got them to vote for me. All of a sudden, I saw myself being elected for a completely new position at a level of governance where I had almost no experience. Not surprisingly, the majority of the elected were men, a tendency that is also detectable in other universities: on a study of general councils in Portuguese universities, the percentage of female representatives is, on the whole, always below 50%, even if higher for the staff (41%) and for academics (31%), than for students (17%) or external representatives (19%) (Oliveira et al. 2014).[11] As these are selected by the elected internal members, this suggests that "the validity and the range of the pluralism of the lists in the effort of ensuring other forms of representativeness" (ibid., p. 86) is questionable.

I am 44. I am in a meeting of a council in University XXX. This is a large and a bit pompous meeting room, with portraits of former Rectors hanging on the wall. All the former Rectors are men. The President of the council is

---

[11]Although Oliveira et al. (2014) refer that the percentage of women elected in my university was 40%, in fact it was only 33.3%.

2 Being Tough, Being Humorous and Being Explicitly Feminist ...

a successful entrepreneur from outside academia. We are in the middle of a discussion regarding who should be invited to become a member of the Board of Trustees. The Board involves people representing the diversity of "civil society" organizations outside the university. My colleagues are identifying possible candidates, mostly men. I suggest that gender should be one important criterion: that we should explicitly think of women to be invited. I give one or two examples. A colleague contests: "gender is irrelevant for the discussion! If there are valid female candidates, it's OK to consider them, but not because they are women!". In his view, he states, "this is a discussion that makes no sense in the University that is, by definition, a place of meritocracy!" – he really means to use the word in a positive way. I interrupt (one is not supposed to), smiling and saying "I am sorry, I am so sorry, but all my life I wanted to say this: [I point towards the pictures and say, in English] I rest my case!". [this is a popular statement in court movies and TV serials]. My colleagues around the room, even those who disagree with me, openly laugh. Gender ends up being recurrently considered in similar debates in the future, at least when I am involved. At least when I am there, nobody uses the "gender does not make a difference" argument anymore. But, of course, they tend to look at me or invoke my name when gender is an issue.

My experience in this board, as well as other more recent experiences in councils or assemblies that involve some degree of institutional power, is that women are generally the minority. Even in fields where women are clearly the majority of professionals or experts, the presence of women tends to be very limited. It is not that women are not welcomed or even supported in those places, it is that, like in my memory above, people have to be reminded to even think of women. This implies that you have to openly advocate *all the time* against "gender maldistribution and gender misrecognition" (Fraser 2007, p. 23). Of course, this does not come without implications. It implies that *all the time* you have to be tough, and *all the time* you have to be humorous—whichever works best for you and the situation—to guarantee that you confront gender injustice. And it is this—the active, systematic and continuous advocacy for redistribution and recognition—that generates both surprising levels of solidarity and astonishing expressions of open sexism. Unfortunately, I found people, inside and out of the academia, who argued for the need to implement the "best European practices" but reacted in sexist ways in relation to women in positions of power—commenting on their looks, referring to their family arrangements. But I also witnessed intense reactions of sisterhood (and brotherhood) from colleagues and people I hardly knew, who were more than ready to argue in favour of gender justice. In this sense, as Watson (2015, p. 416) demonstrates, "laughter (…) has [many times] the capacity to bring about an ironic epiphany" that exposes discrimination.

Being explicitly feminist also has implications in other dimensions of our own career as academics and particularly on the power that each of us possesses. Mistrusting and confronting power should not be limited to mistrusting and confronting the power of "others" but also our own power. This means keeping an eye on your own power and the ways in which you exert it, especially in these days of intense performativity. Concerns with redistribution and representation are not only located on the "outside world", but should consider your own practices within your own research group—especially as the university is "dissolving into the wider world" (Barnett 2000, p. 20), becoming a place that fosters a rhetoric of "excellence" (Readings 1996), "employability" and "entrepreneurship" (Menezes et al. 2018), but with much less actual opportunities for young academics in comparison with those days I entered academia. That is why the metaphor of the "intrinsically disordered nature" of my career made particular sense to me when thinking about this chapter. An intrinsically disordered protein prefers to make multiple connections with diverse others, rather than being focused on one specific target or directionality (Uversky 2013). I trust that these proteins, like myself, believe in the essentially collaborative and collective nature of meaning-making and knowledge construction processes. To remember this at the end of a biographical account of your career might be paradoxical, but it's good to know that you only did it—and that was most of the fun—because you were doing it with others.

References

Arendt, H. (1990|1963). *On revolution*. London: Penguin Books.
Arendt, H. (2001|1958). *A condição humana*. Lisboa: Relógio D' Água.
Baptista, V. R. (2014, setembro). Reflexões sobre a evolução do trabalho feminino em Portugal. In *Plataforma Barómetro Social - Plataforma virtual de reflexão e de análise sobre a sociedade portuguesa e o seu posicionamento no contexto Internacional*, 3.ª Série. http://www.barometro.com.pt/2014/10/05/reflexoes-sobre-a-evolucao-do-trabalho-feminino-em-portugal/. Accessed 4 Feb 2019.
Barnett, R. (2000). *Realizing the university in an age of supercomplexity*. Buckingham: Society for Research into Higher Education and Open University Press.
Billingsley, A. (2017). *Laughing against patriarchy: Humor, silence, and feminist resistance*. Available at http://pages.uoregon.edu/uophil/files/Philosophy_Matters_Submission_Marvin_Billingsley.pdf. Accessed 15 Jan 2019.
Billingsley, A. (2019). *Humorwork, feminist philosophy, and unstable politics*. Unpublished doctoral dissertation, Department of Philosophy, University of Oregon. Available at https://scholarsbank.uoregon.edu/xmlui/bitstream/handle/1794/24550/Billingsley_oregon_0171A_12395.pdf?sequence=1&isAllowed=y. Accessed 14 May 2019.
Bosniak, L. (2002). Citizenship and work. *North Carolina Journal of International Law and Commercial Regulation, 27*(3), 497–506.
Cahill, S., & Densham, R. (2014). *Women, humour and power ...in the workplace: A review of the current literature for Funny Women*. https://www.academia.edu/38284590/Women_Humour_and_Power_in_the_Workplace_A_review_of_the_current_Literature?email_work_card=title. Accessed 8 Feb 2019.
Carneiro, N. S. (2009). *Homossexualidades: uma psicologia entre ser, pertencer e participar*. Porto: LivrPsic.
Charlot, B. (2006). A pesquisa educacional entre conhecimentos, políticas e práticas: especificidades e desafios de uma área de saber. *Revista Brasileira de Educação, 11*(31), 7–18.
Crawford, N. (2003). Gender and humor in social context. *Journal of Pragmatics, 35,* 1413–1430.
Direção-Geral de Estatísticas de Educação e Ciência. (2018). *Perfil do docente 2016/2017*. http://www.dgeec.mec.pt/np4/EstatDocentes/%7B$clientServletPath%7D/?newsId=138&fileName=DGEEC_DSEE_DEEBS_2018_PerfildoDocente161.pdf. Accessed 11 Feb 2019.
dos Santos, C. (1991). *A mulher na Universidade do Porto*. Porto: Afrontamento.

Downing, N. E., & Roush, K. L. (1985). From passive acceptance to active commitment: A model of feminist identity development for women. *The Counselling Psychologist, 13*(4), 695–709. https://doi.org/10.1177/0011000085134013.
European Commission. (2016). *She figures 2015*. Luxembourg: Publications Office of the European Union. https://ec.europa.eu/research/swafs/pdf/pub_gender_equality/she_figures_2015-final.pdf. Accessed 11 Feb 2019.
Faúndez, X., & Goecke, X. (2015). Psychosocial trauma transmission and appropriation in grandchildren of former political prisoners of the civic-military dictatorship in Chile (1973–1990). *Journal of Social Science Education, 14*(2), 26–39. https://doi.org/10.2390/jsse-v14-i2-1446.
Fernandes-Jesus, M., Ferreira, P., & Menezes, I. (2012). Psicologia Política em Portugal: A importância de cruzar fronteiras. *Psicologia Política, 12*(25), 509–530.
Fishman, R. M. (2018). What 25 April was and why it mattered. *Portuguese Studies, 34*(1), 20–34. https://doi.org/10.5699/portstudies.34.1.0020.
Fraser, N. (2007). Feminist politics in the age of recognition: A two-dimensional approach to gender justice. *Studies in Social Justice, 1*(1), 23–35.
Harding, S. (1992). Rethinking standpoint epistemology: What is "strong objectivity?" *The Centennial Review, 36*(3), 437–470.
Hart, M. (2007). Humour and social protest: An introduction. *IRSH, 52,* 1–20. https://doi.org/10.1017/S0020859007003094.
Hofstetter, R. (2012). Educational sciences: Evolutions of a pluridisciplinary discipline at the crossroads of other disciplinary and professional fields (20th century). *British Journal of Educational Studies, 60*(4), 317–335.
Madureira Pinto, J. (1998). Sociology in Portugal: Formation and recent trends. In A. N. Almeida (Ed.), *Terra Nostra: Challenges, controversies and languages for sociology and the social sciences for the 21st century. Proceedings for the ISA Conference for the Lusophone World, Lisboa, Portugal, 1997* (pp. 57–65). Montréal: International Sociological Association.
Marshall, T. H. (1950). *Citizenship and social class and other essays*. London: Cambridge University Press.
Menezes, I., Coelho, M., & Amorim, J. P. (2018). Social and public responsibility, universities. In J. C. Shin & P. Teixeira (Eds.), *Encyclopedia of international higher education systems and institutions*. Dordrecht: Springer. https://doi.org/10.1007/978-94-017-9553-1_361-1.
Menezes, I., & Costa, M. E. (1992). Amor entre iguais: a psicoterapia da diferença. *Cadernos de Consulta Psicológica, 8,* 79–84.

Morais, M. M., & Carvalho, J. E. (1993). *A presença das mulheres no ensino superior em Portugal*. Lisboa: Comissão para a Igualdades e para os Direitos das Mulheres.

Neale, J., & White, K. (2016). The university environment: Opportunities, constraints and challenges for senior women. *Ex æquo, 33*, 17–29.

Nelson, D. (2017). *Tough enough: Arbus, Arendt, Didion, McCarthy, Sontag, Weil*. Chicago: The University of Chicago Press.

Nunes, A. B. (1991). A evolução da estrutura, por sexos, da população activa em Portugal – um indicador do crescimento económico (1890–1981). *Análise Social, XXVI*(112–113), 3.º–4.º, 707–722.

Oliveira, A. C., Peixoto, P., & Silva, S. (2014). *O papel dos Conselhos Gerais no Governo das Universidades Públicas Portuguesas: a lei e a prática*. Coimbra: Imprensa da Universidade de Coimbra. http://hdl.handle.net/10316.2/35053. https://doi.org/10.14195/978-989-26-0939-3. Accessed 13 Feb 2019.

Pateman, C. (1992). Equality, difference, subordination: The politics of motherhood and women's citizenship. In G. Bock & S. James (Eds.), *Beyond equality and difference: Citizenship, feminist politics and female subjectivity* (pp. 14–27). London: Routledge.

Pereira, M. M. (2012). *Fazendo género no recreio. A negociação do género em espaço escolar*. Lisboa: ICS.

Pinto, M. J. V. (1995). A "medida das coisas" entre o Homem e Deus—algumas reflexões sobre o frag. 1 de Protágoras. *Revista da Faculdade de Ciências Sociais e Humanas, 2*(8), 321–331.

Prilleltensky, I. (2008). The role of power in wellness, oppression, and liberation: The promise of psychopolitical validity. *Journal of Community Psychology, 36*(2), 116–136. https://doi.org/10.1002/jcop.20225.

Rappaport, J. (2005). Community Psychology is (thank God) more than science. *American Journal of Community Psychology, 35*(3–4), 231–238. https://doi.org/10.1007/s10464-005-3402-6.

Readings, B. (1996). *The university in ruins*. Cambridge, MA: Harvard University Press.

Ribeiro, N., Ferreira, P., Malafaia, C., & Menezes, I. (2015). The 'Europeanization' of gender policies in Portugal: Transformations in women's access to civil, political and social rights. In M. Barrett & B. Zani (Eds.), *Political and civic engagement: Multidisciplinary perspectives* (pp. 403–419). London: Routledge.

Ryan, W. (1971). *Blaming the victim*. New York: Random House.

Sauzon, V. (2012). Le rire comme enjeu féministe: une lecture de l'humour dans Les mouflettes d'Atropos de Chloé Delaume et Baise-moi de Virginie Despentes. *Recherches Féministes, 25*(2), 65–81. https://doi.org/10.7202/1013523ar.
UMAR. (2019). *Estudo nacional sobre a violência no namoro*. Retrieved from http://www.umarfeminismos.org/images/stories/noticias/Estudo_Nacional_VN_2019_da_UMAR.pdf.
UNI+. (2019). *Estudo nacional sobre a violência no namoro em contexto universitário: Crenças e práticas—2017/2019*. Retrieved from https://drive.google.com/file/d/1ZB_U-I9v1X0o_rvRxXauYIoqQ7HlwvAG/view.
Uversky, V. N. (2013). Intrinsic disorder-based protein interactions and their modulators. *Current Pharmaceutical Design, 19*(23), 4191–4213. https://doi.org/10.2174/13816128113192300005.
Vasillopulos, C. (2014). Through a glass darkly. *Jung Journal, 8*(1), 41–56. https://doi.org/10.1080/19342039.2014.866033.
Veiga, A., Magalhães, A. M., & Amaral, A. (2015). From collegial governance to boardism: Reconfiguring governance in higher education. In J. Huisman, H. de Boer, D. Dill, & M. Souto-Otero (Eds.), *The Palgrave international handbook of higher education policy and governance* (pp. 398–416). London: Palgrave Macmillan.
Vieira, C. (2018, July 4–6). *Carolina Beatriz Ângelo (1878–1911): A visionary woman who challenged the social order of her time*. Paper presented at the European Seminar of the ESREA Research Network History of Adult Education and Training in Europe: "Pioneering Women and Men in European Adult Education (19th and early 20th Centuries)", Paris.
Watson, C. (2011). Notes on the variety and uses of satire, sarcasm and irony in social research, with some observations on vices and follies in the academy. *Power and Education, 3*(2), 139–149.
Watson, C. (2015). A sociologist walks into a bar (and other academic challenges): Towards a methodology of humour. *Sociology, 49*(3), 407–421.
Watts, J. (2007). Can't take a joke? Humour as resistance, refuge and exclusion in a highly gendered workplace. *Feminism & Psychology, 17*(2), 259–266. https://doi.org/10.1177/0959353507076560.
West, C., & Zimmerman, D. H. (1987). Doing gender. *Gender and Society, 1*(2), 125–151.

3

'You Must Wait to Be Asked': Career Advancement and the Maternal Body

Caroline Gatrell

Introduction

Research demonstrates consistently how the route to professor is gendered. It has been shown how structural inequalities within academic systems can make it hard for women to achieve the status of Chair (Fotaki 2013).

It has been argued, for example, that women academics may be judged on their 'maternal bodies' (or their potential for reproduction) rather than on scholarly performance (Fotaki 2013; Gatrell 2013; Greenberg et al. 2019; Tyler 2000; Höpfl 2000). Relatedly, women's commitment to the academy might be questioned due to institutional assumptions that female scholars might prioritize motherhood over employment irrespective of whether they are, in practice, parents. Among women who do not have children (regardless of whether

---

C. Gatrell (✉)
Professor of Organization Studies,
University of Liverpool Management School, Liverpool, UK
e-mail: C.Gatrell@liverpool.ac.uk

they might, or might not, subsequently become parents), the potential for maternity may be sufficient to invoke questions around women's work-orientation (see Gatrell 2013; van Amsterdam 2014; Tyler 2000). Women who do have children are assumed often (whatever their occupation) to be heterosexual and home-oriented, rather than work-orientated (Hakim 2002), supposedly adapting their careers to suit children's (and, if applicable, husbands') needs. Academic women's bodies may habitually be treated as 'other' and as 'lacking' within the masculine oeuvre of the classroom setting (Fotaki 2013; Sinclair 2000; Swan 2005).

On Being a 'Maternal Body'

I began my doctoral research in 1998 when my eldest child was aged one. I became pregnant with my youngest in 2000. I was not in receipt of a grant or fellowship, so I had registered part-time for my Ph.D. in the university where I was employed, gaining a position as a part-time junior teaching fellow to support my studies.

The teaching experience acquired in those early years has always stood me in good stead, and it was helpful to be on-site at the university where I was registered as this enabled me to attend Ph.D. training sessions and use the library. The disadvantages of being on a teaching-only (as opposed to a 'teaching and research') contract, however, lay in assumptions made by some colleagues that part-time teaching fellows with young children were unlikely to achieve a research career ('*she won't ever publish*') as well as the unforeseen problem that the lack of a formal 'studentship' offered less prestige than, say, a grant from the Economic and Social Research Council would have done.

My research topic centred on transitions to motherhood among employed women. I was intrigued by an intellectual mismatch (Mason 2002) between claims regarding a supposed lack of maternal commitment to paid work (Hakim 1996, 2002), and social trends showing how women were more likely, in 1998 than in the past, to maintain continuous employment post-birth (Dex et al. 1998). My Ph.D. focused on how mothers combined pregnancy and new maternity with professional paid work—a topic which I continue to research, and to write about, to the present day (Gatrell et al. 2017).

As I engaged with my Ph.D. research and reflected upon notions of justice and equality at work (Equal Opportunities Commission 2007), I learned how pregnant and newly maternal workers often felt marginalized and out of place in organizations. Feelings among pregnant workers that they should 'appease' co-workers and line managers for combining pregnancy with paid work by, for example, working when unwell were (and still are) common (Gatrell 2011; Longhurst 2001, 2008; van Amsterdam 2014). Women with pregnant and newly maternal bodies are associated both metaphorically and literally with the notion of 'leakage' (Shildrick 1997) as the female body changes shape and begins to produce maternal liquids associated with the baby (amniotic fluid; breast milk). Metaphorically, the pregnant body may be regarded as threatening at work due to its potential for hormonal changes which might (supposedly) invoke the spilling over of emotion, with potential to disrupt apparent rationality of scholarly routine (Shildrick 1997, see also Ashcraft 1999; Greenberg et al. 2019; Höpfl and Atkinson 2000; Miller 2005).

Literally, the bodies of pregnant and newly maternal scholars may be classified as 'leaky' because they grow in size, with maternal 'liquids' such as breast milk posing materially the potential for 'leakage' (Longhurst 2001, 2008; Warren and Brewis 2004). As Höpfl (2000, p. 101) observes, professional organizations such as universities are not places which are welcoming towards women *with 'physical bodies which produce… breast milk and maternal smells'*. 'Leaky' pregnant and newly maternal, breastfeeding bodies, may be associated by colleagues (and sometimes among expectant and new mothers themselves, Warren and Brewis 2004) with unpredictability and discomfiture (Shildrick 1997; see also Acker 2003; Hennekam 2016; Hennekam et al. 2019). Exploring how 'leaky' pregnant bodies may be treated as unwelcome in organizations, sociocultural scholars extend such debates suggesting that pregnant and newly maternal (especially if breastfeeding) bodies may be treated as a source of organizational disgust, or 'abjection' (Tyler 2000). Bodies which toil to grow another body within, while at the same time carrying out organizational duties, may be identified by co-workers as 'taboo' (Gatrell et al. 2017).

Imogen Tyler (2000, p. 290) writes compellingly about her experiences of being heavily pregnant in a university setting, feeling awkward and 'inappropriate' as she attends a philosophy seminar on a hot day. Tyler recalls the sensation of feeling *'heavy and swollen'*, a *'leaky vessel [which] might split apart at any moment…not metaphor but real alien… my body'*. She recounts how the speaker and some colleagues studiously ignored her presence. They evaded philosophical questions about the female body, which might contain another body within itself, Tyler recollecting how: *'my massive pregnant body wants to stand up, to go to the front of the [seminar room], to present itself as a question'*.

In keeping with Tyler's (2000) recollections (see also van Amsterdam 2014; Longhurst 2001), my own experiences of being pregnant while working in a university setting left me with a sense that some colleagues were uncomfortable around pregnancy and new motherhood. In 2000, for example, while I was expecting my second child and in the third trimester of pregnancy, a lecturer colleague parked his vehicle so close to mine that I was unable to open the driver's door of my car wide enough to be able to get in. So I had to go and find the colleague. On moving his car to allow me more space, he asked, not unkindly: *'But Caroline, should you be driving at all? Is it suitable for you even to be here, at the University? Shouldn't you be at home?'*

I recall apologizing to him and driving home with a sense that my pregnant body did not quite fit within the university environment. Through my pregnant presence, I had overstepped an organizational understanding of what was deemed 'appropriate' embodied comportment at work (Tyler 2000, p. 290; see also Longhurst 2001, 2008).

A little nearer my due date, a senior colleague with whom I had regular meetings asked if towels and hot water might be required during our discussions. He expressed anxiety that I might give birth on his office floor and asked when I might begin maternity leave and 'go home'. He indicated his view that 'going home' ought to occur sooner rather than later, from which I inferred (despite the humorous tone of the conversation) that he felt discomfited in the presence of my visibly maternal body. 'Going home', however, was not something I felt keen to do.

My reluctance to begin maternity leave occurred because university decisions regarding whether or not to renew my teaching contract had been 'deferred'. The lack of a renewed contract raised the question as to whether, consequently, I would be offered any paid maternity leave. In response to my colleague's question about 'going home', I thus proposed that I might opt not to take maternity leave at all. If necessary, I warned him, I would plan (as he feared) to give birth in his office and remain at the university, working continuously once the baby was born until the date when my contract expired.

The day after I had made this pronouncement, I received an urgent phone call from the HR department. They informed me that the decision about my contract was no longer 'deferred'; it had been reactivated. My contract would be renewed for a further three years and, as a result, I would receive maternity pay.

In pursuing the reading for my Ph.D., I realized that I was not alone in such experiences. Accounts among and between pregnant scholars, experiencing their bodies as 'out of place' within university settings, showed (and continue to show) how pregnant and newly maternal academics might often feel their presence to be a cause of unease and discomfiture within scholarly settings (Tyler 2000; Greenberg et al. 2019; van Amsterdam 2014).

By the following year, I had given birth to my youngest child and was back at work. I was still working as a junior part-time teacher and trying to finish off my Ph.D., with one baby and one infant in tow. Shortly following my return to work I experienced two encounters which occurred in close proximity and which, looking back, I recall as significant in relation to the journey towards a professorship. Without these two occurrences, I wonder if the path I later followed would have led me to where I am today.

Two Significant Events

The first of these events was hosted by the university faculty which housed the Departments of Sociology and Women's Studies. I was invited to attend an afternoon drinks party in my role as Ph.D. student (as a teaching fellow, I was employed within a Management School). The purpose of this party was to celebrate the circumstance that 20% of professors across the university were women. The speaker at this celebration event was male, and he seemed pleased with this achievement. To me, it did not sound exactly awe-inspiring. The speaker explained how this percentage had been attained (from a previously lower level). He acknowledged that the percentage could be higher, but offered a range of structural and organizational explanations for why this was not the case. As the applause began and glasses were raised, a seasoned and well-known feminist scholar leaned across towards me and said: '*I wonder. It couldn't just be down to good old-fashioned sexism, could it?*' At a subsequent Ph.D. seminar, the women students discussed the occasion and it filled us with a sense of determination. We wanted to expand the 20% by becoming professors ourselves, and we would work hard to get there.

The second influential occurrence took place just a few short weeks after the 'Celebrating 20 per cent' party. This second event was an open seminar, advertised specifically for women and entitled (similarly to this book) 'Making it to Professor'. The Making Professor event attracted a large audience of women (and one or two men) at all levels from across the university. The speaker panel was comprised entirely of women professors who recounted their own experiences of getting to professorial level, outlining the requirements and the hurdles of getting there. Although in later years I attended other, similar events, this first was the most influential because it explained clearly to me, and the wider group of Ph.D. students who attended, what might be possible. If these women professors could make it and were prepared to share with us their experiences, then couldn't we all do it? The session offered a clear indication of what was needed to become professor, providing a list of criteria and a pathway to follow, mapping out the various career stages from being very junior to gaining a Chair.

I came away from that session having learned some key information. First, that for a woman to gain a Chair would be hard work and, probably, doors would not be held open in quite the same way that they might be for some men. Second, I learned that gaining a Chair was not the end-point—once achieved, it could be a challenge to uphold the position in a situation where women might be surveilled closely by others (see Fotaki 2013; Davidson and Cooper 1992). It appears that not everyone is comfortable with the notion of women professors. At the Making Professor event, speakers told of unpleasant behaviours and complaints directed towards them from both staff and some students, often occurring almost immediately after their elevation to professor had been announced. Third, that gaining a Chair was not necessarily open to all men—one of the few junior male colleagues who attended that session whispered to me at the end '*it won't ever happen for me, you know. You have to be "the right sort of chap"*'.

Yet although the session articulated all the difficulties of making it to professor, the fourth and key important point which we all took from the event was that the door to becoming a woman professor might be open, even if this was only a crack—what my late father would have termed: 'the thin end of the wedge'. What was needed, among those of us in attendance, was to get a foot in the door. It might not be easy for women to gain a Chair, but that day we were shown by the speakers who shared with us their experiences that it was could be feasible for women to aspire to this level. And due to the clear explanations offered by the speakers, we now had a sense of which paths we might follow.

In the years that ensued, I used that initial session as a reference point to build on, adding in advice from colleagues along the way. Some of the opportunities that came my way were serendipitous, some were strategic (at least in the sense that I applied for things and metaphorically pushed at the door, rather than hoping it might open). But subsequent to that event, for myself and the others present, a goal was in sight, and we had clear objectives to work towards.

In 2013, I did make it to professor. The observations and 'handy hints' which follow in this chapter are taken from a talk which I have given a number of times on 'Managing your Research Career'—the first presentation of which took place at another session entitled 'Making it to Professor', where I spoke myself, a few weeks after being promoted to Chair.

Developing a Research Narrative

Today, although I continue to develop new theoretical ideas about parenting and work, my research remains as it was when I studied for my Ph.D.: focused on parents and employment with a scholarly emphasis on gender and the body. From an early stage, I learned that what I term the 'maternal body' (a body with potential for childbirth) can evoke emotional, rather than scholarly, responses.

For example, on the first occasion that I presented my research (as a Ph.D. student within the context of a class on 'Shaping your PhD'), my focus on employed mothers proved contentious, student colleagues becoming vocal in their opinions to the point where voices were raised. One man stated '*We've heard enough about women. What about men?*' Another male student suggested that mothers should '*not be at work at all, they should be at home, breastfeeding*'. The class tutor accused the men of '*womb envy*' and suggested we finish the session early; she had had enough. On that occasion, I did not know what to say. I expressed some frustration with these views but without at that point being able to clearly evidence my arguments. Joining me for coffee afterwards, my friend suggested I had (unintentionally) thrown the equivalent of a firework into the seminar room.

On a subsequent occasion a few years later (teaching a session on breastfeeding and employment to a class of sociology students at a neighbouring institution), I found the research area of new motherhood to be the butt of jokes. Some of the male students at the back of the room made crude references to breastfeeding; in retrospect I suspect they may have been embarrassed by the topic: an example of the maternal body as discomfiting or abject (Tyler 2000).

As Özbilgin et al. (2011) suggest, however, when researching a controversial scholarly area, knowledge is everything. Arguments are more effective if grounded in evidence from the literatures, and from your own research. On that occasion, I handled the situation more adeptly—I explained why the research was important and to whom, and how it fitted into the various landscape of sociology, work and health. The jokes and teasing about breasts and leakage developed into an engaging classroom discussion about infant feeding, employment and the maternal body.

In the intervening years, clarity about what interview panels might typically describe as 'your intellectual project' (or what your research is about), has stood me in good stead. I gained my first 'proper' lecturer post in 2007, with Lancaster University Management School. Because I had begun to build up a publication profile (and after applying for several jobs) I was able to move from a teaching only, to a 'teaching and research' lecturer's contract. As a new lecturer, I had a full teaching load and quite heavy administrative responsibilities. During my first term in my new department, the then Head tried to persuade me to move my interests away from bodies, parenthood and employment. She indicated her view that '*we can't recognise your research*' due to genuine concerns that management journals might be reluctant to publish the topics about which I wanted to write. It seemed (in keeping with the observations of Höpfl (2000) and Fotaki (2013)) that the maternal body was not always welcome in the context of management scholarship, perhaps because it was seen as research with potential to disrupt more comfortable and abstract narratives about 'strategy' and 'learning'. In this situation, a focus on what I wanted to do and say in research terms (and having already begun to publish on parenting, bodies and work) gave me confidence to continue. In keeping with the advice from Özbilgin et al. (2011), I had sufficient research evidence to show that the area of research was important and relevant to management studies. I considered that parenting (both motherhood and fatherhood) was under-researched in relation to work–life balance, flexibility and employment. So I put to one side the advice about changing my research approach and kept going in the field where I felt I had a contribution to make. I started to gain acceptances within management (as well as sociology and health) journals, and the departmental resistance to my chosen topic area (due to worries that I might not gain any publications to contribute to various departmental performance measures) fell away.

The reason for mentioning here the above suggestion that I should change research tack is because the act of resisting such pressures assisted me in thinking through and building up a clear research narrative. Thinking back to the early and influential conference on 'Making it to Professor', one characteristic shared among all the women presenters was their commitment to, and clarity about, what their research area comprised. As I prepared my own application for a Personal Chair in 2012, a senior female colleague suggested: '*to be a professor you need to "**profess**" something. Be clear about what it is you are an expert **in**'.*

Writing my application, this advice was not difficult to follow. I was clear about where my research was going, and my publication history aligned with my narrative—the consistent focus was exploring parenting, employment and work–life balance, often through the lens of the body, health and gender. Yet the achievement of this important focus was in many ways serendipitous, rather than strategic. I had an idea from the start about what I wanted to research. I had been reading around various possibilities and was influenced by a senior female colleague who advised me to choose an area '*which burns you up*' rather than one which seems easy or suitable, and my supervisors were supportive of such guidance. However, I did not in those early stages make connections between research emphasis and any hopes I might have had of later becoming a professor.

My research trajectory could potentially have been derailed along the way, perhaps because it led me into sometimes difficult situations, perhaps because others tried to persuade me away from parenthood/maternity towards more conventional management topics or, possibly, because I could have been drawn into roles (such as research associate) where my job was to support the research area of a senior colleague, rather than prioritizing personal interests.

Arguably, the challenge of finding clarity about your own research narrative is ever more pressing, now that most institutions are engaged with key 'performative measures' (in the UK, the Research Excellence Framework or 'REF') which impose disciplinary regimes on academic communities (Knights and Clarke 2013). So, thinking early about where you hope to specialize, and seeking to keep your own research interests within your sight-line is a useful strategy (Murray 2019). Should you decide to change direction this should be as a result of a decision which you own (i.e. something you have chosen, not something you have been persuaded into) and which you have planned, so that at each stage along the promotion process you can make a convincing case as regards what it is you intend to 'profess'.

Added to the strategy of owning your own area of interest, it is important to gain a good understanding of the publication 'currency' in your institution (Murray 2019). Is it books, or papers? Is there a preferred publisher or journal in your department? In the UK, this means understanding what your institution requires for the REF. It is relevant to note here that the REF is regarded by some scholars as narrowing, surveillant and destructive, invoking anxiety among many scholars. As Gabriel (2010, p. 769) observes: '*I doubt that there are many professions whose members are so relentlessly subjected to measurement, criticism and rejection as academics, exposing them to deep insecurities regarding their worth, their identity and their standing*'.

I do empathize with Gabriel's viewpoint; it seems that academics are continually evaluated with regard to both research and teaching, which means that university environments can be challenging. Yet for junior scholars, it is also arguable that performative systems like the REF can provide guidance; a pathway forward. For mothers, or part-time workers, or anyone who is searching for a pathway to make professor, the REF can offer a picture of how you can demonstrate your value and your intellect within your area of expertise. Some departments or disciplines have 'lists' within which journals are ranked in accordance with perceived prestige and status (Management Schools do this). Even if your school/department, or subject group does not appear to hold a formal list, the more senior scholars among any given arena will surely know the leading journals in their field, and which of these to aim for. For me and the junior Management School colleagues with whom I was now working, discovering what was then called the 'Association of Business Schools' journal list (now the Academic Journal Guide) was helpful. It revealed which management journals 'counted', and which were considered less important. As a management sociologist, I was pleased to discover that some health and sociology journals were included on the list. Finding out which key journals are valued in your field can be very useful. If they are not on a list and there is no-one you can ask, look at the publication lists of top scholars in your area to see where they publish. A publication in what is deemed, within your subject area, to be a 'top' journal, can open doors and is worth striving for, so long as you can still write about what is important to you. This not to say that achieving a good publication is easy. However, there are steps you can take to help you develop and frame your submission. Increasingly, doctoral and early career networks put on training events to support scholars in publication. These might be accessed via your own institution or at conferences, via learned societies. Journals too will often organize writing workshops, usually at conferences, which offer relevant and specific advice about what they are looking for from authors. It helps to read carefully recent publications in the journal you are aiming for so that you can join in the debates that are uppermost in readers' minds and, although it might sound obvious, do read the author guidelines and ensure you frame your submission around these. Two very helpful books which elaborate on the publication process, which I have turned to over the years and which offer pragmatic and feasible advice on publication are Delamont and Atkinson (2004) and Murray (2019).

Don't Wait to Be Asked

The management research on women and management suggests that women who seek career progression face a conflict, regardless of whether such advancement is in terms of pay and promotion, or whether it includes access to related activities such as interesting (and CV enhancing) assignments (Bevan and Gatrell 2017). Such conflict lies in the situation whereby women may often be diffident about putting themselves forward, and less likely than equivalent men to ask for increases in remuneration and/or status (Babcock and Laschever 2009). Yet at the same time, it is shown how women who do articulate a desire for additional pay or career enhancement can face penalties, due to being regarded as pushy and over-assertive (Babcock et al. 2003). Bevan and Gatrell (2017) and Bendl (2008) observe how characteristics which might be treated as laudable among male workers (e.g. decisiveness; ambition) may be received differently if displayed by female workers (where decisiveness might be thought of as bossiness; ambition as aggressiveness). Maternal bodies, in particular, are associated with nurturing and care work. I remember being surprised when, as Director of a Masters' degree programme comprising a cohort of mature part-time and senior students (many of whom were 10 years older than I was) the participants articulated the hope that I might be '*a mother hen*' to the group, rather than encouraging them to complete course assignments.

Ramsay and Letherby (2006) observe how, within the academy, women's potential for maternity (regardless of whether or not they are parents) leads to expectations that female academics will take on 'motherly' or pastoral roles within the community, rather than being offered more prestigious assignments which might be allocated to male colleagues. Employed women with children are expected often to suppress their personal ambitions (Hennekam et al. 2019) and to focus their apparently motherly feelings on students and colleagues—sometimes being expected to look after senior male colleagues whose research careers are in the ascendancy (Ramsay and Letherby 2006). Women with no children are expected to have apparently spare time and are assumed to desire an outlet for supposedly under-utilized motherly feelings, prioritizing departmental needs and undertaking pastoral roles in the emotional space which might otherwise have been apparently directed towards children (Ramsay and Letherby 2006).

Undoubtedly, pastoral roles with your school or subject group can be fulfilling and are important for students and colleagues within the academy who need mentoring and support. And it is key that, as their scholarly careers develop, senior faculty should contribute to capacity building within the academy.

Yet at the same time, there is a requirement for scholars to build networks and to take on external-facing roles which build their profile within their field, making contacts and becoming known internationally among like-minded colleagues. If women are mothers of young children, and/or in junior positions with limited budgets, however, this can be a challenge. They might find prohibitive (as did I and some of my junior colleagues) the personal cost of career-enhancing overseas travel and conference attendance. In any case, as Fotaki's (2013) work shows, women academics may in general be excluded from influential 'old boy' networks which lead to important and external scholarly roles (see also Stead and Elliott 2009; Vinnicombe and Bank 2003).

Yet networks, and citizenship outside your department and your university, might be key to achieving promotion.

As a lecturer, I was advised by my then Head of Department that in order to gain promotion to senior lecturer I needed to gain a position on the editorial board of a reputable management journal. On seeking guidance about what I might do to achieve this, he replied: '*Oh, well you can't do anything. You have to wait to be asked*'. Reflecting on this encounter, it occurred to me that I would enjoy the responsibility of being part of a journal team, but I could not envisage anyone asking me to do this. At that time, my children were young and my travel and conference budget limited so my contacts with editors of renowned journals were few and far between. Discussing this problem with one of my Ph.D. students, she suggested I think carefully about which journal I might like to join and simply write to the editor, regardless of whether or not this was the 'done thing'. This I did, crafting a letter and CV, and explaining to the editor of a journal which occasionally published materials relating to my research area, how I could make a contribution as a junior board member. Mentioning my actions to a senior colleague, I was warned that such an approach was a breach of etiquette, which would probably just be ignored.

Two weeks later, a nice note came back from the editor. He invited me to join his journal, as a member of the editorial advisory board. This experience gave me confidence to seek other opportunities, and I began applying for other, similar positions (some of which were advertised, some not), eventually gaining the position as Co-Editor-in-Chief with the International Journal of Management Reviews, a role which I held for six years. These journal roles opened-up opportunities which I had not previously considered. As well as chance to add to my CV and to develop my understanding of what makes a good journal article, I began to meet interesting scholars, not necessarily through attendance at conferences or even in person, but via the process of editing papers.

The journal involvement led to conference opportunities and as my children got older and my conference budget was enhanced, I was able to attend international events—sometimes supported by my institution, but sometimes also by the relevant journal—not just as a scholar, but also as a Journal Editor, contributing to capacity building and mentoring within the academy.

The Ph.D. student who had advised me to ask for opportunities, instead of waiting for these to arrive on my doorstep, had suggested that the worst thing which could happen was that colleagues might simply ignore my request. This I have found, over the years, to be mostly the case. People rarely say 'no' but they might not respond. Sometimes, though, they say 'yes'. In keeping with the Ph.D. student's advice, I decided that it was worth the risk of being labelled 'pushy'. Asking on that first occasion has assisted me in feeling that if an opportunity fits my profile, and I would like to get involved, I will ask. Such pro-active behaviour may have led to further openings. For example, when the role of Doctoral Director within the Management School where I was employed came up, requiring to be filled at short notice, the then Dean and her senior team thought of me—and suggested I apply for this—a role which I enjoyed and was able to make a valuable contribution to the School.

Supportive Networks

Although I was not, early in my career, invited to join the kinds of scholarly networks that might have impressed senior colleagues, I was fortunate to be invited to join informal but well-coordinated (often women-only) groups which were supportive and engaging, and which met women scholars' '*need for a network*' Tanton (1994, p. 19). Such informal networks are key in helping women motivate one another, share information with one another (e.g. about institutional responses to workplace flexibility, or sources of conference funding), and in offering each other specific and reciprocal help, such as reading and commenting on papers prior to submission. In my day-to-day work, I have on one or two occasions come up against colleagues, both women and men, who have been singularly unhelpful. By contrast I find most scholars to be friendly, collegial and interested in sharing scholarship, which is one of the benefits of our job. However, within informal networks (and in contrast to research which suggests that women are sometimes unsupportive to one another, Mavin et al. 2014), my experience has been more in keeping with that described in Tanton's (1994) book, with women at all levels of experience offering encouragement and assistance to each other. While women's voices may be sometimes silenced in the everyday processes of organization (Hamilton 2006), they may be heard and welcomed within such spaces. In the networks I joined, we navigated between us complex issues such as how to manage promotion processes; how to find (or change) a mentor; how to gain access to career-enhancing opportunities and how to manage leaving for, and returning from, maternity leave in circumstances where 'official' support was limited.

Such informal support groups may be found in your own institution, or within learned societies which often run special interest groups and might offer early career streams. If you are not aware of anything you can join, you could always begin a network yourself—perhaps a reading group which can be informal, small and inexpensive, but which could lead to new opportunities for friendship and advice. Or perhaps a writing group which facilitates retreat-style writing as advocated by Murray and Newton (2009) and allows for socializing during writing breaks, encouraging networking and mutual support as well as achieving writing goals. One junior colleague with whom I worked when still a part-time teaching fellow set up a qualitative research forum; we met over lunchtimes once per month, bringing our own sandwiches and taking turns to present. It costs us nothing, and some of us are still in touch nearly 20 years later.

Citizenship

Along with networking opportunities are likely to come openings to be a good citizen within your academic community. This does not mean simply picking up all the work within your own department that nobody else wants to do, which may be expected of women scholars. As noted earlier, women without children are assumed to have 'extra' time (Ramsay and Letherby 2006), while those with children are assumed not to desire career-advancing roles, meaning they are given less prestigious assignments (Gatrell 2005; Blair-Loy 2009).

Rather, the notion of academic citizenship relates to taking on tasks (which can be small at first), which depart from your everyday workload (though if these are benefiting your department, you might be able to seek a 'tariff' for these duties). Ideally, such tasks might offer you a window on the world outside your immediate setting. They could be as simple as organizing a seminar series within your school or group, this allowing you to have some influence on who comes to speak and about what, as well as the opportunity to meet scholars in your research area. Alternatively, you could affiliate with a learned society and offer to chair some sessions at its annual conference, or team up with colleagues to offer a conference stream which gets you 'out there', meeting like-minded people and with a specific role (which in turn enhances the likelihood of your gaining funding). As you look for promotion to the next stages in your career, references from colleagues who know your work and who are employed externally to your institution will be important. The above suggestions can be good ways of making such contacts, some of which can be achieved in cyberspace (e.g. editorial roles) and some with the close proximity of your own home department (e.g. seminar series).

One of my greatest supporters, who provided me with several job references and continued to offer honest and relevant guidance was someone whom I met in such circumstances. I drove him to the station; we chatted over coffee and he became a good mentor and friend—I could have met him at an international conference, but in that situation I got to know him while remaining in my home town.

Maternity and Academic Life Today

My own children are now grown up. However, my own and others' research on parenting and employment suggests that, although university policies may have changed since I was a new mother, maternal bodies are often in practice still treated as 'out of place' with the academy (Greenberg et al. 2009, 2019; Ladge et al. 2012; van Amsterdam 2014; Gatrell 2013; Hennekam 2016; Hennekam et al. 2019). For example, according to Hennekam et al. (2019, p. 13) mothers who fail to downshift their work-orientation (not only in university settings) may be judged harshly, the butt of critical comments, while women who appear to prioritize their babies over career (e.g. through breastfeeding) may find themselves viewed as failing to *'fulfil masculine norms, [this] negatively affecting their career'* as they encounter unenthusiastic attitudes towards the maternal body in the workplace.

Pregnant and newly maternal women are continually under pressure to undertake what I have termed *'maternal body work'* (Gatrell 2013) whereby they are required to present themselves at work as well-dressed 'ideal' employees, apparently in control of their bodies (and by implication their intellect), while at the same time undertaking the physical bodywork required to nurture babies and infant children.

In their autoethnography about managing new maternity alongside their roles as Ph.D. students (at the time of publication having become early career researchers), authors Huopalainen and Satama (2019) adopt a more positive tone in describing the relationship between the maternal body and the academy. They emphasize their resolve and their entitlement to maintain high work-orientation, having been through pregnancy and become mothers. However, their apparently optimistic accounts of managing pregnancy and new motherhood could be interpreted by the reader, conversely, as demonstrating grim determination in the face of obdurate stereotypical masculine-style working conditions, and in the context of limited support from colleagues and family (albeit ameliorated by these authors' close friendship and joint writing). As Huopalainen and Satama point out, ideals in relation both to motherhood and academia *'seem to emphasize full devotion, commitment, professionalization and high performance'*, suggesting that managing infant bodies which *'seep unpredictably out of the times and spaces set aside for them'* (Wolkowitz 2006, p. 91), alongside a full workload and the pressure to publish, must remain challenging for women in the academy. While it is encouraging to see how these researchers value highly their scholarly (as well as maternal) identities, it could be argued that organizational and familial change is slow, with limited (if any?) progress achieved since Knight (1994, p. 147), observed: *in their efforts to ensure that neither their child nor their work lost out in terms of their time and commitment it was the woman herself who bore the brunt* (see also Gatrell 2013, 2017; Haynes 2006; Mullin 2005).

It is not my intention to end this chapter on a depressing note. However, writing a paper such as this one is difficult, since there is the weight of expectation that it may be possible to provide 'answers'. Yet I don't believe there is any easy solution to the problems of being a 'maternal body', with or without children, within academia (see Fotaki 2013). Furthermore, within an area that remains in my view under-researched (motherhood, or non-motherhood, and paid work), it is likely that women's experience of being a maternal body in the academy will differ depending on personal circumstance as they progress their scholarly careers.

For example, black women (while under-represented in research on women and careers) are known to experience lower access to career opportunities than men or white women (Hite 2004), finding the workplace sometimes a lonely place, especially if they are senior and working among mostly white populations (Smith and Nkomo 2003). Professor of Contemporary Art Lubaina Himid CBE, winner of the 2017 Turner Art prize, recounted in a BBC radio interview how *'Someone actually said to me: "black people don't make art"'* (BBC News 2019).

Regardless of whether they have children, lesbian workers may face constant pressures regarding identity management at work (Woodruffe-Burton and Bairstow 2013), and lesbian mothers may find themselves facing acute work-family conflict if they feel unable to be 'out' at work, because this can hinder them from accessing family-friendly initiatives (Tuten and August 2006). And in relation to family health issues the mothers of disabled children can find the experience of combining employment and maternity 'debilitating' (Scott 2010, p. 686) as they struggle to maintain employment and provide care. Broadbridge and Simpson (2011, p. 478) emphasize the need to extend debate about women and equality at work beyond gender, advocating an inclusive and intersectional approach comprising: 'gender *with…*' rather than the more equal footing of 'gender *and…*' race, class, age and/or other key categorizations. From the perspective of a white woman in a heterosexual marriage, I can only acknowledge that my own experiences may be different from those experienced by other women, in different contexts and circumstances (a point also made by Hennekam et al. 2019).

Overall, as Fotaki (2013, p. 1253) observes, the deeply embedded and ingrained structures which perpetuate the *'informal processes of exclusion and devaluation that constitute major impediments to women faculty members' achievements'* are powerful, *'striking at the very heart of the academic enterprise'* and *'with profound implications both on how knowledge is reproduced and on what counts as knowledge'* (Fotaki 2013, p. 1253). Seeking to navigate the complex and often masculine cultures within academia can be difficult, and the continuing inequalities experienced by women scholars within university settings persist (Fotaki and Pullen 2019).

Nevertheless, this chapter is part of a book which seeks to offer ideas about 'How to Make Professor', drawing upon both personal experience and the advice of others. In closing therefore, I seek to make some observations which I hope will be helpful about navigating the academy and the pathway to making professor.

First, being well networked with other women helps, whatever the situation. Of the women with whom I have shared writing and other informal networks, many have offered helpful advice and support which has kept me going over the years. Back in 2005, for example, I was told by a senior male colleague that I would never achieve a 'teaching and research' position because I had not, at that time, published articles in peer-reviewed journals but *'only'* a research monograph which (it was claimed) *'didn't count'*. One of the authors of this edited collection (Murray) advised me: *'just because you **haven't yet**, doesn't mean you **can't** in the future'*—a mantra which has stayed with me over the years and has kept me going when the going gets tough. All the women in the various networks I have belonged to over time have done well and many are in senior roles as scholars, teachers and managers within academia, which indicates the value of such support.

Second, it is important to understand what the 'currency' is, within your own individual context—what matters to your university? And what are your most senior colleagues doing? This can help you focus your strategy in relation to what you publish, and which journals or publishers you are aiming for (see also Murray 2019). Decide what you want to research and write about, and keep closely to these plans. At the same time: bear in mind the 'currency', but don't let the agendas and interests of others derail you. Find space for your own ideas and prioritize what you want to say.

Third—don't wait to be asked! If there is something you would like to do, make your case and put yourself forward. The worst that can happen is that you won't receive an offer—but there is nothing to stop you trying, and then trying again.

Finally—if the going is tough, go easy on yourself. In a world such as that described by Fotaki (2013), the structural inequalities might be challenging (see also Roth 2007). Sometimes women scholars face situations where opportunities may feel closed, workloads unreasonable and family lives are sometimes complex. So, if the career ladder feels sometimes hard to climb don't blame yourself, and don't let others put the responsibility on you. Look for the door which may be open a crack, the tunnel with some light at the end and do your best—you can't do more than that.

I end this chapter with a quote from Professor Lubaina Himid CBE, whose interview on Radio 4's Desert Island Discs is an inspiring if (as she describes it) '*bittersweet*' account of the routes she has taken in achieving her present position as Professor, Turner Prize Winner and Royal Academician. This quote infers that women should keep writing, keep teaching and not give up:

> The world would be a better place if people listened to women. (Himid 2019)

References

Acker, J. (2003). Hierarchies, jobs, bodies: A theory of gendered organizations. In R. Ely, E. Foldy, & M. Scully (Eds.), *Reader in gender, work and organization* (pp. 49–61). Oxford: Blackwell.

Ashcraft, K. L. (1999). Managing maternity leave: A qualitative analysis of temporary executive succession. *Administrative Science Quarterly, 44*(2), 240–280.

Babcock, L., Laschever, S., Gelfand, M., & Small, D. (2003). Nice girls don't ask. *Harvard Business Review, 81*(10), 14–16.

Babcock, L., & Laschever, S. (2009). *Women don't ask: Negotiation and the gender divide*. Princeton: Princeton University Press.
BBC News. (2019). Turner prize: Lubaina Himid told 'Black people don't make art'. BBC News Online. https://www.bbc.co.uk/news/entertainment-arts-48485172. Accessed 2 June 2019.
BBC Radio 4, Lubaina Himid, & Artist. Desert Island Discs https://www.bbc.co.uk/programmes/m0005mfp Accessed 2 June 2019.
Bendl, R. (2008). Gender subtexts—Reproduction of exclusion in organizational discourse. *British Journal of Management, 19*, S50–S64.
Bevan, V., & Gatrell, C. (2017). *Knowing her place: Positioning women in science*. London: Edward Elgar.
Blair-Loy, M. (2009). *Competing devotions: Career and family among women executives*. Boston: Harvard University Press.
Broadbridge, A., & Simpson, R. (2011). 25 years on: Reflecting on the past and looking to the future in gender and management research. *British Journal of Management, 22*(3), 470–483.
Davidson, M. J., & Cooper, C. L. (1992). *Shattering the glass ceiling: The woman manager*. London: Paul Chapman.
Delamont, S., & Atkinson, P. (2004). *Successful research careers: A practical guide*. New York, UK: McGraw-Hill Education.
Dex, S., Joshi, H., Macran, S., & McCulloch, A. (1998). Women's employment transitions around childbearing. *Oxford Bulletin of Economics and Statistics, 60*(1), 79–98.
Equal Opportunities Commission. (2007). *Sex and power: Who runs Britain?* London: Equal Opportunities Commission.
Fotaki, M. (2013). No woman is like a man (in academia): The masculine symbolic order and the unwanted female body. *Organization Studies, 34*(9), 1251–1275.
Fotaki, M., & Pullen, A. (2019). Introducing affective embodiment and diversity. In M. Fotaki & A. Pullen (Eds.), *Diversity, affect and embodiment in organizing* (pp. 1–19). London: Palgrave Macmillan.
Gabriel, Y. (2010). Organization studies: A space for ideas, identities and agonies. *Organization Studies, 31*(6), 757–775.
Gatrell, C. (2005). *Hard labour: The sociology of parenthood*. Maidenhead: Open University Press.
Gatrell, C. J. (2007). A fractional commitment? Part-time work and the maternal body. *The International Journal of Human Resource Management, 18*(3), 462–475.

Gatrell, C. J. (2011). 'I'm a bad mum': Pregnant presenteeism and poor health at work. *Social Science and Medicine, 72*(4), 478–485.
Gatrell, C. J. (2013). Maternal body work: How women managers and professionals negotiate pregnancy and new motherhood at work. *Human Relations, 66*(5), 621–644.
Gatrell, C. (2017). Boundary creatures? Employed, breastfeeding mothers and 'abjection as practice'. *Organization Studies, 31*(3), 239–252.
Gatrell, C., Cooper, C. L., & Kossek, E. E. (2017). Maternal bodies as taboo at work: New perspectives on the marginalizing of senior-level women in organizations. *Academy of Management Perspectives, 31*(3), 239–252.
Greenberg, D., Ladge, J., & Clair, J. (2009). Negotiating pregnancy at work: Public and private conflicts. *Negotiation and Conflict Management Research, 2*(1), 42–56.
Greenberg, D., Clair, J., & Ladge, J. J. (2019). A feminist perspective on conducting personally relevant research: Working mothers studying pregnancy and motherhood at work. *Academy of Management Perspectives*. https://doi.org/10.5465/amp.2018.0087.
Hakim, C. (1996). *Key issues in women's work: Female heterogeneity and the polarisation of women's employment*. London: Athlone Press.
Hakim, C. (2002). Lifestyle preferences as determinants of women's differentiated labor market careers. *Work and Occupations, 29*(4), 428–459.
Hamilton, E. (2006). Whose story is it anyway? Narrative accounts of the role of women in founding and establishing family businesses. *International Small Business Journal, 24*(3), 253–271.
Haynes, K. (2006). Linking narrative and identity construction: Using autobiography in accounting research. *Critical Perspectives on Accounting, 17*(4), 399–418.
Hennekam, S. (2016). Identity transition during pregnancy: The importance of role models. *Human Relations, 69*(9), 1765–1790.
Hennekam, S., Syed, J., Ali, F., & Dumazert, J. P. (2019). A multilevel perspective of the identity transition to motherhood. *Gender, Work & Organization, 26*(7), 915–933.
Hite, L. M. (2004). Black and white women managers: Access to opportunity. *Human Resource Development Quarterly, 15*(2), 131–146.
Huopalainen, A. S., & Satama, S. T. (2019). Mothers and researchers in the making: Negotiating 'new' motherhood within the 'new' academia. *Human Relations, 72*(1), 98–121.

Höpfl, H. (2000). The suffering mother and the miserable son: Organizing women and organizing women's writing. *Gender, Work and Organization, 17*(2), 98–105.
Höpfl, H., & Atkinson, P. H. (2000). The future of women's career. In A. Collin & R. A. Young (Eds.), *The future of career* (pp. 130–143). Cambridge: Cambridge University Press.
Knight, J. (1994). Motherhood and management. In M. Tanton (Ed.), *Women in management: A developing presence* (pp. 141–161). London: Routledge.
Knights, D., & Clarke, C. A. (2013). It's a bittersweet symphony, this life: Fragile academic selves and insecure identities at work. *Organization Studies, 35*(3), 335–357.
Ladge, J. J., Clair, J. A., & Greenberg, D. (2012). Cross-domain identity transition during liminal periods: Constructing multiple selves as professional and mother during pregnancy. *Academy of Management Journal, 55*(6), 1449–1471.
Longhurst, R. (2001). *Bodies: Exploring fluid boundaries.* London: Routledge.
Longhurst, R. (2008). *Maternities: Gender, bodies and space.* New York: Routledge.
Mason, J. (2002). *Qualitative researching.* London: Sage.
Mavin, S., Grandy, G., & Williams, J. (2014). Experiences of women elite leaders doing gender: Intra-gender micro-violence between women. *British Journal of Management, 25*(3), 439–455.
Miller, T. (2005). *Making sense of motherhood: A narrative approach.* Cambridge: Cambridge University Press.
Mullin, A. (2005). *Reconceiving pregnancy and childcare: Ethic, experience and reproductive labour.* New York: Cambridge University Press.
Murray, R. (2019). *Writing for academic journals* (4th ed.). London: McGraw-Hill.
Murray, R., & Newton, M. (2009). Writing retreat as structured intervention: Margin or mainstream? *Higher Education Research & Development, 28*(5), 541–553.
Özbilgin, M. F., Beauregard, T. A., Tatli, A., & Bell, M. P. (2011). Work–life, diversity and intersectionality: A critical review and research agenda. *International Journal of Management Reviews, 13*(2), 177–198.
Ramsay, K., & Letherby, G. (2006). The experience of academic non-mothers in the gendered university. *Gender, Work & Organization, 13*(1), 25–44.
Roth, L. M. (2007). Women on Wall Street: Despite diversity measures, Wall Street remains vulnerable to sex discrimination charges. *The Academy of Management Perspectives, 21*(1), 24–35.

Scott, E. K. (2010). "I feel as if I am the one who is disabled": The emotional impact of changed employment trajectories of mothers caring for children with disabilities. *Gender & Society, 24*(5), 672–696.

Shildrick, M. (1997). *Leaky bodies and boundaries: Feminism, postmodernism and (bio) ethics*. London: Routledge.

Sinclair, A. (2000). Teaching managers about masculinities: Are you kidding? *Management Learning, 31*(1), 68–101.

Smith, E. L. B., & Nkomo, S. M. (2003). *Our separate ways: Black and white women and the struggle for professional identity*. Boston: Harvard Business Press.

Stead, V., & Elliott, C. (2009). *Women's leadership*. London: Palgrave Macmillan.

Swan, E. (2005). On bodies, rhinestones, and pleasures: Women teaching managers. *Management Learning, 36*(3), 317–333.

Tanton, M. (1994). *Women in management: A developing presence*. London: Routledge.

Tuten, T. L., & August, R. A. (2006). Work-family conflict: A study of lesbian mothers. *Women in Management Review, 21*(7), 578–597.

Tyler, I. (2000). Reframing pregnant embodiment. In S. Ahmed, J. Kilby, C. Lury, M. McNeil, & B. Skeggs (Eds.), *Transformations: Thinking through feminism* (pp. 288–301). London: Routledge.

van Amsterdam, N. (2014). Othering the 'leaky body': An autoethnographic story about expressing breast milk in the workplace. *Culture and Organization, 21*(3), 269–287.

Vinnicombe, S., & Bank, J. (2003). *Women with attitude*. London: Routledge.

Warren, S., & Brewis, J. (2004). Matter over mind? Examining the Experience of Pregnancy. *Sociology, 38*(2), 219–236.

Woodruffe-Burton, H., & Bairstow, S. (2013). Countering heteronormativity: Exploring the negotiation of butch lesbian identity in the organisational setting. *Gender in Management: An International Journal, 28*(6), 359–374.

Wolkowitz, C. (2006). *Bodies at work*. London: Sage.

4

Babies Taught Me How to "Do" Academia: Crafting a Career in an Institution That Was Not Built for Mothers

Catherine M. Mazak

It was the first department meeting after I returned from maternity leave, my first meeting as an academic mother. It felt good to be back. The truth was I was desperate for a break from the baby, and I loved my work and was ready to give it my energy again.

On the way out of the meeting, a senior male faculty member pulled me aside. He started asking me very pointed questions about how I had been gone for an entire semester. We are fortunate at my university to have a generous maternity leave policy, and so my February baby meant I didn't have to go back to work until fall.

I explained this carefully, naively thinking he was genuinely interested in our rather wonderful maternity leave policy. When I finished he said, "I wish *I* had 6 months of paid vacation," and walked away.

I stood there, stunned. He was jealous, upset. He made me feel like I had done something extremely unfair to him by giving birth and

---

C. M. Mazak (✉)
University of Puerto Rico, Mayagüez, Puerto Rico

© The Author(s) 2019
R. Murray and D. Mifsud (eds.), *The Positioning and Making of Female Professors*, Palgrave Studies in Gender and Education,
https://DOI.org/10.1007/978-3-030-26187-0_4

caring for my infant. He deeply misunderstood what one does on maternity leave, particularly as a first-time parent. That was the first moment, of many to come, that I felt like the university didn't quite know what to do with a mother professor.

Maternal Narratives and Academia

Narratives of success in academia are fairly lockstep. Get the Ph.D., get the tenure line, get tenure, become a full professor. The challenge for many women is that mothering small children aligns with the most challenging stages of academia: getting the Ph.D. and getting tenure. Mother academics find that the narratives of motherhood and the narratives of success in academia are competing. Adrienne Rich's *Of Women Born* (1976) gives us the term "the masks of motherhood" (p. 239) to talk about the ways that mothers are "supposed" to be. Patriarchal motherhood limits the story lines of women who become mothers, and certainly is at odds with their academic path. These story lines erase the woman who is the mother, replacing her with an idealized, man-focused idea of "mother." In these story lines, mothers do not pursue their dreams and live out their callings. Or rather, they already have, since becoming a mother is the only legitimate dream for women within the confines of patriarchal motherhood.

In their introduction to *Textual Mothers, Maternal Texts*, Podnieks and O'Reilly (2010) argue that "patriarchal motherhood is harmful, indeed unnatural, to mothers and children alike" (p. 17). It is unnatural to prescribe narratives to mothers that insist they cease being people with hopes and dreams and instead live a life wholly in service to their children. The patriarchal narrative of motherhood is exactly at odds with narratives of academic success, which prize solitude and glorify family-less-ness. The work of mothers in academia who want to be successful is to disrupt both these narratives simultaneously. Podnieks and O'Reilly assert that "empowered mothering" has begun to develop in feminist scholarship, but that "we find few models, in literature or in life, of maternal agency in empowered mothering" (2010, p. 18). Mother-scholars are tasked with writing these narratives of empowered mothering every day. These "matrifocal narratives" are a way to break through Rich's "masks of motherhood." As Daly and Reddy (1991) assert, matrifocal narratives "begin with the mother in her own right, from her own perspective," and then "hold fast to a maternal perspective" (p. 3). Through these narratives, we begin to crack through the masks of motherhood, as Rich (1976) suggested, and tell the stories of women who are mothers as powerful agents in their own right. The burden of academic mothers is writing matrifocal narratives of success within academia.

Narratives of academia continue to be patriarchal, as other chapters in this collection have shown. Universities are not designed for pregnant bodies because the very act of being pregnant goes against the glorification of solitude and individual struggle that characterize academia. For the same reasons, universities are perhaps even more poorly designed for mothers. Academic narratives do not have room for the maternal. In *The Slow Professor*, Maggie Berg and Barbara K. Seeber (2016) assert, "Academic training includes induction into a culture of scholarly individualism and intellectual memory…to talk about the body and emotion goes against the grain of an institution that privileges the mind and reason" (Berg and Seeber 2016, p. 2). The image of the scholar, bent low over the desk, working late into the night, tweed jacket with elbow patches slung over the back of the office chair, is a distinctly male image. The scientist who toils away in the lab, tied to her lab bench at all hours, skipping meals and hunkering down to finish just one more grant application, is not pregnant. She is not running out the door at 2:30 p.m. to pick up the kids. In fact, to do so would be considered disloyal and unscientific in the patriarchal culture of academia.

These are the narratives of academia handed to women, and we have to find ways to make motherhood fit in. We are struggling to do so. In fact, the main message that academic women get about being mothers is to hide it. If you are pregnant, hide it as long as possible. A dear friend of mine from graduate school didn't tell her Ph.D. advisor that she was pregnant until six months into her pregnancy. Until then she continued to haul bags of feed to pigs as part of her doctoral research in animal nutrition. She was afraid to tell her advisor (also a woman) of her pregnancy because she knew she would have to stop lifting the 30-pound feed bags and she thought she would be told she couldn't graduate. When she finally could not lift the bags (on doctor's orders), she told her advisor. The solution was that she had to find sympathetic fellow doctoral students to come to do the work for her (for free, because she couldn't afford to pay them and the university wasn't about to).

In her essay, "Scholar, Negated," Jessica Smartt Gullion (2008) writes of the status change she experienced while pregnant in her Ph.D. program. "When I got pregnant," she writes, "my identity changed from burgeoning young scholar to beached whale" (p. 18). Gullion's pregnant body excluded her from the academic narrative. "During my pregnancy, I observed how focus changed from the talents of my mind to the physicality of my body" (p. 19). Further evidence of this shift came when her (feminist scholar) department chair leaned across the desk and fired her from her TA position with the words "I just don't think we can use you" (p. 17). Gullion was in a sociology department, surrounded by scholars who used feminist theory in their work, but none of them could talk to her about motherhood. When she wanted to take a scholarly approach to motherhood, she was shut down. "Theorizing motherhood was unimportant work, and when I began to express interest in doing so, I was further devalued in the eyes of my colleagues" (p. 19). As she tried to write a different narrative for her pregnant body in academia, she just got pushed out.

We are also supposed to hide our motherhood during job interviews. In the Facebook group "Academic Mamas," which has over 14,000 members, someone posts about how to deal with pregnancy, breast-feeding, or revealing they are mothers of small children during the job search process at least once per month. Sadly, the overwhelming advice given is: do not tell them anything until you have an offer in hand. The fear of losing a potential job because the search committee finds out you are pregnant or breast-feeding is real, and profoundly sad. Being a mother makes you somehow less of an academic, less suitable, less dedicated, less reliable. Less scientific? That's the implication. The world warns us of the dangers of being pregnant while on the market. Evangeline Heiliger got a tenure-track offer at Wichita State University which was revoked when she told them she was pregnant and asked about child care (Leiker 2019). The message is clear: We don't want your maternal body inhabiting our academic departments. There is no room for your story here.

A Matrifocal Academic Narrative

In this chapter, I seek to present a matrifocal narrative of success in academia, one that pushes hard against patriarchal maternity, while at the same time revealing how deeply ingrained these patriarchal narratives are in the world of academia. The story is mine. I am a tenured, full professor who got my dream job right out of my Ph.D. Here I trace the ways in which having my three children forced me to shape my working life in a way that not only made me more productive (particularly in research and writing), but also happier and less stressed.

In this narrative, I articulate the particular lessons that having each of my three babies taught me at different stages of my career. Baby one, who came in my second year on the tenure track, taught me how to fit my workday into regular working hours (no weekends!), to write with focus, and to be mission-driven. My second baby, who came the year before I went up for tenure, taught me how to navigate burnout and care for myself. And finally my third baby, who came much later when I was a tenured, full professor, showed me that I was skilled at managing this academic life, that I could manipulate my publication pipeline so that I didn't miss a minute with her *and* still published two books, and convinced me that helping other women to navigate academia was something that I could offer the world.

Baby #1: Learning to Use Focus

I got pregnant the first time by accident. My husband and I had gotten married in 2005, the summer we *thought* we would graduate from our Ph.D. programs at Michigan State. Of course, Ph.D. programs don't always behave exactly as expected. I decided to delay graduation instead of rushing to the dissertation finish line because I won a prestigious dissertation fellowship. My spouse, on the other hand, was delayed because he was the only person in his lab who had mastered the lab techniques, and his advisor couldn't exactly let him go.

That's how we ended up spending the first year of our marriage, and the last year of our Ph.D. programs, 3000 miles apart. I was finishing up my ethnographic case study of language use in a small community in rural Puerto Rico, and he was chained to the lab in Michigan. In May 2006 when he passed his defense and came back to Puerto Rico for good, we were very happy to be together again. And that's how two people who should have known better got pregnant by accident.

I had already landed a tenure-track job at our target institution by then. We were both aiming for positions at the University of Puerto Rico in Mayagüez, and I had gotten one (his would come a year later). The first year on the tenure track is disorienting anyway, but add pregnancy with debilitating nausea to the mix and it is downright dizzying. I was really just getting through the day, chewing gum to prevent myself throwing up as I gave class to three full sections of basic English for first year students. I was exhausted. I remember applying for a large federal grant and having to run signatures—or, more accurately, waddle—to different campus offices while nine months pregnant.

The good news was that our excellent maternity leave plus our completely accidental but excellent baby timing meant that I had six whole months home with baby. It's a good thing, because the parenting learning curve was *way* harder than the tenure-track learning curve. Quickly we learned about our little bundle: She did not like to be put down, and she wanted to be in physical contact with mommy at all times. She was needy, the way little babies are. At six months old, when I went back to work, she was still needy. While pre-baby I had been able to do work-related tasks at any time I wanted (and many times when I didn't want to). With baby around there was no way that I could get work done.

I'll admit that I didn't really want to be working nights and weekends anyway, but even if I did, I couldn't (without hearing intolerable amounts of crying). Did I have a partner? Yes. Did the baby want to be with my partner? Not usually. And so, this baby made something very clear, something that changed my whole worldview: there was nothing going on outside of work that didn't have to do with *her*. And since babies are pretty much unreasonable, demanding blobs until they are three (when it only gets slightly better), she won.

I had to figure out how to fit it all in, as the boundaries between work and home were set firmly. That's when I began to figure out the power of focus. There was no more grace period, no more "spillover" time when work could get done. That meant that I had to focus on what was really, really important in my career and take action on it. For me, I figured out that putting my writing and research at the center of my daily actions made everything else get in line. And I honed working on my writing during my most focused and energetic time of day—right when I got to work—and put off other activities until after the writing was done. I realized that there would never again be long stretches of un-interrupted time to write like there were when I was writing my dissertation (why the heck did I think that writing my diss was so hard? What was I doing with all those hours, anyway?).

When I figured out these focusing strategies, I got pretty darn productive. My colleagues started to notice that I was publishing, and I landed the biggest grant our department had ever seen in that year after the baby. When my colleague told me, "I wish *I* would get paid vacation for 6 months," I was completely thrown. I was so new to motherhood, so new to working and momming, that I just couldn't process what he had said. This colleague had been hired about two years before me. He had published nothing in his five years on the tenure track, complaining that our library didn't have access to the journals he needed. Meanwhile, I had published several articles in nice, solid, mid-tier journals, brought in a $250,000 federal grant, and birthed a human. But he wanted six months of paid leave to get work done.

Maternity leave is not a "paid vacation" (do I really have to say that out loud? Apparently I do). I had a big realization that was solidified in the moment he uttered those words: My colleagues didn't get it. They didn't get *me*. The narrative that I was telling by being productive and also being a mother didn't fit into their worldview.

But even as I was adapting to my new role as mother and professor, I was still very much influenced by the patriarchal narratives circulating in academia. I tried to keep my professor life and my mommy life separate, getting upset when baby was sick and I'd have to miss work. But when baby #2 came along, he taught me that I needed to live academia differently if I was going to survive.

Baby #2: Breaking Down and Burning Out

About three years after the first baby, we had a second one. We planned it this time and were super lucky when our best-laid plans (read: the plans for me to be able to take the longest maternity leave) panned out. A late November baby created a maternity leave that ran into the following summer and combined with a student strike that caused the spring semester to end in late August, which meant that I was with him at home for almost 10 months.

This baby was maybe 10% less needy, but 1000% worse at sleeping. He consistently woke up at 11:00 p.m. *and* 1:00 a.m., and then *for the day* at 4:00 a.m. After ten months, this was getting really, really exhausting. But after so much time out of work, I was excited to get my head back into the academic game. I loved my work and had been away from it for too long. I missed having thoughts (babies prohibit deep thinking). We had gotten a second $250,000 grant and I was excited to get back to running it.

Baby #2 had other plans. About two weeks into the semester that I came back from maternity leave my son stopped breathing. I was nursing him to sleep in a chair in his darkened baby room, practically falling asleep myself, when he suddenly sat up, vomited, and turned a horrible shade of gray. The next 15 minutes was a panicked blur. I pulled my three years old out of bed and made her put shoes on with her princess nightgown. My husband (also an academic) was just arriving home from work and I remember screaming at him that we needed to get to the hospital while I ducked under the garage door, which couldn't open fast enough.

The baby was breathing again as I strapped him into the car seat, but he was still that awful ashy gray-blue. We arrived at the hospital and I scooped him up and ran to the desk. I remember how calm everyone was. No one was rushing to take his vitals. No one came to help. I had to sign in and take a number while the baby flopped in my arms and continued to vomit. This was the beginning of the ten most horrible days of my life.

Over the course of ten days, I only went home for maybe an hour at a time when my husband would stay at the hospital so that I could shower and eat. It was the second week of classes. My husband and I were both pre-tenure. It was 2010 and I didn't have a smartphone, so there was really nothing I could do. I think I called the department and just told them that I was in the hospital with the baby until further notice. All thoughts of the semester dissolved in the blurry exhaustion of caring for the sick kiddo (who was doing better but needed hourly breathing treatments).

When we finally were released from the hospital, I jumped back into the semester with two feet. I was still trying to separate my mommy life from my academic life and was frustrated when I felt like the kids were slowing me down. I was exhausted but I kept doing academia the only way I knew how: at full-throttle. But as soon as I got home from work it was medicines and breathing treatments. Coaxing kids to bed, then crashing myself, only to be woken up at least twice a night by a sniffly baby. I felt like I was on a treadmill set five clicks too fast, and that I couldn't get off or slow down. Brain fog was seriously affecting my work, but I was completely in survival mode, so I hardly noticed.

By late October I was sitting in my driveway, the transition zone between "day job" and "all night job," talking on the phone with my sister about me hospitalizing myself. I was crying, saying I couldn't keep up the pace. I was telling her that the only way out of exhaustion that I could see for myself was to put myself in the hospital, where no one could get at me, and I could finally sleep. Thankfully, my sister recognized a breakdown in progress and convinced me that I could use my sick days to take a leave of absence in the middle of the semester.

So I took sick leave. Right at the worst time of the semester. I remember sitting in my department head's office. At the time he was young and single, and I remember feeling like he would never understand, or that he would push back. He didn't. I took my doctor's note to human resources and I went home and slept. For two weeks I dropped off the kids at day care and went home and forced myself to lie down. I didn't check e-mail. I didn't try to get writing done. I just deliberately rested.

And despite all my internal resistance and guilt, I realized that this was the best possible thing I could have done for myself. The university didn't stop without me. My classes didn't even stop! The program manager of my grant never even knew I was gone—my Co-PI swiftly managed everything in my absence, as she had when I was on maternity.

When I had to miss the second week of class to be in the hospital with my son, I didn't blink an eye. But when I needed to take a leave to prevent myself from ending up in the hospital, I resisted. That's because as academics, as Berg and Seeber put it, "to admit to struggle undermines our professorial identity" (2016, p. 2). The experience I had parenting my second baby taught me that even though academia was trying to push my maternal narrative out, trying to make me act exactly like a childless, white male professor, ignoring stress and burnout, I had to push back. I had to live my academic life as the professor *and* mother that I truly was. I had to push back against the patriarchal academic narrative and the patriarchal maternal narrative and create my own way: whole, complete, both mother *and* academic. This meant doing academia differently.

Baby #3: Ratchetting up the Maternal Narrative in Academia

Six years went by. I got tenure; I became a full professor. And then, because life is like that, the sudden loss of my father-in-law reminded us of the shortness of life, and of what you leave behind. Nine months later, when I was 40 years old, baby 3 was born.

By this time, I had changed my approach to academia entirely. If a child was sick, I stayed home from work. I told my students "today there is no class because I'm caring for my sick child." We made up the work electronically, or I added office hours for one-on-one attention for those who wanted it. I openly talked about being pregnant, instead of trying to hide it. My senior seminar students knew that I fought nausea by eating goldfish crackers constantly throughout class. At the end of the semester, they gave me a t-shirt from their graduating class and a box of goldfish crackers. I never apologized for taking care of my children. I purposefully wove my maternal narrative into my academic work.

And I got really good at planning my maternity leave. This time, a mid-September baby, plus six years of accumulated sick days, meant that I spent almost an entire year home with baby. I also was a much more experienced academic writer, and I had cleared my pipeline very purposefully so that I was not working on anything while on maternity. I had two edited volumes that were submitted in their final versions right before baby came, and an academic article got accepted in the highest-tier journal I had ever published in then as well.

Of course, the way that academic publishing works, all three of those things came out the semester I got back from maternity leave. And again, there was no narrative for this in academia. I had deliberately planned this: clear pipeline by submitting everything right before baby arrives, then be able to completely relax with baby without unfinished projects looming over me. In order to accomplish this, I used the skills of finishing projects and manipulating my pipeline that I had honed over the course of my thirteen years in academia. To me, this was no big deal. It was just getting to spend what I knew would be my last maternity leave delightfully detached from academia.

To my colleagues, of course, this was baffling. One of my senior women colleagues, a woman who I adored beyond words, who was an academic mother and now had grandchildren, pulled me aside in the hall and congratulated me on my publications. Then she said, "So you used your maternity leave to write your books." I was taken aback, since this represented not only a grave misunderstanding of how maternity leaves work but also of how book publishing in academia works (i.e., it takes a long time). "No," I said, "I breastfed the baby and slept as much as I could over my maternity leave." She looked at me with round eyes and said, "How did you do it?"

This was a pivotal moment for me. How *did* I do it? I certainly didn't learn how to get my writing done as a professor doing a million other things in graduate school. How did I write books and plan my publication pipeline, and teach a 3/3? And then I realized: *If I could articulate how I did it, then I could teach other academic women how to do it, especially mothers.*

I hadn't felt a creative burst so explosive since graduate school. What if I could actually impact how women experience academia by talking about what no one ever talks about: how to get your writing done amidst all the chaos? What if instead of flailing around, feeling guilty that they never get to their writing, or too overwhelmed to start, academic women actually had a place to go to ask questions and learn what has worked for others? What kind of legacy would *that* be? The thought of it completely lit me up.

That moment marked a shift in my career. My job at the University of Puerto Rico was becoming less and less dreamy, as the fiscal crisis worsened and the threatened budget cuts and tuition hikes finally became a reality. I still loved being in the classroom and mentoring students, but the spark and drive I had pre-tenure had faded as the university had become less and less supportive of anything other than classroom teaching. But my family was very committed to Puerto Rico; we weren't going anywhere. So I started creating online ways to help academic women write and publish more, connecting with women all over the world through social media and meeting with them via Zoom. I began to run academic writing retreats in Puerto Rico, and I created online courses about writing and publishing.

The more I worked with academic women, especially mothers, the more I saw firsthand how the narrative of academia hurts them. These women are doing groundbreaking research, yet they are taught to question themselves and doubt their abilities at every step of the way. Their institutions overburden them with service commitments, their colleagues bully them. The more I work to support women to write and publish more, the more activist I get about changing the culture of academia.

Conclusion: Maternal Narratives of Resistance

If we want academia to be different, to be a place where the patriarchal narrative of motherhood is no longer the default narrative, we need to change it ourselves. Structural change in institutions is famously slow and arduous. If we are going to augment the number and types of narratives acceptable in academe, we will need to push back from the bottom up. Berg and Seeber "see individual practice as a site of resistance" (2016, p. 6) and call for these individual practices to push back against the neoliberal university, the university of fast capitalism. They argue that "individual professors' well-being has far-reaching effects" and that "addressing individual professors' stress has political and educational ramifications" (p. 4). I agree, and I see my work from now until retirement as spreading the message that women can do academia differently and still be successful. I'm on a mission to teach women how to experience academia within narratives that they write themselves. These rewritings are profound acts of resistance.

If we do not include women, and mothers, in the narrative of academic success, humanity suffers along with those individual women. Keeping women out keeps us all behind, as does pushing women to do academia in exactly the same way that the white men it was built to educate have been doing it. We need women's voices and women's stories, mother's voices and mother's stories as part of knowledge-making across academic fields. When I help academic women write and publish more in my courses and workshops, this is what I'm teaching them: how to arrange your academic life so that the amplification of your voice, your message through writing and publication is at the center of your career. This alone is a push against the narrative of women in academe. *Take up space. Raise your voice. Your work matters.*

References

Berg, M., & Seeber, B. K. (2016). *The slow professor: Challenging the culture of speed in the academy.* Toronto: University of Toronto Press.

Daly, B. O., & Reddy, M. T. (Eds.). (1991). *Narrating mothers: Theorizing maternal subjectivities.* Knoxville: University of Tennessee Press.

Gullion, J. S. (2008). Scholar, negated. In E. Evans & C. Grant (Eds.), *Mama, PhD* (pp. 16–19). New Brunswick: Rutgers University Press.

Leiker, A. M. (2019). Professor candidate claims WSU retracted job offer after she disclosed pregnancy. *The Wichita Eagle.* Retrieved from https://www.kansas.com/news/local/crime/article223843430.html.

Podnieks, E., & O'Reilly, A. (2010). *Textual mothers maternal texts: Motherhood in contemporary women's literatures.* Waterloo, ON, Canada: Wilfrid Laurier University Press.

Rich, A. (1976). *Of women born: Motherhood as experience and institution.* New York: W. W. Norton.

5

Writing Myself into an Academic Career

Rowena Murray

Context

This chapter is not an analysis of discriminatory contexts. It's not about them; it's about me.

Some scene-setting may help with understanding my experiences in my context. My academic career has mostly been at UK universities, although I also had visiting positions in other countries. In the UK, academic careers go from Lecturer, to Senior Lecturer, Reader, Professor and some staff progress to other senior posts. 'Professor' is the most senior academic post, normally associated with research, publications, funding and strategic institutional, national and/or international roles.

How many women professors are there in the UK? According to the UK Higher Education Statistics Agency (HESA 2018), in 2005/06 almost 50% of academics on the first-level grade (Lecturer) were women.

R. Murray (✉)
School of Education, University of the West of Scotland, Ayr, UK
e-mail: r.e.g.murray@btinternet.com

© The Author(s) 2019
R. Murray and D. Mifsud (eds.), *The Positioning and Making of Female Professors*, Palgrave Studies in Gender and Education,
https://doi.org/10.1007/978-3-030-26187-0_5

- 2005/06 16.7% of professors were women.
- 2006/07 17.5%.
- 2013/14 22%.
- 2017/18 26%.

These figures (which do not include women who progress in other senior roles) show that things are improving, little by little, year by year. At the time of writing, around 30% of professors are women.

However, destructive forces continue to work against academic women's careers in the UK as elsewhere: calculated and spontaneous 'micro-inequities' (Aiston 2015), 'cultural sexism' (Savigny 2014), under-valuing of women's research, compared to men's (Larivière et al. 2011), 'subtle gender biases' (Nielsen 2015, p. 386) and harassment (Valentine 1998). While men and women face the same pressures to publish, there are 'personal costs, in the form of health concerns and work-family conflict … more so for women than for men' (Richard et al. 2015). All of these have been part of my experience of working in universities.

Being in This Context

In this context, from the start of my academic career in the UK in 1987, I knew that women's applications for promotion to professor were likely to fail. In fact, at that time it was rare for a woman to reach the level of Reader (the level before Professor), and in my case, it took many years.

To convey my experience of context, I use four quotes, said to me at different points in my career between 1987 and 2019. To me, they represent the voicing of gender discrimination throughout the career I was trying to build. They are just words. But for me they were, and still are, markers of discriminatory beliefs and practices, and I have to admit that these—and many other 'words' said to me over the years—had a real impact on my confidence, my sense of self-worth, my motivation to apply for promotion and, sometimes, they affected everything. However, I also felt, well, I'll just show you what I can do: I will carry on with my work in spite of your barriers and put-downs.

Having said that, I must make it clear how vulnerable I felt, how debilitating the anxiety was, how the fear of the next undermining attack dissolved my sense of my ability, and how hard I had to work to make sure that all of these did not change how I behaved and who I was.

The first marker of discrimination I have chosen is denial, not denial of gender discrimination, but denial of the fact that it would affect my career. This quote was said by a sympathetic, collegial male academic who knew me well. I was talking about how gender discrimination was likely to impact on my career, and he replied: 'Surely *you* don't experience discrimination?' For me, this type of response meant that when I talked about the gendering of academic advancement—even with someone I trusted—I could be corrected. I could be positioned as about to circumvent systemic discrimination. It did not apply to me. Thus, my understanding of discrimination was flawed, perhaps emotional?

Yes, we could debate these points, but I found it was, in fact, difficult to articulate and evidence discrimination in my career, so I was not effective in these debates. While it might not have been the speaker's intention, he successfully invoked the individualising argument.

The next marker of discriminatory thinking was the downgrading of the publications I was beginning to produce: 'What you are doing is not research; it's scholarship'. While I was and still am happy to debate the many meanings of 'research' and 'scholarship', in context—at a formal meeting, with senior people present—this explicitly downgraded my research, in terms of the values of the time, to something lesser, called 'scholarship'. This had a direct effect on the perceptions of my work and provided a rationale for overlooking it. Because the speaker held a powerful position, I felt powerless to challenge this overt undermining, particularly in that context. What was the point of challenging them, I thought? Because I was motivated to write in spite of all this, it has been suggested that the put-down was helpful—it motivated me to write. Correction: it was not helpful. Being devalued increased the pressure to perform until, I remember saying, I felt like I was hanging on by my fingernails. Yes, I kept writing, but I had no hope that it would improve my working conditions or promotion prospects. The currency of writing had, after all, been devalued.

The next marker of discrimination downgraded not only my work but also my field: 'So you do academic writing ... *about* academic writing?!' Out of context, this sounds like intellectual curiosity. In context, it showed that not only had this person not bothered to check my profile online, but the rhetorical question suggested that although I was established in this field, it was not really a field at all. This made me despair of achieving recognition for my work, although I did not depend on this person's recognition at this stage in my career. Again, the onus was on me to construct a credible account of a profile that was already out there for all to see. This was not just about my work; I felt I was being reduced, belittled.

The strangest of what I take to be discrimination markers was a warning about what I presented as indicators of my research success. When I described its impact, my retreats, my books, the Keynotes, my national and international status, the blurted response was, 'Don't be a guru!', but I was already a professor! Being a professor was contrary to this person's view of me—do not profess ... stop professing ... stop writing all these books ...—was, I think, the message. This was absurd, but, again, it worked, to some extent to make me question myself. Was it me? Was I doing something to make these people feel they had to undermine my work—that is also absurd, but probably not far off the mark. It was, and still is, disturbing to know that my successes can have this impact on people in authority.

In case it seems like I got off lightly—that these were only casual remarks said to me from time to time—here is a list of *some* of the long-term undermining strategies used on me:

- Interrupting at various types of meeting, in front of peers and senior staff
- Ridiculing my work
- Stating that the impact of my work was due to other factors
- Belittling my research and scholarship
- Constant criticism
- Unmerited criticism
- Criticism at key meetings with key staff
- Criticism in front of senior staff

- Criticism at first meetings with new HoD, VC, Dean etc.
- Criticism of me at meetings I did not attend
- Constant undermining amounting to harassment by email
- False accusations: e.g. I was not accountable or I was doing too much external work
- Marginalising my work, even when I delivered targets and helped others to do so
- Not sharing information with me
- Hostility and/or lack of support needed to do the job—administration and academic
- Not acknowledging achievements
- Physical aggression—pointing, shouting, accusing me in public spaces
- Excessive monitoring/overbearing supervision by colleague not my line manager, followed by accusation that I was refusing to be accountable
- Reconstituting my success as failure
- Attributing my success to others
- Isolating—creating impression that I isolated myself
- Lack of support from management and HR on my complaints
- Being accused of doing one/some of these things to colleagues who did them to me.

I have to add that I was never the only one experiencing all of these, and I might not have been the only one affected by them. There could have been a ripple effect, since many of these acts were performed in public spaces at work and were witnessed by others.

To anyone who finds these actions trivial—and I understand that some seem trivial—I suggest that they spend a year experiencing all of these, learning, in fact, to anticipate all of these on a daily basis. Then, they will have an idea of what it's like to be faced with full-time unremitting, unearned hostility and negativity. To fully understand the effect of this undermining, however, they must experience daily criticisms—for a year—of their work in both formal and informal work settings, such as review, research assessment and applications for promotion. Over time, without respite and intensifying year on year, they will find that it is unbearable.

Of course, no one is going to volunteer to experience this. Of course, anyone who has not experienced this will think I am exaggerating, or that I was weak, for not fighting back. Of course, I was strong in attempting to work with and against this undermining, and over the years I became skilful at doing so, but it wore me down. Moreover, having to work against all this is a distraction from real academic work, which is its purpose, of course.

Of course, no one would ever admit to doing any of this to me. In fact, it is the reverse. Each of these actions would be described in very different terms by those who performed them. This is, for me, how the 'barriers' to my career progression operated. Training or confidence building or networking might help me to endure this culture of undermining, but they would not change the attitudes and behaviours of those who were undermining me. It was clear from what they said, when challenged, that they saw this as the right thing to do. They had done nothing wrong; I had done nothing right. They had nothing to 'admit' to.

Nor is it the case that I experienced all of these all of the time, but I lived just about every working moment knowing that I would, sooner or later, possibly both. It was as if it was in the air that I breathed. So, I was in that sense experiencing undermining all the time.

My context was, therefore, not a series of episodic put-downs, but a chronic culture in which—statistics told me—I had limited prospects of career progression at any university. For me, it was not just that there were 'barriers' to my career progression; it seemed that I was up against a set of practices deployed by many people—almost like a game plan for putting me down, holding me back and making me want to leave. It worked, to the extent that I did want to leave, but I needed to make a living, and I still had a sliver of motivation to do so in a university. I had, therefore, to find a way to work within that culture if I were to progress in an academic career.

Perhaps it does not happen to all women in academia in exactly this way. Perhaps there are environments where undermining is not systematic. But I hear of so many incidences, these patterns of behaviour, things that are said to women, that it's almost like there is a playbook for gender discrimination.

In this context, what could I do? How could I retain my self-worth? My confidence? How could I challenge those who undermined me and disregarded the national and international profile I had built?

Writing Myself into a Career

To begin with, in this context, I desperately searched for a way to survive—nothing more, nothing less. I had to publish—otherwise I was going nowhere. I had to develop a profile in my field—beyond my context. I had to write. For all this, I had to 'retreat' from this context. I actually felt that I was not going to be able to function in the context I described in the previous section. In fact, I felt I was losing the will to live in that context. This is why I set out to develop an alternative environment that was collegial, compassionate, creative and safe—for me and for others.

At first, I created writing groups to bring together people who wanted to write and talk about writing. This gave me a new way to do the part of my job that involved helping academics and students and to meet institutional targets, such as Ph.D. completions and publications. A support group was what I needed most.

Then, I ran writing retreats, following Sarah Moore's lead (Moore 2003), and I created a new format, Structured Writing Retreat (SWR) (Murray and Newton 2009). Through writing about all of this, I created a profile and a body of research in the field of academic writing, and with that came collaborations and invitations to work in other places, to grow my external profile.

The Social Writing Framework

I now analyse my experiences using the Social Writing Framework (Fig. 5.1) that I developed to explain the components of a SWR (Murray 2015). (I will not describe the functioning of writing groups and retreats, since I have written about them elsewhere [Murray 2015, 2017, 2019], and because this chapter focuses on my career.)

Fig. 5.1 The Social Writing Framework (*Source* Adapted from Murray 2015)

My Social Writing Framework consists of a large inner circle and many smaller circles arranged around it. The inner circle represents the social, physical and cognitive components of SWR, and the smaller circles represent components of social writing. The smaller circles are not lined up with the social, physical and cognitive domains because, I argue, relationships between them are too various to capture in that way.

The framework shows the writing process *as* a social process. It represents writing in terms of potential relationships with and between concepts, places, people and objects. Its purpose was to bring all these elements and relationships into our understanding of 'writing'. Writing is not just about text, but about creating writing-oriented contexts.

I will explain how I used the framework to analyse my career and will argue that this analysis shows my growing agency over the past twenty years, achieved in groups that I created, not just through my personality, resilience, luck, intellectual acuity, allies or mentors. All of those played a part, but in this chapter I focus on what I did. With this focus, the framework is not just a model for achieving productivity, though that is obviously essential; here, I reconfigure it as a model for developing and sustaining self-efficacy—the belief that I could achieve my goals—through social writing. I argue that I would not have developed self-efficacy if I had not created writing groups and retreats.

This is not to say that agency and self-efficacy are constants; for me, they are products of social writing. This is where I perform and sustain my self-efficacy and help others to do so. Social writing is, therefore, more than a mechanism in my career; it is a way of making my career meaningful for me and useful for others.

Before I start my analysis, I must acknowledge a risk in this argument. I have been warned that I could be seen to overstate individual agency, and, in fact, that the concept of individual agency is problematic, since it implies that the individual can—and should—overcome systemic discrimination herself. My response is that I do not intend to understate the power of systemic discrimination. The forms of 'retreat' that I created were in response to the literally—physically and mentally, for me—overwhelming power of discrimination and the relentless undermining I experienced. In fact, while I claim agency in developing social writing, these are not *individual* activities; they were, and are, group activities, increasingly attended by women (Murray and MacKay 1998; Morss and Murray 2001; Murray and Newton 2009; Murray 2012; Murray and Kempenaar 2018). So, I find it impossible to overstate the power of the retreat environment in my survival, development and progression as a female academic.

In order to build the argument that social writing was a key component, I used Fig. 5.1 to reflect on the components of social writing in relation to my career progression. I set out to map my experiences using the components of the framework. This identified three phases: (1) I ran writer's groups, (2) I created Structured Writing Retreats, and (3) I built a profile in the field of academic writing through my research and publications about this work.

I used the Social Writing Framework to see if I could break down these three phases into their components. I did this several times, and I came up with different versions of my career each time. However, I could see themes and patterns in these analyses. The result of my analysis might be a unique—i.e. specific to me alone—account of career progression, or it could be something more: a way to explore agency in writing—key for academic careers.

The following three sections explain what social writing involved and how it helped me progress as a writer and in my career—this is how I wrote myself into my career. Each section focuses on what I needed most at a stage in my career. This is not to say that I breezed through promotion processes, since there were blocks, but that I managed to take control of my career—and, to some extent, my feelings about it—through social writing. Without writing there could be no career; without social writing I would not be a Professor.

Phase 1—The Social Component

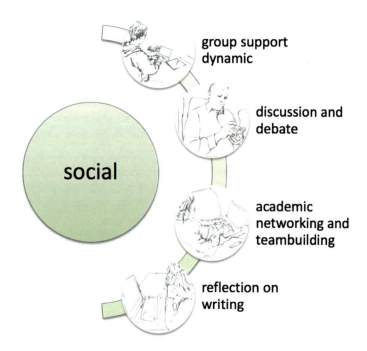

For the first part of my analysis, I focused on my first writing groups. At that time, what I needed most was support. I simply invited like-minded people, people I knew were interested in writing more and/or struggling to write at all, to meet in my office for 90 minutes' writing every week or two. I took the initiative in creating a space where they and I could write, talk about writing and achieve success in publications and other outputs.

The green circles mapped the components of this phase, signifying an emphasis on the 'social' components that were crucial for me at that time: *group support dynamic, discussion and debate, academic networking and team building* and *reflection on writing*.

The group support dynamic was what I most needed because I was already acutely aware of discriminatory values and practices that could limit, even damage, my career and my well-being. I had an overwhelming sense of threat in my context and was not able to write. There was no space for writing at work, and no time for writing in my role—I did ask and was told no. Having found that I could support individual writers, forming a writer's group seemed like a logical step. Everyone who chose to attend the writing groups felt the benefit of writing in this way. Academic-social processes came with meeting regularly to write, such as intellectual exchange, thinking, ideas, sharing readings, reflecting on the writing process and problem-solving.

For me, while it felt very positive to be writing with other people, this was a way of efficiently doing my job by supporting more writers at one time, rather than one by one. More importantly for me, writing in the group helped with my anger, anxiety and frustration about the workplace—not by discussing it, since we did not, but by providing an alternative space. I drip-fed my knowledge about writing into discussions, and at the same time, I learned from other writers. I discussed this work with senior officers, linking it to, for example, their aims for Ph.D. completions and research assessment. I ran workshops, gathered data, presented it at conferences and published articles about this work.

Discussion and debate about writing processes and the subjects we were writing about increased through writer's group meetings. We had more opportunities to talk about our work and our writing and about different ways of doing both. We observed that there was no space in our departments for talking about writing-in-progress and all that that involves. More importantly, in this space we could rehearse arguments we were developing in our papers and chapters, which helped us clarify our writing and anticipate peer review.

For me, having a space for constructive debate with colleagues was a novelty. In these discussions, I learned how to strengthen my papers about writing strategies that I 'knew' helped people across the disciplines. In this way, I consciously positioned myself as a research-active academic and research leader. This counteracted fears and anxieties I still had about other positionings of me and my work.

Academic networking and team building are important in academic careers, but how do we find time for them? The writer's group was immediately a network and a team in the sense that we had that feeling of working together while we worked on our individual writing projects. We were all in the same boat—in a good way. It was reassuring to know that others found writing challenging, and that we could quickly find solutions to the challenge.

For me, this meant that I had not only an alternative space for writing and doing my job, but also an alternative set of colleagues. Growing a network outside of the work context is, after all, a key part of research. Meeting regularly strengthened this effect. Getting to know each other's work and knowing that we could safely talk about it in this context was an important part of the mindset I needed to produce high-quality writing for highly competitive journals. Even when I was writing books, it was helpful to have critical friends, and it boosted my confidence and concentration—in the act of writing—knowing I had access to their critique, comment and ongoing support. Support was still an important function of the group for me.

Reflection on writing was not about navel-gazing; it was the very opposite. In this safe, yet intellectually attuned context, our talk about writing was spontaneous yet focused on our projects. Because we met over a period of months or years, we were able to reflect on the 'life span' of writing projects—the highs and lows, the tricky moments, the short cuts, the mountains and molehills—topics that were not routinely discussed in other contexts, but which increased our understanding of what we needed to do to achieve our goals.

For me, it was key to hear other people's reflections on writing. I knew a lot about writing, but I didn't know what they knew. This gave me insight into the academic paradox: that academics know a lot about writing, but may not be able to do all the writing they want to—myself included. I began to develop my interest in what people actually did when they wrote, what they thought, where and when they wrote—the specifics. These social components of writing were therefore the most important for me early in my career. This is not to say that other components were not in play, just that they were not as important when I was struggling to survive in academic contexts.

Phase 2—The Physical Component

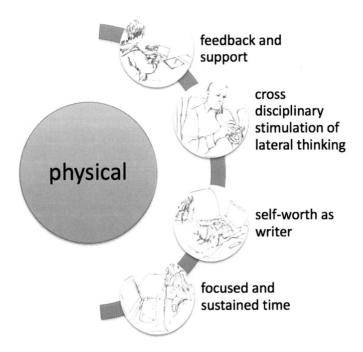

In the next stage of my career, I was spending more time in writing retreats and researching and writing about what went on in these spaces. For this phase, I selected the purple circles in my analysis, though the green ones were still in play. The purple circles convey a shift from the urgent need for 'social' support towards the 'physical' dimension of the framework: *feedback and support, cross-disciplinary stimulation of lateral thinking, self-worth as writer* and *focused and sustained time.*

This theme is about constructing environments for writing that cater for well-being, rather than intensifying pressure. It became clear that this was a crucial component of writing, for me and for many others.

Feedback and support continued, but I moved beyond the desperate need for supportive colleagues, perhaps because I had formed several groups of them. This is not to say that all writing retreats ran smoothly, since there were intermittent challenges there too, but generally, writing retreats were a haven, but it was never just a haven; there was also critical, mostly constructive feedback on writing and on the retreats themselves.

For me, self-worth was boosted by the awareness that I had moved beyond the need simply for support and the realisation that we could use writing retreats to do intellectual work.

Cross-disciplinary stimulation of lateral thinking was a feature of the Structured Writing Retreat that I created, in which the fixed programme of writing time slots and breaks allows time and space for comparing experiences, intellectual cross-fertilisation that we did not routinely find in other contexts. Often people would talk about how much they enjoyed finding out about research in different disciplines. Lateral thinking may have been facilitated by the change to writing practices imposed on participants by the retreat structure. Because we were all writing together, on our individual projects, over a period of three days, there was space for sharing observations about changes in writing behaviours, attitudes and concepts. As facilitator, I made it one of my jobs to stimulate discussion of these issues.

For me, a writing retreat was an alternative environment, where cross- and interdisciplinary discussions took place almost all of the time. Because participants were all working on their writing, they all had that in common. They could all talk about that, and in the course of doing so, other strands emerged: we talked about research methods and ethics and other, broader experiences, including career progression.

Self-worth as writer seemed to increase quite rapidly for those who chose to attend writing retreats. They reported increased confidence and reduced anxiety in relation to their writing. Some adopted my retreat strategies for other academic roles. Since more women than men by far attended retreats, this was a way of developing the attributes that were frequently associated with leadership, but in relation to writing specifically. I realised that there was limited benefit in developing a woman academic's self-worth if she did not develop self-worth in relation to her writing, since publication would be the/a key criterion in decisions about her career progression.

For me, these retreats were spaces for developing and sustaining my self-worth as a writer. It may seem strange to say that I lacked self-worth as a writer, given that I was already publishing books and articles, but in contexts where my worth was routinely undermined and devalued, I saw the benefit of these other contexts, and that is why I continued to run retreats—for my benefit and others'. This might sound like running away, but I did work in 'the context' too—chairing a women's committee, teaching Women's Studies, joining the Management Development for Women team etc.—but I was under no illusion that these activities would protect me from systemic discrimination. In fact, it was mostly the opposite.

Focus and sustained time were what people in academic contexts craved. Even when I was not asking about time—in interviews about writing retreats, for example—they talked about 'time'. The problem of making time for writing—everyone understood that it was about prioritising, and everyone knew the importance of publications for institutions, but few admitted to the need to change writing behaviours. My solution was to create a place where writing was privileged over everything else. Unplug. When academics did this, they were incredibly productive. It was quality time for quality writing. But this type of space was not generally provided on campuses. We created our writing time and space.

For me, this was also about work-life balance, I could write for hours a time, regularly losing track of time, forgetting to eat, etc., but I wanted to create a way of regularly prioritising writing. If there was no way to do this on campus, I had to create a space where writing was the only task. This worked so well that I gathered more data, presented it at conferences, published journal articles and wrote it into new editions of my books. This analysis of how I adjusted the physical environment reveals how important it was for me to create alternative spaces for writing. This was the point in my career when I realised that I was not just supporting others' writing but, in doing so, playing a research leadership role. For women academics, there seemed to be additional benefit in having a place to process some of the 'counter measures' in their careers. Not everyone talked about this, but I began to introduce the topic to conversation. Running retreats over several years, in several countries, gave me a body of experience in this leadership role, along with an emerging track record and national (Scotland and UK) and international profile in writing, and there were other achievements at this time, thanks to this environment.

Phase 3—The Cognitive Component

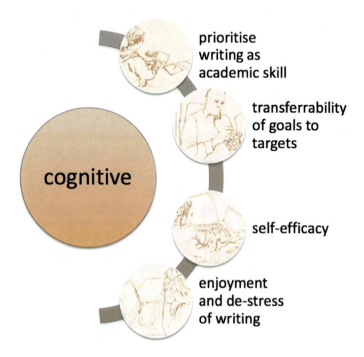

By the time I was promoted to Reader and then professor, I had developed a profile in my field. While the green and purple components were still in play, it is the orange circles that I choose to characterise this phase. These components reflect my shift towards the cognitive domain of the framework: *prioritising writing as academic skill, transferability of goals to targets, self-efficacy* and *enjoyment and de-stress of writing*.

This is not to say that I had not been working at the cognitive level before this point, but that I was able to make more time and space for my writing plans and goals—at one or more Structured Writing Retreats per month from 2015—and was more and more routinely using goal-setting and monitoring to maintain my self-efficacy. I learned about behaviour change, and this was reflected in my publications at the time, so that I had a better understanding of the concepts and was better able to explain their importance to writers attending my groups, retreats and workshops. This is how I self-consciously, deliberatively developed self-efficacy and helped others to do so, in relation to their writing. I used various conceptual frameworks to develop understanding of academic writing and published on these too.

Prioritising writing as academic skill did not mean teaching academics how to write; it meant privileging writing over other tasks. This involved designating time and space for writing, but this was not widely practiced. This was the context in which writing retreats were so valuable, why they were and are so popular and effective. This raised the question of whether we could integrate this way of working in other academic contexts or do our writing away from the heat of competition and the culture of gender discrimination.

Transferability of goals to targets—by supporting writing a university can boost its research standing. In our context, such extrinsic motivators held significant power, and we saw subjectivity deployed at various levels in deciding whether or not our publications would 'count' in research assessment and promotions, and this could be demotivating. We were aware that extrinsic motivation was not enough. We needed intrinsic motivation, where our own values were brought into play, in relation to our publication targets, for example.

Self-efficacy, the belief that we can achieve our own goals, may seem self-evident for academics. Of course, we knew what we had to do. We had our writing 'goals'. We knew how to achieve them. When I suggested that academics make their writing goals specific—in terms of numbers of words and minutes—it seemed simplistic or 'mechanistic' to some. But those of us who attended writing retreats found that goal-setting and monitoring the extent to which we had achieved our goals developed our self-efficacy, and if we didn't do that, how would we have developed self-efficacy in relation to writing? I made the principles of self-efficacy a more explicit part of my retreats. These were not new concepts; they were well established in other areas (such as health promotion), but they were challenging to people who had never used them in relation to their academic writing.

For me, these concepts were familiar from my sports background, though I knew that would not be enough to persuade others to adopt them. However, the concepts had a good fit with my SWR model. Evidencing their impact strengthened the case for using them in my writing and in helping others with theirs. The concept of self-efficacy helped to explain how my retreat model worked and increased my confidence in using it.

Enjoyment and de-stress of writing will be irrelevant, to some, and writing stress will seem unavoidable. This phase in my career was about not only reducing stress, but about producing and disseminating as widely as possible the evidence that writing retreats can reduce writing-related anxiety (MacLeod et al. 2012).

For me, I relaxed into the role of leading retreats and developing understanding of academic writing. Because I had at least one retreat a month, I did not experience as much stress about writing as I used to. I developed confidence that I would get my writing done at that month's retreat. I knew that this did not guarantee success—'writing' at retreats included revise-and-resubmit and re-writing after rejection—but I developed confidence in working through these contested stages in writing.

Linking my activities, my research outputs and others' outputs from my writing retreats, which I gathered and reported on regularly, to university targets was a way of making the case for writing retreats, not just for their own sake, not just to reduce anxiety—crucial as that was—but also to benefit institutions. To my surprise, I found that this was another failing argument, but I felt it was important to continue to make it. I kept sending information about outputs and benefits to senior officers across the university.

I continued to create dedicated writing time and space at my retreats, writing workshops and writer's groups in various forms and venues, including, with a select few, my own home, which is where I am writing this chapter. More recently, Lucy Hinnie adapted my model of SWR for Twitter, as RemoteRetreat, thus increasing its accessibility.

In this analysis, I have represented my career in terms of what looks like a progression from social to physical to cognitive components of the Social Writing Framework. This is not to say that it was a planned progression. Yes, I had plans. No, they did not succeed in getting me promoted until I had applied and been rejected several times. Nor am I recommending it as a step-by-step recipe for 'making it' to professor.

By creating alternative spaces, I was able to retreat from contexts where words, values and actions were more likely to inhibit my writing and, thereby, to limit my career progression.

How I 'Made' It

All I did was create environments where I could write. However, in these spaces I could also help others to write, which was important to me, and I developed knowledge about academic writing.

There are, of course, counter-arguments. For example, it will be argued that all of this applies equally to men, but statistics tell a different story: men are still more likely to be professors, and research explains how this happens (Larivière et al. 2011).

There will be resistance to my implicit critique of context: 'Ideological, structural or intellectual critique is frequently met by strategies that individualize and pathologize those who complain' (Barcan 2013, p. 8). My analysis could be reconfigured as my pathology: in fact, I set myself up for that when I said, 'This is not about them; it's about me'. However, this chapter builds on other critiques: performativity in education workplaces can be harmful (Ball 2003), there is a need for self-care (Ball and Olmedo 2013), we can invent remedies (Hey 2004), and writing retreats are an alternative to extreme competition and individualisation (Acker and Armenti 2004; Moore et al. 2010).

There will be pushback against what may be seen as my whining—of course the academic world is competitive, of course there are disagreements, and of course there is pressure—it is the nature of the beast ... the very essence of academic work. Yet my analysis focuses on solutions to current problems. Even if we disagree about the context 'problem', you would think we could agree about the value of trying (and funding) these solutions, but I doubt we will, particularly when it comes to decisions about resources. The question remains of how systemic change can be achieved by retreating from the 'context'.

Am I bound always to be in opposition? As a woman professor, I continue to be an anomaly. It has worked for me to create spaces where I am not anomalous, not in the sense that I am surrounded by women professors—probably not in my lifetime—but in the sense that I can focus on my writing, and all that that means. It is both as simple and complex as that. Creating spaces where I can do that has helped me to develop in many ways—it's not just about churning out text—and as long as discrimination and undermining persist, which they do for me still, I will have a use for writing retreats and will continue to run them so that others can benefit in similar ways. This spreading of benefit is my motivation for creating a Training for Retreat Facilitators, so that others—again, mostly women—can develop the knowledge and skills for creating retreats, do their writing and progress in their careers.

Now, I have decided to work half-time at a university and half-time independently, which means running writing retreats and workshops through my company. This arrangement allows me to concentrate on my writing and continue to support others. It means that I no longer have to collect information about outputs and outcomes for an institution, but continue to listen and learn about what seems to be helping. The next steps are podcasts, audiobooks, ebooks and using social media to increase the reach of this support.

This independence takes me away from undermining cultures, though I can still see how they impact on others, which strengthens the argument for social writing.

Conclusion

As I used the components of the Social Writing Framework to analyse my career, it became clear to me that these were the components of my progression to professor. These components were needed not to 'help' me write, not to solve a writing 'problem', but to combat forces working against my writing and against my career progression.

Social writing was my response to environments in which I worked. Intensification of what I see as social and intellectual assault led to the consolidation of my social writing model. Initially, I was only aiming for survival, then I wanted to develop new contexts for writing and then it became a field of knowledge in its own right.

As I said at the start, this is not to claim a causal connection between my 'agency' in creating these environments and becoming a professor. I constructed the agency to create alternative spaces in which I could do the writing I had to do and, for some of the time, the writing I wanted to do.

I do not offer social writing as a recipe for success, although it is handy for aspiring women academics that this alternative mode of writing—and achieving through writing—already exists. Social writing now takes many forms. There are many variations (Haas 2014).

Nor am I saying that social writing puts a stop to destructive actions and words or limits their impact on me. It does not. Nor does it change discriminatory values and practices. In fact, sometimes I felt it intensified them, when individual and group successes at writing retreats seemed to inflame them.

Given how effective social writing was for me, it is perhaps astonishing that there were no countermeasures. In fact, there were. Funding was cut, powerful people undermined the benefits—'I hear great things about the retreats, but I hope there comes a day when people don't need them'—and lists were drawn up of things I was not doing because I was 'only' running retreats, and there were many other responses that took no account of my regular reports of the outputs and benefits of social writing for individuals and institutions.

Some will argue that I was privileged in being able to—allowed to?—develop agency in my career, but describing my route to Professor, as privileged is wilfully to ignore the desperation, despair and distress I experienced along the way—as explained in the section on 'Being in this context'. Alternative spaces were necessary inventions not just for my career progression, but also for my health and well-being.

Finally, I started this chapter with the words, 'this is not about them … it's about me' because it is about how I created alternative spaces for writing in contexts where they were needed. As long as there is systemic discrimination, these spaces continue to be needed in many contexts. So, while this chapter is about me, it is, of course, also about them.

References

Acker, S., & Armenti, C. (2004). Sleepless in academia. *Gender and Education, 16*(1), 3–24.
Aiston, S. J. (2015). Whose academy? Gender and higher education. In J. Case & J. Huisman (Eds.), *Investigating higher education: A critical review of research contributions* (pp. 80–96). London: Routledge-Society for Research into Higher Education.
Ball, S. (2003). The teacher's soul and the terrors of performativity. *Journal of Education Policy, 18*(2), 215–228.
Ball, S., & Olmedo, A. (2013). Care of the self, resistance and subjectivity under neo-liberal governmentalities. *Critical Studies in Education, 54*(1), 85–96.
Barcan, R. (2013). *Academic life and labour in the new university*. Farnham: Ashgate.
Haas, S. (2014). Pick-n-mix: A typology of writers' groups in use. In C. Aitchison & C. Guerin (Eds.), *Writing groups for doctoral education and beyond* (pp. 30–47). London: Routledge.
Hey, V. (2004). Perverse pleasures: Identity work and the paradoxes of greedy institutions. *Journal of International Women's Studies, 5*(3), 33–43.
Higher Education Statistics Agency. (2018). hesa.ac.uk. Accessed 7 Feb 2019.
Larivière, V., Vignola-Gagne, E., Villeneuve, C., Gelinas, P., & Gingras, Y. (2011). Sex differences in research funding, productivity and impact: An analysis of Quebec University professors. *Scientometrics, 87*(3), 483–498.

MacLeod, I., Steckley, L., & Murray, R. (2012). Time is not enough: Promoting strategic engagement with writing for publication. *Studies in Higher Education, 37*(6), 641–654.

Moore, S. (2003). Writers' retreats for academics: Exploring and increasing the motivation to write. *Journal of Further and Higher Education, 27*(3), 333–342.

Moore, S., Murphy, M., & Murray, R. (2010). Increasing academic output and supporting equality of career opportunity in universities: Can writers' retreats play a role? *Journal of Faculty Development, 24*(3), 21–30.

Morss, K., & Murray, R. (2001). Researching academic writing within a structured programme: Insights and outcomes. *Studies in Higher Education, 26*(1), 35–52.

Murray, R. (2012). Developing a community of research practice. *British Educational Research Journal, 38*(5), 783–800.

Murray, R. (2015). *Writing in social spaces: A social processes approach to academic writing*. London: Routledge-Society for Research into Higher Education.

Murray, R. (2017). *How to write a thesis* (4th ed.). Maidenhead: Open University Press-McGraw-Hill.

Murray, R. (2019). *Writing for academic journals* (4th ed.). Maidenhead: Open University, Press-McGraw-Hill.

Murray, R., & Kempenaar, L. (2018). Why do women attend writing retreats? *Gender and Education.* https://doi.org/10.1080/09540253.2018.1557321.

Murray, R., & MacKay, G. (1998). Supporting academic development in public output: Reflections and propositions. *International Journal for Academic Development, 3*(1), 54–63.

Murray, R., & Newton, M. (2009). Writing retreat as structured intervention: Margin or mainstream? *Higher Education Research and Development, 28*(5), 527–539.

Nielsen, M. W. (2015). Limits to meritocracy? Gender in academic recruitment and promotion processes. *Science and Public Policy, 53*(3), 386–399.

Richard, J. E., Plimmer, G., Fam, K.-S., & Campbell, C. (2015). Publishing success of marketing academics: Antecedents and outcomes. *European Journal of Marketing, 49*(1/2), 123–145.

Savigny, H. (2014). Women, know your limits: Cultural sexism in academia. *Gender and Education, 26*(7), 794–809.

Valentine, G. (1998). 'Sticks and stones may break my bones': A personal geography of harassment. *Antipode, 30*(4), 305–332.

6

Academic Fluidity? An Unconventional Route to the Professoriate

Jackie Potter

Opening

I am a professor. Say it again. Say it slowly. I am a professor. I enjoy it and marvel at it. The strangeness, the aloofness, the otherness of the term in relation to me and my work but not anymore. It seems such a strange destination to have arrived at because of the career journey I have taken. I have made specific choices at key junctures that I knew at the time were taking me away from a traditional academic career even though I continued to work in higher education.

In this chapter, I'm going to retell three 'moments', as remembered and somewhat fictionalised to preserve anonymity of institutions and key influencers, that were all tipping points—places in my career when I had to explicitly confront and deal with the ambiguity in my professional arena about whether the work I do is fully compatible with conventionally held views of academic activity. In each case the

J. Potter (✉)
Oxford Brookes University, Oxford, UK
e-mail: jpotter@brookes.ac.uk

stories are associated with moving, or beginning to think of moving, from one higher education provider to another. There is a great spectrum of Higher Education Provider diversity and, on reflection, I see now the extent of that variation among the institutions where I have worked. The variation, most easily plotted in terms of the extent of the institutional orientation to teaching or research, and in terms of the historical roots and longevity of the university, influences how those institutions manage recognition and reward for academic work. As a result, at the times of my first two stories, the moves I have made have challenged me to take opportunities that have led me to believe I was leaving academic life (as I knew it) and taking on roles that could not be adequately recognised and rewarded as such. This included firstly, leaving a research-only role for a teaching and research focused role in an aspiring higher education college when, at the time, I had no experience of teaching. My second moment charts my move into a professional services role in academic development, to lead support for student and staff learning, at a time when the nature of that work as academic or not was unclear across the academy and, as a result, was determined locally by senior leaders in individual universities. The final move I chart is back into the heartland of the academy as a professor. I explore aspects of the work I had done previously, in roles not conceived of as academic, that were influential in enabling that recognition process and therefore allow me now to occupy a role acknowledged as encompassing both academic and professional leadership.

I have used narrative to bring to life the moments of transition and change, from one discipline to another, from one university to another, and to act as objects to anchor the ideas under discussion here. Fyffe (2018) uses narrative retelling to explore the transition to work as an academic developer. She comments that *"accounts of coming to academic development are distinct but remarkably similar"* (p. 357) and reports from Fraser (1999) that the majority of people arrive (to academic development) with extensive teaching experience after a first career. It is not my intention to theorise or legitimise my story, although I will use theory and models in the text, but instead to use my story as an example that might demonstrate how, by following your ambition and desire, that may nonetheless lead you away from disciplinary research, you can still find new and better-fit opportunities for recognition and promotion within the ever-diversifying higher education enterprise.

Leaving the Ivory Tower

Conceptions from the last century viewed the higher education enterprise as distant from society, as focused on the pursuit of new knowledge through pure research and admitting some students to study to regenerate the academy and sustain it, and to populate some key professions. Contemporary notions of (UK) higher education as a public good, where applied research benefits society and it is valued and understood by the public, and where many, diverse graduates leave with employability skills to take on well-paid roles in a service economy has been a revolution that has taken place in less than a lifetime—in mine. I studied as an undergraduate in the mid-1980s when fewer than 5% of 18–21 year olds went to university: we were considered elite although times were starting to change. Later, when I was working in a university following my postgraduate studies, the changes to higher education were happening with more speed.

In 1995, I was pregnant and had a child. I was on a two year fixed-term post-doctoral research contract for a national funding body and working in a research-intensive university science department in the UK. I was, by virtue of serendipity, the first researcher in the country, supported by that research council, to be eligible for maternity leave. This was owing to a recent change in the law, the number of months I had already worked on the contract and those that would remain after the birth. It was a stark reminder of the fate of many who had gone before me and had had no such support and it shocked me. It perhaps helped explain why only two of the academics I had met during my own studies were women: I had studied in the UK at research-intensive universities as an undergraduate and as a postgraduate researcher in the 1980s and 1990s. I was lucky, pregnant in the right window of my funded project and a funding body that was an early adopter of the new law. In fact, I was told proudly that I was the first woman to receive maternity leave from them.

> *I believed that starting a family as a woman and undertaking research were not easily compatible because it was commonly expected that as an early career researcher you needed to undertake one or two fixed-term research contracts, ideally in different research groups, before applying for a permanent (tenure-track) academic role. When I went back to work a few months after the birth of my child I returned as a part-time worker on a precariously short, fixed-term contract with a very new sense of the responsibility I now carried to provide for a new life. It wasn't long before I started looking for jobs but deep inside, I felt that I hadn't 'done my time' to get a job in the research-intensive university sector I was familiar with so I cast the net wider and applied for a role at a university college – a part of higher education I knew very little about. They were enthusiastic about appointing me to a lectureship as I had research credentials – something many of their staff lacked and they knew that they would need to change in the longer term as they pursued their goal of achieving the status of a university. I moved into a largely teaching role and found my research area, which required international fieldwork, was difficult to sustain: funding bodies repeatedly rejected my grant applications. I worked hard to become a good teacher, it was difficult work– I found it to be emotionally and intellectually challenging - and I also enjoyed it tremendously. Over the next 8–10 years, I applied the investigative approach from my research background to the day-to-day work I was involved with as a teacher. I had some success with teaching development grants and enjoyed that scholarship work. I sustained a portfolio of extended teaching commitments across undergraduate and postgraduate courses, including PhD supervision, and a mixed research portfolio in my discipline as well as undertaking scholarship research into student learning. I accepted a range of exciting Faculty and institution-wide roles to lead curriculum and teaching and learning developments. The college secured its university title. I was under more pressure to secure disciplinary research funding and follow a more research-based route to academic success but it was no longer what I relished about the job.*

During my employment as a post-doctoral researcher I had developed an internal sense of confidence and competence. These attributes are described by Åkerlind (2008) in her four category model as a key, first developmental stage for early career researchers who are growing to independence (for example, following dependence or inter-dependence as student-researchers with supervision.) She recognises that this stage can also be occupied by researchers later in their career when they, for example, change research direction or topic. It was, I believe, this confidence, that allowed me to (perhaps misguidedly) believe that I could apply and be successful in a fuller academic role and led to my application for a lecturer post in a college of higher education.

I mourned and grieved for my lost confidence when I took on my new teaching-focussed academic role. I opted in for all the development opportunities I could and in those days it was not a requirement to undertake any form of academic development to become a university educator in the UK, even in a teaching-focussed institute. The exposure to theory to make sense of my practice was elucidating and exciting and I relished formal classes. More than the formal learning however, my development as a university teacher is peppered with wonderful memories of questioning and coming to understandings through the conversations I held with more experienced colleagues in coffee room conversations and department staff meetings. Roxå and Mårtenssen (2009) talk about the value of significant conversations and networks and of sincere conversations based on trust and intellectual intrigue. I was privileged to have these in abundance and rapidly developed a series of stances towards teaching that increasingly acknowledged the primacy of focusing on student learning and indeed my own learning though my interactions with students. Åkerlind (2004) describes four conceptual categories, hierarchically linked, as ways academics experience or understand being a (university) teacher using phenomenography. I look now at those categories and recognise that journey to increasingly complex, learner and learning centred appreciation of teaching as a practice and a purpose. I hadn't read her work then, but at the time of my personal growth and learning to become an effective educator, John Biggs published his (1999) book, and I remember as I read it, and colleagues did too, we celebrated that here was an explanation of what we were talking about when we discussed and tried to express the purpose of our teaching—to promote quality learning.

Alongside my developing skill and enthusiasm for teaching, and for supporting learners and learning, I started to undertake investigations as well as to innovate with new approaches to teaching practice. Slowly, and with many false starts, I embarked on a trajectory where I undertook investigations for the satisfaction of increasing my own personal knowledge and practice and more latterly to inform a group of others in my shared disciplinary context where I would open up my investigations for their involvement, scrutiny or evaluation. In this way, I embarked on the earliest stages of the scholarship of learning and teaching. I was reading and informed by the developing literature on teaching scholarship from the United States and later by Ashwin and Trigwell (2004) who model the purposes, processes and outcomes of investigations. As I made more public my teaching activities, my teaching philosophy and my aspirations for my learners, the number and range of conversations and conversation partners increased to include those from outside my department but within the discipline and, in particular, who were involved in establishing the then emerging learning and teaching subject centres. This was a national initiative by the UK funding council to develop teaching and learning in UK higher education. They stood for a decade as a cornerstone that enriched the scholarship of higher education teaching in the UK by brokering collaborative learning through events, grants and the encouragement to write to share practice. They occasionally employed me to run workshops for academics in my discipline in other universities on aspects of teaching practice and my understanding of how people learn. The opportunities and experiences I gathered within my institution were available to me because of the tremendous growth and ambition of it during those years. They increased my confidence and I came to believe that not only did I have something of value to share with academics about my own practice, I had the skills to support their learning based on my learner-centred conception of teaching as enabling others to, *"think critically and originally, to question existing knowledge, explore new ideas, see new dimensions and become independent learners"* (Åkerlind 2004). My teaching philosophy was the foundation for my next career step.

Moving to the 'Other Side'?

The staff of a modern university occupy a diverse mix of roles. The simplistic, binary divide of staff into academic and non-academic roles (more commonly now described as professional support staff) does little to expose the ragged and fragile boundary between academic and other professional work. Celia Whitchurch (2008a) describes blended professionals: those who have mixed backgrounds and portfolios comprising elements of academic and professional activity. Notwithstanding the blurring of work and function, the type of contract on which an individual is employed is also be a critical sign of how a role is conceived and deployed in universities. Devecchi et al. (2018) explored experiences of managing change and of leadership among academic and professional services staff in the UK. They cite an interviewee in their research who exposes the inconsistencies at the boundary, "*I would consider myself an academic although I'm not on an academic contract*" (p. 19). They state that strong archetypes of academic and professional services staff persist in universities despite the creation of new roles (that challenge these) and work by Whitchurch (2008b) that challenges the binary division and describes a moving picture, akin to a kaleidoscope, of administrators, managers and other professionals.

I took on another role and responsibility within the University in 2003 and my new boss asked me, "what's your ideal job?" I didn't reply. I didn't know but I did know that it wasn't doing the broad variety of work that comprised my current academic portfolio of teaching, research, knowledge exchange, academic administration and service to the university. I was feeling stretched, tired and undervalued. I felt pulled in so many directions and when I looked around me, to see what was expected further of me to achieve promotion, I saw that I would need to be spread even more thinly across a wider variety or projects and areas of activity. I started to look at the jobs available weekly in the Times Higher magazine. I didn't look at academic jobs like mine but at jobs I'd never really noticed before. Academic management jobs, professional services jobs. These jobs held expectations to manage and lead others, were associated with more responsibility (and money) and they were not linked clearly to the academic promotion pathway. I had never realised so much variety existed and that there were so many of those jobs! I started a scrapbook and for the jobs I liked the look of. I would annotate the advert commenting on what was appealing to me about the role, what relevant strengths I had and where I had more limited experience.

My best friend listened to my reflections and said to me, "you'll need to update your CV. I can help you." I accumulated all the fragments and pieces of work I had undertaken, I sifted and sorted them and created order and sense and in doing so, and with her help, I rewrote myself as a capable, experienced science academic with considerable administrative experience. I applied to be Head of Department but was not successful and found I was relieved. In 2005, I applied to establish a new centre to develop the academic capabilities of staff and students in a research-intensive foreign university. "I've found my ideal job!" I told my old boss. They offered me the job but they would not accept that the job was an academic role. The only reason that bothered me at the time was because of the implications for my pension – I took the job anyway; it was, after all, ideal. It turned out to be very nearly so. A collegiate university and a role that I cherished to manage a Centre for student and staff learning. I was not academic but I worked in a scholarly way to embed practices in the university and introduce changes. I undertook small educational research projects and published those and other practice-based studies alone, with students and with colleagues, some of whom were academics and some were not. I was in transit: moving from my science discipline to create a new identity through the study of higher education learning and aspects of higher education management. I was learning fast and still perhaps practising as an academic although I was not an academic anymore.

There are not only archetypes for academic and professional services roles, there are also institutional archetypes and the research-intensive institutional archetype is among the most recognisable and enduring. It was to this type of university that I moved and while they could not accommodate my new role as an academic one that is, on reflection, quite possibly an outcome of how the role came into being: from the stable of learning and development in Human Resources. In contrast, their main research-intensive university competitor had grown academic development from a base of academic workers offered secondments and roles on equivalent contractual footings. The role I occupied was new to the university and was mine to fill and develop without much institutional expectation of what it might look like or deliver. Unfettered by a conception of how it ought to be undertaken based on a previous incumbent, the university and I created a space that fitted well to the model of a blended professional described by Whitchurch (2008a). I directly transferred a good deal of my academic knowledge and approach to work into the new role. One specific example was the way I used scholarly writing as a common mode of communicating for example when working with academic colleagues and proposing new approaches they could incorporate into their academic practice or synthesising current knowledge on a topic, when suggesting new policies to committees and in my approach to bidding for money to undertake new project work. I remember noting at the time that I had referenced my first committee paper for the university (on research-informed teaching) as extensively as I would an article for publication. It was the purpose and the audience for the persuasive argument that I was making that had changed and it changed the way I saw writing and academic writing. From something necessary, difficult and individually completed at the end of a project, it became something necessary and purposeful, interesting and engaging, and collaborative between writer and readers and sometimes among writers. This was a transformative insight that allowed me to develop my professional writing for institutional purposes and also my academic writing and scholarship journey within my new discipline of academic development. This latter writing was based entirely on my practice and it was written, as before within my science discipline, to inform a group of others in my shared disciplinary context where I would open up my investigations for their involvement, scrutiny or evaluation. My disciplinary community had changed from academics within the sciences to a new community of academic developers, largely working in my new country. I transferred the approach of writing to expose my practice—the innovations and the challenges in my work—based on notions of its utility to the audience (see Pesata 2007). It was also a way to articulate my developing capability as I started to 'find my feet' in a new profession that occupied an academic space, and with it the notions academic endeavour of not only teaching others but of also researching and writing about that practice to one's own community. In the same way, I had researched and reported on the teaching practice in my science discipline, I now researched and reported on my development practice as an educational developer. I now see that my practice of research had not matured although my role had changed. In relation to the model of Ashwin and Trigwell (2004) I was still undertaking evaluation of practice and had not developed agency as a researcher in my new academic space. Although I was mirroring and modelling academic work (Green and Little 2015) I was yet to accomplish fully undertaking scholarship research—categorised by Ashwin and Trigwell (2004) as work embarked on to create public knowledge that is verified by those outside that context and will inform a wide audience. I was still talking to people like me about my practice and work.

Blended professionals can feel isolated from both the academic and professional spheres. Some interviewees in Whitchurch's (2008a) study reported a feeling of outsider status despite their appointment being made because of their mixed backgrounds and portfolios. I had the fortune to join a community of national academic developers who felt united by a common professionalism in their support for the academic development project and a desire to write about their work and engage in scholarship. Many were also undertaking academic qualifications in educational research to support their own personal transitions into this emerging profession—my way to embrace the need to 'credentialise' my work was to seek professional recognition from the relevant professional body, the Staff and Educational Development Association. Within my institution there were a wide number of third space professionals that I worked with, in the research and grants office, in learning development and careers and in access and participation: I felt a strong sense of community with those people on joint projects where our work intersected.

As before when I made the move to teaching-focussed academic from researcher, I found that the move from teaching-focused, scholarly academic to academic developer was one that required a good deal of learning fast on my part. There were still the sincere conversations (sensu Roxå and Mårtenssen 2009) with likeminded colleagues. However more of them were now dispersed across institutions and in different countries. The largest arena for learning was in the field of management and leadership. In making my move to this new country, new institution, new discipline, this professional contract and blended professional role, I had taken on responsibilities to manage people and resources and to lead through shaping institutional policies and practices. I have been learning to be a manager and a leader of Centres that support staff and student learning ever since.

Under Review

In my lifetime working in higher education there have always been reviews of higher education as governments seek to elicit from the sector better value and outcomes for the economy and society as a whole. As the sector comes under closer scrutiny and needs to adapt to an increasing range of expectations so universities themselves review and refresh their purposes and priorities, their educational and research offers and the structures that enable them. Centres that lead on staff and student learning development are not immune to such reviews. Periodic snapshots of such Centres in the UK have been commissioned by the Heads of Educational Development Group (HEDG). They show the variation in units' structures and functions and the way those frequently change (Gosling 2008) although nearly 60% of Heads of Centres' interviewed in 2011 felt that the institutional environment for educational development was more favourable that five years earlier (Jones and Wisker 2012). Although the academic development project is now universally accepted universally as a key service in a UK university (and is increasingly found in other countries around the world) there is fluidity to the shape and form of Centres that provide it, in how they are aligned to academic work and to other third space professionals. Most recently there is a case of a UK university offering the service of academic development not through a Centre (which was disbanded to reduce costs) but by coalescing an offer from a complement of substantive role holders and associates embedded in the academic structures led by a senior university leader (Taylor, forthcoming).

In 2014 I am flown back to the UK after an accident on holiday. It will be at least four months before I can get back to my job leading a UK Centre and for now, it is rest and recovery. As I get stronger, I consider my options for phasing back to work and make a suggestion to the Pro Vice-Chancellor (Student Experience). She agrees and as a result, I spend three months focused on writing grants and bids for external funds to develop institutional academic development work and, in collaboration with other universities, a national project. I have a good success rate and, as a result, the breadth of my work expands and I get involved in educational research based in the institution and with the national project alongside my usual activities. The Centre is on a high and it comes as a surprise that we are to be reviewed: there are no criteria put forward against which we will self-evaluate our work and the seniority of the University review panel members is both striking and worrying to me. There is no external panel member. My boss tells me there is nothing to worry about. I turn to my networks and professional body for thoughts on how I might lead my team to approach this. It seems that reviews are not usually good news for people in Centres. Centres come and go and reviews are often the precursor to a Centre going. People who run Centres are sanguine about the comings and goings of Centres and their own roles as Centre leaders. As I look at it, I realise that Centre leaders move around—new Centres are created at the same rate as others are disbanded. That feels comforting although I am comfortable already where I am. The review marks the beginning of a slow process of an increasing spotlight on my work and the work of Centres like the one I'm leading. The importance of work like ours has developed nationally now as a result of changes to the ways higher education is refocusing on teaching excellence and student outcomes. No-one seems to know if these Centres are academic or if they are not.

The review happens. There is no feedback, no summative judgement just a record of the conversations I, and my team, have had with the review panel. Nothing happens. We carry on, we do good work, perhaps some of our best work, until the new, planned structure and governance is explained to us and the existing Centre is disbanded. A new Centre is formed, new lines are drawn and I apply for the role of leader. It is offered to someone else and I am not surprised or disappointed. My husband says we can move anywhere—he knows I enjoy leading support for student and staff learning, whether as an academic or not. Weeks later, shortly before Christmas in 2017, my ideal job is advertised. There is one Centre that formed my academic capabilities as a teacher twenty years ago and sustains an international reputation built on longevity, external consultancy and ground-breaking research and publications on teaching in higher education. It now needs a new leader. I apply and that University recognises my work for scholarship and academic leadership of learning and teaching as a route to the professoriate.

I'm undertaking more research. My research work is now characterised strongly by working with others. There are two types of research projects that I'm involved with. That which uses the university as the site for study and is important to inform future practice in it. The work is undertaken collaboratively with academics in the university. They are from different disciplines and I am now firmly from the discipline of academic development and educational research: my science background last explicitly played a role in my scholarship many years ago (see Potter 2009). Although we are working together, sometimes on varied sub-projects, the liaison with the funder is my responsibility. I feel a responsibility to my colleagues and to my institution to make sure the research is translated into action that will impact positively on student learning and staff academic practice—that it will have a practical and near immediate benefit on students and staff. I am, as Handal (2008, p. 56) describes it, *".. a person in the academy who is actively and purposefully engaged in contributing to change—change of aspects of the academic culture and the practice of academics within it."* By contrast, when I am working with colleagues from other universities on national research projects I do not carry the weight of responsibility for the application of the research into local change. Although I am still aware of the varied dispositions I might adopt as an academic developer (Land 2004) I do not feel the same tensions of undertaking academic development 'insider work' (Lee and McWilliam 2008). I see a clear distinction between these two forms of research I undertake and each of them informs a different aspect of my identity. On the one hand, I am contributing to disciplinary knowledge in the fields of student education and academic development and with this comes a sense of academic identity (as described by Taylor 2008). On the other hand, I am working as someone looking to create change for the academic community and this creates a sense of being an outsider of that community, a position Whitchurch (2008a) describes as a common space occupied by blended professionals.

I am not, however, a professor because of a strong and sustained research profile but instead because of my contribution to teaching and learning activities and leading developments to improve student (and staff) outcomes. Practices, such as externally examining, organisational change projects and policies to improve the student experience, developing and providing scholarly development opportunities for students and for academics for a range of universities and contributing to the work of professional bodies have been continuously part of my roles throughout my career and it is this that has particularly been acknowledged. I have joined a university that recognises five routes to the professoriate, extending the range of valued activities and achievements, from the traditional route of research, whether pure or applied. Although it is other achievements that have allowed me to be recognised by the academy, the research work that I have completed and my relationship to research, best summarises my career most clearly for me. This charts the shift from one discipline to another, the development of a scholarly approach to teaching and learning to an increasingly public and accountable series of research projects on a range of topics comprising the scholarship of teaching and learning and approaches to educational change and leadership in higher education. It charts an academic identity that has been made and remade, questioned and challenged and that now finds legitimacy in a discipline, academic development, that is itself contested as a legitimate academic subject. Academic development was described recently as cultural work, where deliberate attempts are made to develop and disrupt an organisation and that is a dynamic, constructive and critical activity (Stensaker 2018). If there is truth in this, it might be reasonably argued that adopting research or research-like practices to enable evidence-based practice could be a fundamental survival strategy to work alongside the academic community who prize research, evidence, curiosity and rigorous inquiry so highly.

Across my career to date, the sense of movement and change, in the academy at large and in the individual institutions and Centres where I have worked, has been a constant feature. Delanty (2008) describes institutions as increasingly fluid, multilinear; more akin to processes and as in constant motion. He suggests they don't just respond to change but have 'change built into them' (p. 127). In these changing institutional contexts, identity work for individuals is on-going and identity is constantly under construction (Taylor 2008) with any individual capable of having multiple identities at one time (Delanty 2008). In the last section of this chapter, I want to introduce and explore the concept of my identity as an academic as fluid and contextual and particularly contestable as it sits at the boundaries of academic and professional activity. I want to introduce the term academic fluidity.

Academic Fluidity

I have an academic title and role. I enjoy privileges and take responsibilities associated with that (see for example, MacFarlane and Burg 2018). I also hold a professional management title and that too comes with privileges and responsibilities, or perhaps the visibility and accountability that Whitchurch (2008b) describes as arising from an ethos of partnership to deliver modern administrative and management roles. In this section I reaffirm how my identity, now, as a professor and as a leader of a professional service in a university, does resolve the dissonance I have felt in other roles and times around being an academic that does professional work and being a professional that does academic work. My work is multi-faceted but is always shaped to be delivered within the academic community and for the academic community. As a result, I am always alert to the value the academic community places on different work—on the prestige economy of the various academic activities – and alert to recent research work on the gender differences in how prestige may be accrued or valued (Kandiko Howsona et al. 2018). My route to the professoriate has been unconventional and has not had research as the cornerstone to support success. However, research and contribution to the knowledge economy, feature heavily in my definition of self at all stages of the career 'moments' I have considered here. Taylor (2008) describes disciplines as rich sites for the creation of identity and the link I feel between knowledge creation and my own identity, across the disciplines I have identified with in my career, is strong. When I first moved from my science discipline to professional work at the margin of academic acceptance, I encountered my first experience of academic fluidity. I am defining academic fluidity here as personal, professional academic identity that is shaped and defined as a result of undertaking various work practices, irrespective of contract types and roles, and through interaction with others in the academic environment, including students, managers, academic and professional services staff. Academic fluidity is the changing sense of self that emerges in an individual from task to task, from environment to environment, and in contact with different people. The key feature of academic fluidity is that the persons' sense of identity is mutable and changes.

Academic fluidity is influenced by the interaction of others. For example, it would be entirely within my grasp to move from feeling, acting and being academic in all my previous roles and indeed my current role to not feeling, acting or being so within the same working day while attending to other work activities or in the company of different others. This perception of fluidity transcends roles I have held, contracts I have been employed on and the disciplines I have been part of. What is common is that the sense of identity, as academic or professional, shifts in response to my surroundings, most notably the people I am with and the work activity I am doing.

Identity is shaped in contrast to others, through positionality, by making distinctions between the self and others (Delanty 2008). Within communities of others I can feel like them or unlike them, often as a result of my responsibility or part to play in the action going forward. For example, in a group of academic colleagues planning a symposium, I identify with them as an academic. When working with academic developers on cross-institutional research, I relate to my colleagues in academic development as academics too. By contrast, when attending a committee to present statistics on participation rates in academic development activities, I do not feel like an academic engaged in academic work. I wonder do other academics feel academic fluidity when they are engaged with academic administrative work or take on leadership and management responsibilities? Is the issue here simply that the conception of academic work is too simplistic? Perhaps the strength in the concept of academic fluidity, and the associated impact of looking closely at activities and interactions with others, is the resulting attentiveness to the multiple facets of identity and, as a result, an increase in self-understanding, and acceptance of the self. I would propose that this comes from seeing the complexity and environmental responsiveness of identity in routine work and activities.

As universities have changed and become more entrepreneurial, commercial and accountable to society and government, so have the expectations of the routine activity undertaken by academics as well as an increase in the number and diversity of third space professional roles that work with academic colleagues in partnership. My career has taken place against this backdrop of change to the academy: some of the roles

I have held have come into existence as a result of individual universities developing responses to those changes. Across my career, it has been increasingly important to sustain an agile and responsive sense of identity. The notion of academic fluidity helps me explain this at the margins of academic and professional services work and in the transition from discipline to discipline. What is clear is that while academic fluidity, this notion of identity shaped by surroundings, creates change in the perception of self, some things remain immutable. In particular it is clear that my values have been steadfast and are at the core of driving my career ambition and career decisions, both at the key 'moments' narrated here and in making smaller choices inbetween.

References

Åkerlind, G. (2004). A new dimension to understanding university teaching. *Teaching in Higher Education, 9*(3), 363–375.

Åkerlind, G. (2008). Growing and developing as a university researcher. *Higher Education, 55*(2), 241–254.

Ashwin, P., & Trigwell, K. (2004). Investigating educational development. In P. Kahn & D. Baume (Eds.), *Enhancing staff and educational development* (pp. 117–131). London: Kogan-Page.

Biggs, J. B. (1999). *Teaching for quality learning at university: What the student does*. Buckingham: Society for Research into Higher Education.

Delanty, G. (2008). Academic identities and institutional change. In R. Barnett & R. di Napoli (Eds.), *Changing identities in higher education: Voicing perspectives*. Abingdon: Routledge.

Devecchi, C., Mansour, H., Allen, N., & Potter, J. (2018). *Leading change together: Managing cultural change across the higher education workforce*. London: Leadership Foundation for Higher Education.

Fraser, K. (1999). Australasian academic developers: Entry into the profession and our own professional development. *International Journal of Academic Development, 4*(2), 89–101.

Fyffe, J. M. (2018). Getting comfortable with being uncomfortable: A narrative account of becoming an academic developer. *International Journal of Academic Development, 23*(4), 355–366.

Gosling, D. (2008). *Educational development in the United Kingdom: Report to the heads of educational development group.* HEDG. http://www.hedg.ac.uk/ico/wp-content/uploads/2016/02/HEDG_Report_final.pdf Accessed 15 May 2019.

Green, D. A., & Little, D. (2015). Family portrait: A profile of educational developers around the world. *International Journal of Academic Development, 21*(2), 135–150.

Handal, G. (2008). Identities of academic developers: Critical friends of the academy? In R. Barnett & R. di Napoli (Eds.), *Changing identities in higher education: Voicing perspectives.* Abingdon: Routledge.

Jones, J., & Wisker, G. (2012). *Educational development in the United Kingdom: Report to the heads of educational development group.* HEDG. http://www.hedg.ac.uk/ico/wp-content/uploads/2016/02/HEDGFinalReport2012.pdf. Accessed 15 May 2019.

Kandiko Howsona, C. B., Coate, K., & St Croix, T. (2018). Mid-career academic women and the prestige economy. *Higher Education Research and Development, 33*(1), 533–548.

Land, R. (2004). *Educational development: Discourse, identity and practice.* Maidenhead: The Society for Research into Higher Education & Open University Press.

Lee, A., & McWilliam, E. (2008). What game are we in? Living with academic development. *International Journal of Academic Development, 13*(1), 67–77.

MacFarlane, B., & Burg, B. (2018). *Women professors as intellectual leaders.* London: Leadership Foundation for Higher Education.

Pesata, T. (2007). Troubling our desires for research and writing within the academic development project. *International Journal of Academic Development, 12*(1), 15–23.

Potter, J. A. (2009). Starting with the discipline. In R. Murray (Ed.), *The scholarship of teaching and learning in higher education.* Maidenhead: Open University Press and McGraw Hill.

Roxå, T., & Mårtenssen, A. (2009). Significant conversations and significant networks—Exploring the backstage of the teaching arena. *Studies in Higher Education, 34*(5), 547–559.

Stensaker, B. (2018). Academic development as cultural work: Responding to the organizational complexity of modern higher education institutions. *International Journal of Higher Education, 23*(4), 274–285.

Taylor, C. (Forthcoming). The distributed academic development team: A case study. In J. Potter & C. Devecchi (Eds.), *Delivering educational change in HE: A transformative approach for leaders and practitioners*. London: Routledge SEDA Series. Due to be published 2020.

Taylor, P. (2008). Being an academic today. In R. Barnett & R. di Napoli (Eds.), *Changing identities in higher education: Voicing perspectives*. Abingdon: Routledge.

Whitchurch, C. (2008a). Shifting identities and blurring boundaries: The emergence of *third space* professionals in UK higher education. *Higher Education Quarterly, 62*(4), 377–396.

Whitchurch, C. (2008b). Beyond administration and management: Changing professional identities in UK higher education. In R. Barnett & R. di Napoli (Eds.), *Changing identities in higher education: Voicing perspectives*. Abingdon: Routledge.

7

My Personal Journey on the Pathway of Resilience

Sarah Skerratt

Resilience *has no meaning* except in relationship to more or less desirable outcomes. It is defined either in terms of having approximated *desirable* outcomes, or having distanced oneself from *undesirable* outcomes. (Kaplan 1999, p. 30; emphases added)

My Desirability Framework

Kaplan's assessment of the resilience concept has impacted on my thinking, both in terms of my on-going analysis, and in reflecting on my own personal and academic journey thus far. His subtext of who decides what is "desirable" and "undesirable" has fuelled my life in multiple ways and particularly the extension of "desirable for whom". Although I remained unaware of this framing in the literature until

---

S. Skerratt (✉)
Scotland's Rural College, Edinburgh, Scotland, UK
e-mail: Sarah.skerratt@sruc.ac.uk

© The Author(s) 2019
R. Murray and D. Mifsud (eds.), *The Positioning and Making of Female Professors*, Palgrave Studies in Gender and Education, https://doi.org/10.1007/978-3-030-26187-0_7

relatively recently, I have been living out these meanings in my early and subsequent career and personal choices.

Who decides? Aged 22 I decided I would become a Professor by the age of 50. This became my very private, desirable outcome. On my 50th Birthday, I achieved this, reflecting on how this had taken 28 years of deliberate, sometimes pragmatic, steps towards my goal. I have achieved this goal in spite of others with power and influence in my life desiring other outcomes for me, and pressuring me towards those. And in the four years since gaining my professorship, I have learnt that what was desirable for *me* is misunderstood, and indeed undesirable, for (some) *others*. I have also discovered that resilience, which is my inner "pilot light", a fire-that-will-not-be-extinguished, is also immensely subjective and contested externally (what others may think is right for me) and in the resilience field of literature.

A Summary of the (Community) Resilience Literature

To unpack this further, I will first dig a little into the literature around resilience, as it remains a contested concept. Figure 7.1 shows a timeline of evolution, particularly in relation to community resilience. There is consensus that research around community resilience began with earlier thinking in maths and physics (in relation to what makes materials strong and resilient) and ecology (the characteristics of ecological systems). Key concepts included: the ability of materials to "recuperate and maintain" their integrity and shape (Gordon 1978), and to "absorb and maintain" shocks from outside while keeping their form and function (Holling 1978, 1986; Holling et al. 1995). The starting point was that systems are subject to external shocks, with resilience relating to how well those systems could adjust and recover from such shocks—or "bounce back". This has, largely, remained the dominant way of thinking about resilience for the past 40 years.

Subsequent *community* resilience research has been undertaken across environmental sciences, engineering, sociology, psychology

7 My Personal Journey on the Pathway of Resilience

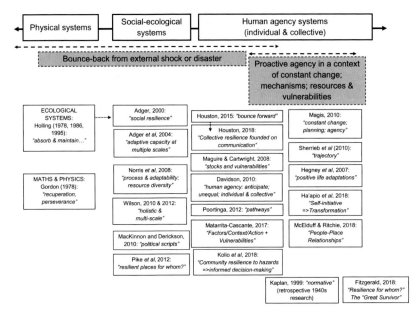

Fig. 7.1 40 years of resilience research (1978–2018) (Adapted from Skerratt [2013])

and economics, resulting in no single, over-arching definition (Koliou et al. 2018). The focus is on how well communities can plan for, resist, absorb and recover from hazards that are both man-made and natural, with an emphasis on three priorities: reduce the impacts, reduce recovery time, and reduce future vulnerabilities. Learning and adaptation are critically important (Folke 2006), with the ability to reorganise and change being seen as a fundamental aspect of "adaptive processes" (Cutter et al. 2008).

Resilience is also described as: being able to harness capacity in a positive direction of travel (Norris et al. 2008); the use of community resources by community members to thrive in an environment of change, uncertainty, unpredictability, and surprise (Magis 2010); the ability to function amid crisis (Cohen et al. 2013); the ability to collaborate and learn with relevant stakeholders (Kuir-Ayius 2016); and collective, interactive behaviour (Houston 2018). Resource diversity enhances community resilience (Folke 2006); resource dependency reduces it (Adger 2000), as does vulnerability and social vulnerability (Matarrita-Cascante et al. 2017).

Key factors that enhance community resilience are described using varied terminology:

- "*Capitals*": social, economic, natural and cultural capital (Roberts and Townsend 2015);
- "*Resources*": natural, built, human, cultural, social, political and financial (Magis 2010);
- "*Strengths*": people–place connections, values and beliefs, knowledge, skills and learning, social networks, engaged governance, a diverse and innovative economy, community infrastructure, leadership and a positive, change-focused outlook (Berkes and Ross 2013);
- "*Capacities*": economic development, social capital, information and communication, and community competence (Norris et al. 2008).

Resilience is not fixed, but rather a process. Present resilience is not a predictor of future resilience, since what are considered as assets or resources may not be relevant in a future situation (Amundsen 2015). Further, resilience resources may be deployed successfully in some instances and not in others Kaplan (1999), such that "competence in resolving issues in one developmental period does not predict later competence in a linear, deterministic way" (p. 64). Community resilience can therefore be seen as ability over time, rather than a fixed outcome (Norris et al. 2008).

Managing resilience over time brings in the really important concept of "human agency", which focuses on how humans imagine, anticipate, act individually and collectively (Wilson 2012; Pendall et al. 2010; Davidson 2010). Resilient communities are able to anticipate and plan for events before they occur (Brand and Jax 2007). However, human agency is "distributed unequally" (Davidson 2010), with no individual or community starting from the same place.

This thread of inequality also emerges around who is benefiting from the concept and practice of resilient communities. In summary, there is a push towards what has been termed the "great survivor"

(Fitzgerald 2018), where the community "rolls up its sleeves", "gets stuck in", "does not give up" and is applauded for doing so. Resilience is positive, benign and desirable (Fitzgerald 2018). However, such self-reliance is also seen as a way to transfer responsibility away from the State, with the "implicit suggestion that the organisation or individual should stand 'on one's own two feet'" (White and O'Hare 2014, p. 946), and a "sink or swim strategy where not all communities will survive" (Lowndes and Pratchett 2012). A growing number of researchers argue that community resilience is not occurring in a vacuum, but is very closely connected with what is seen as "desirable" and "undesirable" within policy, with consequent winners and losers.

My Journey Away from Undesirable Outcomes Towards Desirable Outcomes

A key finding throughout the literature, not only in relation to communities, but in research into childhood resilience and resilience of children into adulthood, is the ability to reach out. To know your limits; where you end; where you need to be picked up, guided and strengthened by another. Those who more-than-survive are the ones who do not rely only on their inner resources, but (particularly in crisis) create webs of support and inspiration, sharing the journey as fellow humans.

I grew up in central England in the 1960s and 1970s, bubbly and eager to see what was around every corner, under every rock and in every cupboard. Masses of curly auburn hair, a constant dimpled smile, a musical ear. I loved life and the living. Far from idyllic, however, as a life of extreme and repeated childhood abuse of all kinds from age six to 14 led to extraordinary confusion, distress, phenomenal headaches for weeks on end, self-harm, and an attempt to end my life in my teens. I found faith, and people of faith, although that was not without its own abuse. I have since moved on from that faith; however, I am without doubt that, without connecting to this group of people, I would have migrated to the streets aged 15 due to extreme fear and self-loathing.

Classical music was my very early refuge. My desirable outcome—to be an opera singer—was my chosen career from the age of nine, and I trained and joined choirs to make sure I could reach that goal. But this was made impossible since much of the abuse took place in that musical world, such that even now, 40 years on, I cannot reconnect with classical music because the body remembers, even if mentally and spiritually I have distanced myself from the horrific experiences.

My daily survival depended on my resilience. But what amazes me about the child, teenage and newly-into-adult Sarah, is that I kept reaching out to others, even though to do so had meant unimaginable humiliation, gut-wrenching physical and emotional pain, with days and nights of extreme darkness. I kept trusting others, and even now my *modus operandi* is to trust someone until they show me I cannot or should not, rather than the reverse. I am fascinated, confused yet relieved that my hard-wiring has chosen that response, though at first glance it's far from rational.

At 18, in the midst of home-based manipulation, I made it to the University in Manchester. At this point, I still had my faith, which at Uni gave you an instant network through the Christian Union. However, I always felt an outsider and fraud, because, having experienced the things that had been done to me as a child, I was not "pure" as I believed my friends to be. "Sin" was always writ large, and I dared not disclose my past in such a setting. The perversion of the perpetrator is such that you believe you are the one at fault, and it took me many more decades to know that this is The Big Lie.

At Uni, I *loved* to study, learn and understand. I'd been pushed (with others at my Grammar School) to go into sciences, because that's how you would get a job. I had an aptitude for languages and music, but instead it was Geology and Geography for me. Three-dimensional maps were impossible for my brain to compute and draw, but I excelled in other aspects of geology—mainly memorising the beautiful cross-sections under the microscope, like mini-universes. In my final year, I "discovered" human geography, planning, policy, and I was hooked—trying to understand people on a grand, population scale and how we manage our environments in ways that help or hinder people's life chances. It was mind-blowing that an actual discipline existed that

7 My Personal Journey on the Pathway of Resilience

focused on the intricacies of collective human behaviour linked to physical spaces and places. I felt that I had found my "home". In one class, one of my pals told me of a Master's in Development Studies, with a Scholarship opportunity. I applied straight away and was successful.

This was the most stimulating year at Uni and has never since been eclipsed. I had become fascinated by disciplines and perspectives that were at odds with one another while each equally convinced that they had *the* answers. In this field, the core modules I selected were Agricultural Economics—focused on the rational and therefore predictable behaviour of "homo economicus", and Social Anthropology—a discipline which celebrated "the insider's view from the insider's perspective", respecting (and holding in tension) multiple world-views. I cherished walking from a debate in one Department on development approaches, crossing the road, and hearing diametrically opposing (and perfectly rational) explanations from eminent professors in the other Department. I listened, respected, questioned, argued and learned. I made up my own mind and was encouraged to do so. I felt extremely privileged, and at the same time felt I was learning something immensely valuable that would set me on my journey. That's when I decided to become a Professor by the age of 50. Perhaps it was awe at those Professors who opened my mind; a celebration of the diversity of knowledges and how they could co-exist; and that I wanted to be an author, in my own small way, that promoted such diversity of narratives and voices. If I could, I would. I had been shown the possible.

In talking with my supervisors, I realised the next step was a Ph.D. Some of my pals in the Hall of Residence (which held the scholarship) were doing their epic Ph.D. studies, and I talked long into the night with them about the philosophies and ontological frameworks they lived inside for years on end, the flashes of insight, the setbacks, the sheer thirst to understand and articulate complexity through simplicity. I became utterly fascinated by "systems thinking", realising how everything is connected, and how we needed multiple perspectives if we are to understand complex phenomena. I was convinced this "space" was for me, so I went "PhD-hunting", applying to a small number of institutions, saying this is what I had learned thus far, and this is what I wanted to learn and become.

I went to one interview, where it became clear that they wanted me to be a quantitative analyst in Agricultural Economics. I could not see how this would allow me to articulate the rich, contradictory nature of people's voices. I didn't know then that I was passionate about qualitative work—I didn't know the labels or the theory. I just had an inner drive that made it clear to me I had to study how people think and articulate their thoughts, how they make decisions and justify them, identifying what drives them and shapes their world. Perhaps in understanding others, and finding the tools to understand others, I would then understand my own "world" and life all the more.

I heard back from Edinburgh University and came to Scotland for an interview. The date for arrival in Edinburgh coincided with the Departmental trip to a local island in a small boat. I do not have sea legs. So, while trying to make my best impression on the Professor who would be interviewing me the next morning, I felt extremely nauseous and much was out of focus. I was nonetheless offered the Research Assistant position, and the person I shared the office with back in the late 1980s is still a dear friend now. He had arrived a few weeks before and managed to negotiate the amazing salary of £7000 per year—a fantastic amount of money to me as a student.

The Ph.D. formed the evaluation part of a government-funded programme of on-farm environmental schemes that farmers could choose to opt into. We were to generate evidence as to why farmers (male) did or did not participate. I had been inspired by the (sadly now late) Dr. Ruth Gasson, who had pioneered research in the 1970s, rather heretically, into farm *household* decision-making, that is, arguing that it is not only the man in isolation who makes on-farm decisions, but that decisions are made jointly with other family members. Ruth's was a very niche area at the time, pre-dating what we would come to call Gender Studies. I felt it imperative to pursue this angle myself, even though it lay outside the remit of the government-funded work.

During the first year of my Ph.D., however, things didn't go smoothly. I was given increasing amounts of teaching to do, and my then Ph.D. supervisor wanted me to move into something called Expert Systems computer programming, rather than remain at the more ethnographic end of the analytical spectrum. The stress was immense, since

I was just a lowly researcher, and he was an established Dr, soon to become Professor. I felt I was holding on by the thinnest of threads to my own rationale, to Ruth Gasson's initial work. We battled, and finally, because I wanted my Ph.D. so much, I decided to leave my secure post and work part time to pay for my keep. I cleaned flats in Edinburgh and remember really low points when I wondered if this journey was worth it. But again, I had reached out and asked for help, was able to buy an old bicycle which saved vital pennies on bus fares, managed to get a study room in the Uni library, and even a loan for a computer (a Dell 386, with a floppy disc drive—how I loved that machine as it held my ideas that I typed in day after day).

I was so determined to get my beloved Ph.D. that I also went to see my former supervisor's boss and asked for a different supervisory team. I was able then to have two supervisors, one in Social Anthropology (who had also been at Manchester University) and one in Agricultural Economics. I was thrilled to have two such inspiring Professors as supervisors, which meant the interdisciplinary approach once again became possible, allowing me to delve into the "messy" stuff of decision-making and individual's rationales.

My Social Anthropology Prof was inspirational. I remember an occasion when one of my hour-long supervisory sessions focused on the fact that I had used the word "autonomy" to describe the behaviour of those I was analysing. The interrogation was challenging, humbling and opened my eyes to yet more ways in which we can label people, their stories or experiences according to *our* understandings—in ways that make sense, but only from our perspective. It is rational to do so, to want to short-cut to an explanation and close-down the inquiry, but that does not respect the person who gave you their story.

I was fortunate that my other supervisor Professor put me forward for Research Council funding for additional fieldwork, which enabled me to spend a winter in the study area in Scotland. I gathered valuable data on how farming *families* made land-use decisions; how farmers and farmers' wives disclosed different things depending on whether their spouses were in the room with me; and the importance of children and parents to decisions. Probably the key aspect I learnt was to be myself. I am not from a farming background, and the farmers would occasionally "test" me, for example, by asking how much I would pay for that cow or that ewe. I was embarrassed by not knowing, but decided instead to tell them I had no idea, and to teach me how to make such an assessment. I did receive three marriage proposals while on fieldwork; I put it down to the fact that I am trained listener, and the gentlemen were isolated individuals who rarely saw folk, particularly females. Looking back, as researchers, we had no "lone-working" policies for working on farms; and I do remember seeing extreme isolation and poverty in many farmer's kitchens—images that have never left me and motivate me still.

Interestingly for me, it was only when I got my Ph.D. that I felt I could walk with my shoulders back, in the corridors of the Social Anthropology Department. I had done my Ph.D. fieldwork in Scotland, and so had not gone through the rite of passage of fieldwork in oft-quoted Papua New Guinea or an African country, where I would have been visibly different and at a loss language-wise. So I was always treated as "second-class" by the other Ph.D. students, as my ethnography was not seen as sufficiently demanding and a wee bit fake. I did emphasise that I had grown up near a city in England and spoke a different language to the farming families I was researching—but to no avail!

Three years researching one subject gave me the need for variety. I therefore decided to set up my own research consultancy, which I ran for several years. My first job was helping a rural charity—firstly in evaluating their provision and direction-of-travel, and writing them a report. All good so far. They then asked me to stay on to help them prepare for the Royal Highland Show—the biggest rural event on the Scottish calendar that attracts around 200,000 visitors per year. I was making cotton-wool sheep for a children's height chart and painting countryside scenes. That was a low point, as I remember thinking "Why did I bother with all that sacrifice for a PhD when I making cotton-wool sheep for a living?"

Work picked up, and I engaged with a diverse set of clients, focusing on agriculture and rural issues across the UK. One piece of research was a turning point in my life and shaped the direction of my subsequent career. I was interviewing people in poverty in rural north-west

England. I had a hire car, and reasonable expenses were covered. I drove to this small, former industrial town and interviewed a house-bound lady in her 70s, who could hardly move yet insisted on making me a cup of tea and gave me biscuits. I began to ask her about her living conditions, the poverty, the challenges she faced. She was extremely open, proud and unashamed, as she should be. I listened for an hour or more, and drove away in my paid-for vehicle, eating my paid-for sandwiches. It was then I decided that anything I did, from that moment on, had to make a direct difference to those I was "studying". Otherwise, I felt I was extracting data from people in challenging circumstances and choosing then not to help with the knowledge they had passed on to me. I was just leaving her where she was.

I then searched for work that would "make a difference". This became my "desirable outcome". However, I began to discover that, if you are wanting to climb the ladder towards a professorship, interdisciplinary work is already viewed as the lesser of the sciences (compared with single discipline science). If you then add a focus on thoroughly applied work, engaging with stakeholders, policy-makers, prioritising translation of science into impact, this was downgrading the science even more. I am writing of the 1990s, when "excellence with impact" was definitely not in common parlance. I remember going to one interview at a northern England university and being humiliated at interview by the leading-light Professor telling me I was clearly a "jack of all trades, master of none" due to the breadth of my experience, with his career advice being to specialise above all else. This was a severe knock-back to me for many months, as my firm belief in a systems approach due to the complexity of reality in the social world, meant I could not be a reductionist scientist. I wasn't critical of that per se; it just wasn't right for me. I repeatedly received signals that I was reaching for something that was viewed as "undesirable" in mainstream academia, particularly if *en route* to becoming a professor.

While running my consultancy, I was offered work that took me back into the farm household decision-making field, with colleagues in France. This was an amazing year working with computer modellers who were seeking to integrate ethnographic findings into predictive Agent-Based Decision Models that also demonstrated the importance of farmers' own networks—formal and informal. We paid for the key agricultural adviser (from the area where I had carried out my Ph.D. fieldwork) to come and critique the model, and learnt so much from his decades of experience. I was also invited out to Brazil, to assess why farmers were using their own trusted networks in preference to the state-sponsored advisory service—to understand their rationale in order to improve the way formal advice was being implemented.

On returning to the UK in the early 2000s, I felt that I needed to broaden my research scope beyond the agricultural community to the thousands of others who live and work in rural areas, and so began to look at wider rural community resilience. At that time, digital connectivity (particularly at the time of the Millennium) was seen as the answer to most rural problems, because it would lead to the "death of distance" and the "end of geography", by linking everyone and making place-based constraints obsolete. This was a fascinating time to be working in the digital space—bringing together people's own experiences of digital technology in rural areas and comparing them with the hype and aspirations of the telecoms industry and related policy statements. (This same juxtaposition continues almost 20 years later.) I returned to Scotland in 2005 to pursue this theme.

Then came another key moment in my career which proved essential in moving towards my desirable outcome of becoming a professor. Until this point, I hadn't grasped the nettle of writing for peer review. Although I enjoyed writing creatively, I also did not want to be part of a reward system that placed such an emphasis on paper-writing and the review process. I was concerned more with impact, and writing up the reports, than in seeking peer recognition within my academic network. I also resented having to do so. At the same time, I knew I had to face this unknown landscape, with no idea where to start and struggled with the idea of expressing myself within the structure of an academic paper. I was so fortunate that the university I had just joined was hosting Prof Rowena Murray (one of the co-editors of this book) to run a series of Writing for Publication Workshops as well as Writing Retreats. With Rowena's support, I wrestled my mind into this new (for me) way of writing, and managed to begin crafting, and enjoying, paper-writing. Although I had been reading and critiquing papers for years, I had never seen that as possible for me. Without this intervention and guidance, I would have been thwarted in reaching my bigger work/life-goal.

Around the same time, I was then asked to join a Higher Education Institution which wanted to broaden its focus beyond the farm gate to include "wider rural community" issues. Approximately one million people live in rural Scotland. "Rural" and "farming" are often conflated, which is a gross oversimplification, since there are multiple non-land-based enterprises in rural areas, plus the public sector accounts for c. 50% of all rural employment. Representing the complexity of rural people's lives was a challenge I was keen to accept.

I found myself in a totally new situation: a permanent research position. The previous eleven years, post-Ph.D., had been contract-based. I now found myself with the opportunity to be strategic, to see outcomes through, and to reflect on what those outcomes could and should be—and for whom. My characteristic way of being (and working)—to reach out, network, learn, understand other's viewpoints and rationale—kicked in, and I soon realised that I needed to represent two themes through my research. Firstly, the complexity that is rural—tell the story of what rural looks like, but more importantly why, and what that means for different people. Secondly, generate new data and new understandings of the rural that is usually under the radar—difficult to see, either because we don't want to know about it, or because methodologically it presents a challenge. In a nutshell: I needed to find out what was not working and for whom—and how this matched or mismatched the policy rhetoric and resource in Scotland.

I established a reporting series where we took the temperature of rural Scotland across a series of priority topics. We produced new evidence with commentary on why this mattered. We presented compelling evidence for change. We worked with multiple stakeholders across public, private and charity sectors to point to evidence of different types and from sources that we ourselves could not access. We generated change in policy, raised issues on the national agenda around rural poverty, disadvantage, isolation and remoteness, rural homelessness, youth life chances. I wanted to "myth-bust" the rural idyll, because I knew, from the anecdotal evidence I was gathering through my one-to-one meetings, that people's lived experience is not an idyll.

Then came another significant moment for me. As part of the preparation for one of our biennial reports, I met with the youth coordinator for one of the local councils. I had been doing some work with Scottish Women's Aid (SWA) on the extent to which their safety programmes for women and children in domestic abuse situations could be realised in a rural setting (e.g. "safe houses" are not necessarily safe because everyone knows where they are). I was meeting the youth worker to talk about their partnership approach (with SWA) to supporting young people. The adviser explained that, because they cover a rural area, they have only small numbers of young people who are self-harming—too small to trigger help from central government. The perverse wish therefore became that *more* young people would self-harm, in order to reach the threshold that would trigger the required central support. I wondered how this could ever be acceptable as a desirable outcome, but it *was* a necessary and undesirable thought if help was to be delivered to those in need.

Way back in my Ph.D. days, we were taught about "anthropology and autobiography"—the way in which your own life story affects what you research and how you research it. Back then, I had an inkling that this made sense, in terms of wanting to understand the other—how they made their decisions, what motivated them to be as they were, what drove them. I could see why I needed to know that—to make some sense of my own past.

As I grew to know more about the dearth of services and support in rural Scotland (and in most rural areas, as I work internationally), and the severe challenges that many people live with on a daily basis, I began to remember my own earlier life, which directly impacted on me until I finally broke away from home in my mid-20s. I wondered how on earth I would have managed in a remote rural setting; who I would have been able to reach out to; and frankly, whether I would have survived.

This undoubtedly shaped my growing confidence in using a social justice lens to examine how national policies were being experienced in rural areas, particularly focusing on the government's intended consequences of empowerment and resilience. I explored the extent to which discontinuities exist between the policy vision and rhetoric and people's on-the-ground realities. Evidence shows that the empowered are becoming more empowered, and I wrote of "Darwinian development" where those who can work the policy and project system will become stronger, potentially to the detriment of those with already-fewer resources. This matters, because the normative "desirable outcome", from government's perspective, is for resilient and self-reliant communities to meet their own needs and solve their own challenges. Possible, perhaps for those who can, but what about for those who cannot?

The Professor Moment

At this point, in 2014, I was nominated for a professorship. I was 49, so the timing was auspicious. However, because my research was multi and interdisciplinary, and because I had chosen to spend so much time working in partnership with policy-makers, charities, local government, private sector (in transdisciplinary research), I felt I would not stand a chance, largely because my peer-reviewed publications record was not (as I saw it) "up to scratch". I had that same imposter feeling as in the corridors of the Social Anthropology Department—that my work was not part of the authentic canon that is the gold standard of academia. My focus on making a difference, seeking out what was below the radar—had this cost me my larger "desirable outcome" that I had set my heart on over two decades prior?

I reached out to my career mentor, a very successful female professor. I sent her my CV and asked for a meeting to work through it. I remember it well—the dread beforehand, aware of all that I had not achieved, all that I would not be able to show; the sense of upcoming embarrassment over a short coffee. Instead, the Prof said that my reaction was actually quite gender-typical, being extremely aware of what I perceived as shortfalls, rather than being able to look back and catalogue my successes, unique contribution, steps forward that would not have happened without me. She red-penned my CV, shifting sections around, being justifiably harsh in her critique of how I had simply given an account of what I had done but not what I had achieved. Without her input, I would have said thank you for the nomination, but I am not ready. And I would never have been ready. Instead, my mentor enabled me to see that, while I had not taken what might be termed by some a "conventional academic route", my journey was still valid, impactful and of professorial merit.

I worked very hard on my submission and CV, writing and re-writing, struggling to portray myself in a positive light, mindful of the "jack of all trades" dismissal and other undermining ghosts from my past. The period from submission to receiving the decision from the external assessors was long; time definitely expanded over those intervening months. On hearing their positive decision, I wept; I'd done it, despite everything. And I had done it with a team of supporters, friends and colleagues along the way. I had reached out throughout my life; I had not travelled alone.

My On-Going Drive to Profess

This validation gave me added impetus to continue looking deeper, behind the "green and pleasant land" rural façade. Due to my own personal challenges in childhood and into early adulthood, I specifically wanted to learn more about the impacts of isolation and remoteness on people's mental health in rural Scotland. I had taken decades to disclose my past; I wanted to understand others' (lack of) opportunities for disclosure of all conditions, concerns, anxieties and fears—in a rural setting, and implications for mental well-being. I formed a partnership with a leading Scottish mental health charity, as although I am a rural specialist, I am not a mental health specialist and had concerns of moving unschooled into such a sensitive area. Together we carried out focus groups and a survey, producing the first report of how hundreds of people who experience mental ill health also experience rural life in Scotland. Their narratives were raw, particularly from young people who sugar-coated nothing. Their stories are real, now, as I type; amongst many things, we read: "don't tell me that a beautiful view makes me well".

When people tell you of their deep pain, you then have a choice. To analyse, write the report and/or paper and move on. Or to do something with what you have been privileged to learn. Working in partnership, we have been able to do the latter, influencing national and local policy, creating a national forum which is affecting change, creating action research which is currently working in rural communities with those experiencing mental ill health to identify their community-based approaches, and generating new partnerships for change.

It's a small contribution to a much bigger challenge. For me, this is what being a professor is about. This is perhaps what being a professor can allow. I remember, soon after becoming a professor, I was talking with a colleague about how I felt no different, but that some other people were seeing me differently, and expecting more from me. She said, "Well now that you are a professor, you can simply profess". This made me laugh, and—while obviously remaining responsible and evidence-based—it did make me relax and think, well, yes, I *can* speak and comment; I have been researching this for 30+ years; I can have a legitimate voice.

My passion for speaking out for those under the radar continues. Only last week, in my role as Chair of our Equality, Human Rights and Inclusion Committee, I met a representative of DeafScotland. She told me how, in Scotland's "central belt" (the area that includes our two major cities of Glasgow and Edinburgh and the bulk of our 5M population), there is one British Sign Language interpreter for every 200 people who need that interpreter. While sitting in our meeting with her interpreter, she said there were 199 people without their need being met, at that same moment. In rural areas, the number without an interpreter is far greater.

Imagine, for a moment, the layering effect: you are deaf, suffering domestic or child abuse, experiencing mental ill health, and living in a rural area where services are centralised, public transport is minimal or absent, networks are sparse, life is lived in a public space and stigma persists. How, *how* can resilience be supported?

We have a wealth of literature around community and individual resilience: How does it translate into the daily, layered lives of those below the radar? We have laudable policies that seek to engender and support resilience within communities: How can they touch people's layered realities?

A fundamentally important way forward is to keep generating lived-experience data and to remain assertive about its validity and relevance. Within the hierarchy of policy evidence, small qualitative data sets sit at the bottom in terms of trustworthiness; in the formal analytical language, they are termed "suspect". If you are also presenting qualitative evidence about "the darker side of rural", from those who are disenfranchised, marginalised, experiencing loss, abuse, suicidal thoughts and feelings, fear, who are homeless, drug-dependent, with little/no/declining support—it is much easier to dismiss these findings as small, suspect data sets that don't corroborate national Big Data and Randomised Control Trials.

This strengthens the need to *profess*, on the basis of triangulated rigorous evidence, in order to push for social justice for those off the radar and the invisible. We must also endeavour to generate evidence focused on those who are "in plain sight" but whom we may not see. When we carried out the rural research with the national mental health charity, Support in Mind Scotland, we were surprised that the majority of survey respondents who reported self-harming, depression, suicidal thoughts and feelings, were in employment. Surprised, because the "traditional" image of those experiencing such conditions is also one of being unable to work. So, as I type, we know there are hundreds of people in this position in rural Scotland.

Freedom from and Freedom to...

Guidance from my Social Anthropology Prof supervisor, which still motivates me 35 years on, is that people are so inherently complex. You and I know how complex *we* are as individuals, and if someone tries to reduce us, categorise us (even through tick-boxes on a survey), we refuse, as we are aware of how we do not fit neatly into any box. So it is with anyone you or I meet, and anyone about whom you or I collect data.

This truth has added resonance for me. After the conclusion of many years of attempting to seek legal justice for the abuse in my past, I was given the legal conclusion that the jury would not believe me, because I am "too high-functioning". I was speechless and felt fury on so many levels, for myself and thousands of other adult survivors. This serves to re-emphasise that we can truly know no-one's hidden story unless we take the time to listen. Much remains hidden in plain sight.

I do not plan to conclude my chapter, because my hope is that this is simply an update for now, and that there will be more; that I will have the chance to continue. So in the meantime, a parting thought: resilience has been defined simply, yet profoundly, as "freedom *from*, freedom *to*" (Pratchett 2004). In 1987, I set my desirable outcome of becoming a professor by the age of 50, marking out a path that was *freedom from* so much that had almost crushed me and put out my light. Increasingly, I am using my privilege to *profess*, as *freedom to* speak out for others who cannot disclose, whom we cannot see or hear unless we choose to be attentive, and whose paths we are privileged to cross.

References

Adger, W. N. (2000). Social and ecological resilience: Are they related? *Progress in Human Geography, 24*(3), 347–364.

Amundsen, H. (2015). Place attachment as a driver of adaptation in coastal communities in Northern Norway. *Local Environment, 20,* 257–276.

Berkes, F., & Ross, H. (2013). Community resilience: Toward an integrated approach. *Society and Natural Resources, 26*(1), 5–20.

Brand, F. S., & Jax, K. (2007). Focusing the meaning(s) of resilience: Resilience as a descriptive concept and a boundary object. *Ecology and Society, 12,* 23.

Cohen, O., Leykin, D., Lahad, M., Goldberg, A., & Aharonson-Daniel, l. (2013). The conjoint community resiliency assessment measure as a baseline for profiling and predicting community resilience for emergencies. *Technological Forecasting and Social Change, 80,* 1732–1741. https://doi.org/10.1016/j.techfore.2012.12.009.

Cutter, S. L., Barnes, L., Berry, M., Burton, C., Evans, E., Tate, E., et al. (2008). A place-based model for understanding community resilience to natural disasters. *Global Environmental Change, 18,* 598–606.

Davidson, D. J. (2010). The applicability of the concept of resilience to social systems: Some sources of optimism and nagging doubts. *Society and Natural Resources, 23*(12), 1135–1149.

Fitzgerald, A. (2018). Querying the resilient local authority: The question of 'resilience for whom?' *Local Government Studies.* https://doi.org/10.1080/03 003930.2018.1473767.

Folke, C. (2006). Resilience: The emergence of a perspective for social–ecological system analyses. *Global Environmental Change, 16*(3), 253–267.

Gordon, J. (1978). *Structures.* Harmondsworth, UK: Penguin Books.

Holling, C. S. (1978). Resilience and stability of ecological systems. *Annual Review of Ecology and Systematics, 4,* 1–23.

Holling, C. S. (1986). The resilience of terrestrial ecosystems: Local surprise and global change. In W. C. Clark & R. E. Munn (Eds.), *Sustainable development of the biosphere* (pp. 292–317). Cambridge: Cambridge University Press.

Holling, C. S., Schindler, D. W., Walker, B. W., & Roughgarden, J. (1995). Biodiversity in the functioning of ecosystems: An ecological synthesis. Cited in Perrings, C., Mäler, K. G., Folke, C., Holling, C. S., & Houston, J. B. (2018). Community resilience and communication: Dynamic interconnections between and among individuals, families, and organizations. *Journal of Applied Communication Research, 46*(1), 19–22. https://doi.org/10.1080/00 909882.2018.1426704.

Houston, J. B. (2018). Community resilience and communication: Dynamic interconnections between and among individuals, families, and organizations. *Journal of Applied Communication Research, 46*(1), 19–22. https://doi.org/10.1080/00909882.2018.1426704.

Kaplan, H. B. (1999). Towards an understanding of resilience: A critical review of definitions and models. In M. D. Glantz & J. S. Johnson (Eds.), *Resilience and development: Positive life adaptations* (pp. 17–84). London: Kluwer Academic and Plenum Publishers.

Koliou, M., van de Lindt, J. W., McAllister, T. P., Ellingwood, B. R., Dillard, M., & Cutler, H. (2018). State of the research in community resilience: Progress and challenges. *Sustainable and Resilient Infrastructure.* https://doi.org/10.1080/23789689.2017.1418547.

Kuir-ayius, D. (2016). *Building community resilience in mine impacted communities: A study on delivery of health systems in Papua New Guinea.* Unpublished doctoral dissertation, Massey University, Palmerston North, New Zealand.

Lowndes, L., & Pratchett, L. (2012). Local governance under the coalition government: Austerity, localism and the 'big society'. *Local Government Studies, 38*(1), 21–40.

Magis, K. (2010). Community resilience: An indicator of social sustainability. *Society & Natural Resources, 23*(5), 401–416.

Matarrita-Cascante, D., Trejos, B., Dongoh Joo, H. Q., & Debner, S. (2017). Conceptualizing community resilience: Revisiting conceptual distinctions. *Community Development, 48*(1), 105–123. https://doi.org/10.1080/155753 30.2016.1248458.

Norris, F. H., Stevens, S. P., Pfefferbaum, B., Wyche, K. F., & Pfefferbaum, R. (2008). Community resilience as a metaphor, theory, set of capacities, and strategy for disaster readiness. *American Journal of Community Psychology, 41,* 127–150.

Pendall, R., Foster, K. A., & Cowell, M. (2010). Resilience and regions: Building understanding of the metaphor. *Cambridge Journal of Regions, Economy and Society, 3,* 71–84.

Pratchett, L. (2004). Local autonomy, local democracy and the 'new localism'. *Political Studies, 52*(2), 358–375.

Roberts, E., & Townsend, L. (2015). The contribution of the creative economy to the resilience of rural communities: Exploring cultural and digital capital. *Sociologia Ruralis, 56,* 97–219. https://doi.org/10.1111/soru.12075.

Skerratt, S. (2013). Enhancing the analysis of rural community resilience: Evidence from community land ownership. *Journal of Rural Studies, 31,* 36–46.

White, R., & O'Hare, P. (2014). From rhetoric to reality: Which resilience, why resilience, and whose resilience in spatial planning? *Environment and Planning C, 32,* 934–950. https://doi.org/10.1068/c12117.

Wilson, G. A. (2012). Community resilience, globalization, and transitional pathways of decision-making. *Geoforum, 43*(6), 1218–1231. https://doi.org/10.1016/j.geoforum.2012.03.008.

8

Actively Constructing Yourself as a Professor: After Appointment

Beverley Anne Yamamoto

My story is set in Japan, in the city of Osaka, where I have been working for the past 13 plus years in a leading national research university. I have been living in Japan for much longer. When I came to Osaka in January 2006, seven years had passed since I had gained a Ph.D. in East Asian Studies from the University of Sheffield in the UK and I had considerable experience working in part-time (adjunct professor) positions in a number of Japanese universities and in one UK university. This was my first full-time position. I had a high level of Japanese proficiency and modest accumulation of research experience and publications. I entered as a lecturer (*koshi*), one step above entry level[1]

---

[1]Faculty positions and commonly used English translations are as follows: *joshu* or assistants, non-teaching positions largely in science faculties and supporting the research activities of the laboratory; *jokyo* or assistant professors, largely non-teaching positions found in arts and humanities faculties and often supporting a department or office; *koshi* or lecturer/associate professor,

---

B. A. Yamamoto (✉)
Osaka University, Osaka, Japan
e-mail: bevyamamoto@hus.osaka-u.ac.jp

© The Author(s) 2019
R. Murray and D. Mifsud (eds.), *The Positioning and Making of Female Professors*, Palgrave Studies in Gender and Education,
https://doi.org/10.1007/978-3-030-26187-0_8

and on a limited term contract. I was relieved and grateful to have any full-time position at a leading research university. As I struggled to create a career path for myself, I witnessed male colleagues with fewer publications and less teaching experience enter tenure track positions at grades above me. Indeed, this was the norm. However, against the odds, I gained my professorship at Osaka University in April 2013. This chapter is less about how I reached professor position and more about how I *became* a professor after appointment.

Just as gaining the doctorate is the start of a process of recognizing yourself and being recognized as a scholar, getting the professorship is not an end point, but a new beginning. As I see it, you are not a professor at the moment you receive the title; instead you have been awarded a platform from which to begin actively constructing yourself as one. But what does this mean exactly? Where do you look for mentoring and leadership roles when you are a minority member of faculty as female and foreign? If language is a primary means through which we construct, negotiate, and communicate identity, what kind of 'identity work' (Howard 2000) is involved in *becoming* a professor after appointment? In a highly conservative East Asian cultural setting, to what degree should I assert my Western values as a leader? These are some of the questions I grappled with and continue to grapple with as a woman professor here in Japan.

In this chapter, I seek to throw light on the ongoing and accumulative process by which I have constructed myself as a professor over the past six years. I have already written about the route to becoming a professor elsewhere (Yamamoto 2017a) and will only lightly retread some of this ground, albeit hopefully from new perspectives. What I explore here is the *process*, which is still ongoing, of feeling comfortable in my

---

may have some teaching responsibilities, can be part of a graduate student supervisory team, but not as a lead, often hired to help run an office within a faculty; *jun kyoju*, one rank below professor and has full teaching and research portfolio, has decision-making powers as a committee member and a member of the faculty senate; *kyoju* or professor in addition to teaching and research portfolio, can lead committees and graduate supervisory teams at doctoral level.

position and using the full potential of the professorship to further education, research and to create a collegial work environment supportive to all those around—academic and non-academic staff and students. This process is non-linear, and there are days when I feel I am making a difference and others when I feel defeated and overwhelmed. Drawing on self-reflection rooted in a social constructionist approach where attention is also paid to the physicality of embodiment, I hope to highlight not only the distinct features of my positioning here in Japan, but also the shared dynamics of constructing an identity as a woman professor that are voiced by other contributors to this volume.

The Context in Broad Brush Strokes

This section provides a brief overview of the Japanese university context that forms the backdrop to my story. It touches upon the diverse and hierarchical nature of the university system and the inherent gender biases and inequalities in wider society that it both reflects and reproduces. The chapter highlights the growing number of women studying at university level in Japan and how this has not been met with a significant increase in female faculty generally and less still at senior levels. It will also note the push toward 'internationalization' in the leading Japanese universities and how this has translated into a growing population of international students, especially at graduate level, but only modest increases in foreign faculty, especially at more senior levels.

The Diversity of the Higher Education Sector

Japan has a highly diverse higher education system with four kinds of higher education institutions: 4-year universities, 2-year junior colleges, Colleges of Technology and Specialized Vocational Colleges. Universities sit at the top of the hierarchical arrangement of these institutions.

The university sector itself is also diverse in terms of mission, scope and funding. A small proportion (86 in total) are funded at a national level (legally National University Corporations—NUCs), and these are generally the most competitive for entry. The seven former imperial universities are the most prestigious of the NUCs. Osaka University, a former imperial university, is generally regarded as third from the top in this hierarchy, although this position is not unchallenged. There are also public universities that are funded at a municipal level (92 in total) and they form a middle tier. Finally, there are a wide variety pf private funded universities (603), many of which are struggling to meet quotas for student enrollment and face survival issues (Yamamoto 2017b). A few private universities, however, such as Keio and Waseda, are in the elite tier of universities and have competitive entry. I have worked in national, public, and private universities in Japan and each would have provided a different environment for the professorship.

Systemic Gender Inequalities

Globally, there has been a dramatic rise in the representation of women among the undergraduate student body, and Japan is no exception to this trend. In the OECD report *Education at a Glance* (OECD 2015), it was noted that 'From outright exclusion and discrimination in educational institutions less than a century ago, girls and young women have conquered schools and colleges.' It was also remarked that 'The numbers are astonishing,' with women making up 58% of 'the six million students across OECD countries graduated from a higher education institution with a bachelor's degree' in 2013 (OECD 2019). While an OECD member state, it would be overly optimistic to say that 'girls and young women have conquered schools and colleges' in Japan.

The overall gender gap in Japan has closed considerably with many more women going on to university today compared to even 10 years ago, but not to the extent seen in other OECD countries. In 2018, the advancement rate to a four-year degree program stood at 56.3% for men and 50.1% for women (Gender Equality Bureau 2019). While Japan is getting closer to reaching parity in terms of university entrance, women are greatly underrepresented in the top universities.

As of May 1, 2018, less than 20% of the undergraduate students at Japan's top-ranked university, University of Tokyo, were female and there is a decreasing trend (University of Tokyo 2019). Likewise, at Osaka University, women made up just 32% of the undergraduate student body as of May 1, 2016, *down* from 35% in 2011. In medicine, only 17% of students on the 6-year MD program were female, and only 9% of undergraduates in engineering science were female in 2016 (Osaka University 2019).

Women have a harder time getting into top institutions for a variety of reasons, including gendered expectations on the part of those advising students, but also biased and sometimes illegal university entrance exam policies. An extreme example of the bias against women came to light in August 2018 when it was discovered that Tokyo Medical University had, since 2010, a policy of deducting between 10 and 20 points from the scores of female candidates wanting to enter the Medical Doctor program to ensure that women medical students amounted to no more than 30% of the intake. Following this, it came to light that other top medical schools had been similarly 'adjusting' scores in order to control the number of females entering programs. The reason given for this illegal activity was, the stereotyped perception, that female students were less likely to practice long term as doctors once they qualified (*Japan Times* 2018). It is important to add that there was a media outcry about this practice, and the heads of these institutions were forced to apologize and takes steps to redress the situation. Nevertheless, frequent sexist gaffs by senior politicians and others in leadership attest to the reality that for many men in positions of power women are still regarded as light or support players. Where women reach more senior positions, it is generally in areas regarded as suitable for women. This can reinforce rather than challenge the gender binary. So the only female vice president at Osaka University is in charge of gender equality promotion.

With a heightened media interest in gender inequality in Japanese universities recruitment policies as a result of the above scandal, a matriculation ceremony speech at Tokyo University in April 2019 by feminist and former professor of sociology, Ueno Chizuko,[2] added fuel to the fire and gained widespread coverage. She noted, the above-mentioned trend, that the ratio of female to male undergraduate students at the University of Tokyo had actually declined in recent years. Having risen to the level of full professor herself at the University of Tokyo, she spoke about the hardships she had faced in such a male-dominated institution (*Japan Times* 2019). Her speech focused media attention on the steep climb faced by talented female faculty to be treated on the basis of something even approaching equality with male colleagues. I wonder if this is the kind of speech those in power expected when they invited Professor Ueno to speak.

Professor Ueno was instrumental in my journey to Osaka University. Our paths crossed early on in my career when I focused on her writing for a graduate module I taught at the University of Sheffield. Later, I translated one of her books, *Nationalism and Gender*, which received considerable acclaim (Ueno 2004). Professor Ueno also provided me with a two-year visiting researcher position at the University of Tokyo in order to support my career. As a leading female academic and feminist sociologist in Japan, her support gave me credibility and confidence. Indirectly, she helped me gain entrance as an academic to a full-time position in a former imperial university, the ivory tower of the academy.

A Very Sticky Floor

Women are greatly underrepresented as academic staff and as leaders in the elite NUCs and private universities. Most universities now have affirmative action gender policies, but we are waiting to see the positive outcome of these. Osaka University is not alone among the top-ranked universities to see a decline in the ratio of female to male students at undergraduate level over the past five years. Top-ranked universities continue to represent an elite field (Bourdieu 1993) that is male dominated, despite the rhetoric of breaking down gender barriers.

---

[2]Following Japanese convention, I am using surname followed by given name for my colleagues here.

8 Actively Constructing Yourself as a Professor: After Appointment 161

To understand the steep gradient that female academics have to enter and then navigate a career path in leading universities in Japan, I will briefly focus next on the structure of faculty positions and the variations in contract status in national universities. Japanese national universities are relatively top heavy with associate professors and professors than, for example, would be usual at a UK university. At Osaka University in 2018, there were 933 professors, 827 associate professors, 58 lecturers, and 1189 assistant professors. Only professors and associate professors have voting privileges in the faculty meetings or can lead committees (Osaka University 2019).

The relatively large number professorships should help women reach this positions, but that is not the case. In 2018, only 75 (8%) of the 933 full professors at Osaka University were female. In the year I became a professor, 2013, there were a total of 60 women professors (6.7%) out of a total 891 (Osaka University 2019). Women get stuck in entry-level positions such as assistants (*joshu*, largely supporting laboratory work in science faculties), assistant professors (*jokyô* usually no teaching, but play a heavy support role to the running of a research field or helping individual professor), and lecturers (*kôshi*, who may have a light teaching role, but are generally hired to support a particular office within a faculty, such as career support, evaluations, or international exchange). With a heavy administrative/management support work load, it is not always easy for entry-level staff to find time for research.

Contract basis is also important. The majority of faculty positions are *sennin* or regular posts, and most of these are tenured from the beginning rather than contract based, although this is changing. Lower-level positions are nearly always contract based, and it is challenging to move into a tenured position. In addition to *sennin* positions, large research universities usually have a variety of *tokunin*, or specially appointed faculty positions. Generally, these contracts are limited and not renewable beyond a specific period. My faculty, the School and Graduate School of Human Sciences, has just this year created a tenure track system to make it easier for high performing junior staff working on contract to move to tenured positions. This is to be welcomed and could make a difference to women wanting a career in academia.

While the Japanese Ministry of Education, Culture, Sports, Science and Technology (MEXT) reports that there has been a steady rise in the proportion of full-time faculty members who are female, the figure remains low by international (OECD member country) standards. As of 2018, 24.8% of full-time faculty in universities were female, up from 16.2% ten years earlier in 2008 (MEXT 2018). Not surprisingly, the more prestigious the institution the lower the proportion of female full-time faculty. In the research focused national universities, only 16.3% of full-time faculty were female in 2018. While 57.8% of entry-level assistant (*joshu*) positions were held by women in national universities in 2018, only 9.4% of full professors were female. Less than 2% of university presidents and 11% of vice presidents were female that year (MEXT 2018).

At Osaka University, only 14.2% of full-time faculty were female as of May 1, 2018. As noted above, only 8% of professors were female (Osaka University 2019). Osaka University has never appointed a female president, but the past two presidents both appointed one female vice president in a newly created position to promote gender equality in the university (ibid.). Very few senior leadership positions, including Deans and heads of programs, are female. Japanese universities love matriculation and graduation ceremonies. When the leadership sits on the stage, it is a sea of Japanese older males with their caps and gowns, even though many young women head up to the podium to receive degree certificates. Senior leadership continues to be a bastion of male privilege.

As Director of the Human Sciences International Undergraduate program, Deputy Director of the International College and Chair Holder of the newly established university-wide project the UNESCO Chair in Global Health and Education, I am what the Japanese call a *reigai* or exception. On occasions, I feel the confusion and discomfort of some colleagues. Wearing these various senior leadership level hats, I have a range of decision-making powers. Nevertheless, there is a caveat here, in that I have leadership positions for projects that are somewhat peripheral to the mainstream educational and research work of the university. This is despite the centrality of internationalization to the university mission.

8 Actively Constructing Yourself as a Professor: After Appointment

Internationalization of education was not my specialism when I entered the university, indeed my Ph.D. was in East Asian Studies for a research on teenage pregnancy and abortion in Japan. My long-term interests have been sexuality, gender, and health focusing on young people. However, the opportunity to contribute to the internationalization of education agenda was offered to me and I took it. I worked hard, contributed at the level of practice and research. This is the route that led me to a professorship. Today, in this area I have considerable influence, but in more mainstream avenues of university life my 'voice' is somewhat muted. Establishing the UNESCO Chair and linking my research to the sustainable development goals has meant that I am now getting senior-level attention for something other than internationalizing the university. But I need to backtrack a little here.

My Entry into Osaka University

I entered Osaka University in a post very much designed for women—a limited contract, no route to promotion, and one with a heavy care element. I was appointed as the person responsible for the Office of International Exchange (OIE) in the Graduate School of Human Sciences. The OIE was created to provide a service for international students and faculty and to support outgoing study abroad students. It was *sennin* rather than project based, which gave me some small advantage in terms of status, but the contract was for a maximum of five years (3 years, renewable for 2 more years). Several sympathetic and supportive male colleagues early on expressed surprise that I had been appointed in an entry level *koshi* position given my experience, however, that was the position I applied for and one I also knew I was lucky to get.

I had been selectively applying for full-time positions for close to a year both within and outside Japan. I had two young children, bilingual, and mixed heritage, whose educational needs I needed to consider and a husband who had no mobility unless he quit his job, which was not financially viable even if we had considered it a good idea, which we did not. So for me, getting the job at Osaka University was a huge achievement and it provided a window of opportunity for myself and my family. It was an opportunity that I was determined to use. Indeed, I was extremely happy with the appointment, and I felt that I have been provided with an environment where I could be creative, productive and happy. This does not mean I lacked consciousness of everyday forms of discrimination or was blind to how closed the tenure track would be to me unless I had senior level support. These were a given and something I knew I would have to deal with.

I was not fully aware, however, of how unique my positioning was as a foreign woman trying to carve a career pathway in an elite Japanese university in a field that was not connected to English language teaching. This has become evident to me as I have talked to many other (male and female) foreign academics with good research backgrounds who had resigned themselves to language teaching positions rather than one in their disciplinary field. The possible temptation of fast track promotion to a professorship through a language teaching position had been there for me, too, but I worked hard to gain my Ph.D. and I was stubbornly determined to teach in my field and not outside it. I also aimed for a research-intensive university as, again, this is why I had worked so hard to complete my Ph.D.

The challenges I would face to create a career path for myself at Osaka University emerged only slowly. I was very determined and worked very hard to show those around me that I added value to the faculty. There were times where I felt that my judgement might be wrong, that I was naïve, and would not be able to move from contract to a tenured basis, but I received sustained support from several colleagues, including two female professors, professors Muta Kazue and Kimura Ryoko. Both were feminist scholars and they invited me to work in research projects with them, leading to a jointly authored volume on gender and war memory. They continuously supported my efforts to be moved onto a regular tenured track. They were both role models for me and mentors.

I was also supported by two non-Japanese, male colleagues who as men had experienced something akin to a glass escalator rather than the sticky floor (although I am sure, they would not see it this way), but they always listened when I needed to unload my own frustrations of being stuck there. I had received good advice from one; that if

I continued to get research funding and publications, the obvious discrepancy between my position and my performance would become too obvious to be ignored. He said my colleagues would find it emotionally burdensome to not improve my contract position and status. This was the Japanese ethic of rewarding those who persevere. In my case, it did work, but it required a post to be made available or created for me. This was something I could not do myself, but needed a patron.

My professorship is, in particular, thanks to the efforts of Professor Hirasawa Yasumasa who was a mentor and role model for me from the point I entered Osaka University. He continued to push for my promotion even when his own health was undermined. He worked to create a post that was tenured and would allow me to gain a professorship. As an outsider, I could not have worked the system in my favor without his ongoing, strategic support. He also ensured that I took over as Director of the Human Sciences International Undergraduate program, rather than helicoptering in a Japanese faculty member. I had been associate director from the beginning so this should have been a given. I became the Director of the program the same day that I took up my professorship. As Director, I also became Deputy Director of the International College.

Professor Hirasawa's maneuverings meant that from the moment I became a full professor I was in a senior leadership position that required I manage an international undergraduate program, the staff and budget connected to this program, and Chaired relevant committee meetings. It also meant I had regular meetings with the executive leadership of the university. This was definitely a learning process not just for me, but also for colleagues. I was frequently the only foreigner in high-level meetings and often the only female academic in the room.

Becoming a Professor: A Double Translation Process

I became a professor on 1 April 2013. It had the feeling of that April fool moment when I wondered whether I was going to wake up and find I was back in an entry-level contract position. With the fight to have my contribution recognized on an equal basis at an end, at least in terms of positional status, I wondered who I was as this female professor. The title was there, but it did not fit my own sense of who I was at that time. I also felt I had to re-think my strategy. Before the professorship, I would readily challenge colleagues when I felt that the voice of international students or staff, or that of women, was not being heard or considered. Now that I was a professor a direct challenge would not be appropriate as it could be viewed as a harassment. I found myself moving to the position of facilitator rather than agitator.

Constructing an Identity as a Leader

As we all know, academic work is generally divided into three areas: education, research, and administrative-/management-related activities. The process of constructing my new identity, it was the administrative side that posed the biggest challenge. Instead of being a committee member, I was now also a Chair. Committee meetings are highly ritualized activities in any country, but Japanese meetings take this to a new level. They are often based on strict hierarchy with the Chair tightly controlling content and interactions. There is much use of honorific language and set phrasing that moves the meeting from its beginning through to the middle and finally to its end. The main Committee that I had to Chair, the Committee on the Promotion of Internationalization of Education (CPIE), was made up of members with some kind of international background, which should have made life easier, but I was initially deeply uncomfortable about how to *be* a Chair. My Japanese proficiency was sufficient to allow me to make a tolerable attempt at modeling the Chair leadership style of my colleagues, but it would not have been sustainable emotionally for me. It would have been too stressful. Initially, I was not clear how to do meetings differently so they worked for me and my colleagues. Lack of example was an impediment.

I had not attended a committee where either a foreign and/or female academic chaired the meeting. So I had no image of how I could do things differently in this particular institutional, cultural setting.

My image of those who Chair meetings in Japan was of leaders who were male, Japanese, senior members of the faculty, who had years of practice of not only performing, but embodying authority. Imitation was something I only briefly considered as an option in my mind, so it came apparent I had to find another way of *being* a leader.

The first thing I did when Chairing was to invite the administrative staff to join us around the table and to introduce themselves, rather than to sit anonymously on tables outside our circle. Although administrative staff are not committee members, they play a very important role in advising on protocol, regulations, and practices. I wanted these staff at the table and free to speak.

In the early days, I think my style would have been viewed as chaotic by many in the room, but over the years CPIE has become more fluid in the way we discuss issues. I definitely prefer a democratic and fluid leadership style. It has taken time not only for me, but also for my colleagues to be confident about my style of Chairing. It helps that CPIE has also become notably younger, with more junior colleagues with considerable overseas experience joining the Committee.

Embodying the Professorship

I grappled with two particular questions when I first had to take leadership roles as a full professor: How could I, with my foreign (Western) and female body be seen to *embody authority*; as a feminist academic concerned with issues of equity and social justice, *what kind of authority* did I want to embody? As I look back, I realize that an ongoing dialogue around these questions with myself was part of the process of constructing myself as a professor.

Jill Blackmore talks about the 'disciplined but disruptive body of powerful women' (Blackmore 1999). Even today, with all the titles I now possess I find it very difficult to see myself as a 'powerful woman.' This image does not fit how I think about myself. As I have some degree of control over specific budgets, Chair hiring and promotion committees and practice decision-making power in a myriad of other ways, this reluctance to define myself as powerful reflects, in part, my own awareness of the precarity of my position. While on occasions it is obvious, most of the time it remains hidden just below the surface, but I know that my authority is dependent on the patriarchal benevolence of those who powerbase is built on the more solid one than mine; that of elite, academic, male social and cultural capital.

Body Matters

Blackmore notes, the body is central to the act of performing leadership, but citing Foucault adds that it is also the site both of production and internalization of various disciplinary regimes enforced through institutions' (Blackmore 1999). Being tall, taller in fact than most of my colleagues, has helped me gain a certain presence that I have found valuable since becoming an academic leader. I could use my height as a conscious point of resistance to being placed in a 'feminine' box. I literally stand above many of my male colleagues and, if necessary, could impose my presence even at the same time I was being located on the margins. Standing tall and confidently was part of the process of *becoming* a professor.

Appearance, while a relatively superficial aspect of leadership, is also highly symbolic negotiation that is part of the performance of embodying authority. Japanese culture demands you blend in rather than stand out. A commonly articulated Japanese proverb is that the nail that sticks out gets hammered in. Japanese society demands conformity and uniformity; it is the route of least resistance. My height, blond hair, and Western looks mean that there is no point of 'least resistance' in terms of my physical presence. I could temper this with culturally appropriate mannerisms and dress, but I felt that my added value to the university was to create tensions that would open up the space for non-conformity. Many of my female colleagues did take the route of minimizing difference from the masculine norm by dressing in conservative colors and wearing trousers, with a shirt and jacket. Particularly, female aspects of the body are covered (up). They can blend in with male colleagues who choose loosely fitting suits or jeans and shirts. This was not the route I took and became more and not less daring with dress once I had the professorship. This was one of the freedoms of authority.

Once I became a professor, inevitably, I monitored my own dress to always look professional, but largely with eye-catching dresses and jackets. I covered my body with garments that marked me clearly as a woman. This was part of the process of creating a comfortable space where I was expressing myself rather than mimicking others. It backfired on me on a number of occasions where at meetings or symposiums people who did not know me mistook me for an international student or foreign visitor, rather than a professor. In fact, there was often incredulity on such occasions that I was a professor at a leading research university. However, the disorientation that my appearance, my presence often caused could be used as a moment to assert rather than subordinate myself. It was a statement—hey guys I am here and (as much as possible) on my terms. It was a resistance to the ongoing danger as a foreign, woman professor of being ignored, trivialized, or compromised. My appearance was a statement about all three.

Authenticity and the Task of (Re)-Defining Success

In Bostock's fascinating investigation of women academics at the University of Cambridge, she notes that her informants all 'talked about the vital importance of knowing what you stand for, the values that drive you and the work you are passionate about' (Bostock 2014). In expanding on this she concluded that, a 'focus on authenticity helps you ask yourself deeper questions about the legacy you want to leave and what you want to be known for'. The women she interviewed made the point that 'an individual cannot view themselves as successful without understanding the values that underpin such a judgement' (Bostock 2014).

I had to construct myself as a professor in an academic space where many everyday norms of interaction were more stylized and regulated than I was comfortable with even after many years living here; they felt 'unnatural' for me to emulate. To *become* a professor required a degree of transformation of habitus, to draw on Bourdieu, but I felt real limits to the extent to which I could reconstruct my own 'embodied disposition' (Jo 2013).

Bourdieu defined habitus as is 'systems of durable, transposable dispositions, structured structures predisposed to function as structuring structures' (Bourdieu 1990, p. 53). The habitus of many of my colleagues, creating 'structuring structures,' that were too tight for me and potentially conflicted with my Western informed ideas of democratic and equitable processes. This is not to deny the dedication of most of my colleagues working in Human Sciences to values such as social justice, equity, and peace. If habitus 'functions at every moment as a matrix of perceptions, appreciations, and actions' (Bourdieu 1977, p. 83), there were many occasions when I had to override my own 'common sense' notions of what was 'right' and 'authentic.' A Japanese ethic takes truth as something that is contextually based and created by groups. One person in a group cannot be right if she or he is the only one articulating that value or ideal. My Western ethic is strongly invested in the idea that one person can speak the truth or articulate what is right even in the face of a group that has reached a completely different consensus. As a woman professor in a Japanese university, I had to grapple with these two ethical systems.

Rooted within these two ethical systems were different ideas around gender and authority. If habitus is 'an embodied disposition, which influences the actions an individual takes' (Jo 2013), which produces different patterns of social practice, becoming a professor involved complex and sometimes painful negotiations with myself. Clearly, my habitus as a British woman raised in a lower-middle-class family in London would be different from that of my colleagues raised in various locations in Japan, many of whom have enjoyed consciously or unconsciously the 'patriarchal dividend' of being male elites in a highly gendered society (Connell 2005).

In order to be socially sensitive, I needed to act, think, and respond in ways that I had not been socialized to do. Sometimes I felt my version of events was the authentic one, but only to have this challenged by colleagues who inhabit a world where reality is constructed differently. With a strong desire to listen as well as to be heard, to understand as well as be understood, the internal battle has been when to assert my reality—one where women have as much right to self-expression, fulfillment, finding out how much they can achieve as men—without being arrogant or dismissive of the cultural sensitivities of the culture that has provided so many opportunities for me.

Support and Knowledge Sharing Across Borders

As my career progressed, I gained support from academic networking across borders with other successful female academics. As I grappled with new challenges, I found some of the most important conversations I had at this time were with these women. Most were working at leading institutions in the UK. We were in very different cultural locations, but there was much shared experience as women working in the academy.

One person who I had ongoing conversations about being a woman professor was Rowena Murray, one of the editors and authors of this volume. Over a number of years, I invited Rowena to work with our graduate students to increase their writing output. In the evenings after writing retreats and intensives, over wine or dinner, we would talk at length about our experiences as women professors. These conversations allowed me to articulate my own sense of mission as a leader in the academy and to have that legitimated. To hear similar values and ideas expressed was a validation of my own. I felt less marginalized and more sure of myself.

The writing workshops, as academic practice based on collegiality and an ethic of care, allowed me to better theorize my approach to teaching and research. We published an article reporting on and theorizing our experiences running structured writing retreats and structured writing days together for students in Japan (Murray and Yamamoto 2019). Many hours were spent discussing how to support our own work and that of our graduate students through social writing; how to use our leadership positions to nurture collegiality; how to do leadership. The process of creating a nurturing academic space not only improved my performance as a researcher, but also positively informed my role as a supervisor of graduate, especially doctoral, students.

Networking is a necessity in academic life to exchange ideas and information, but for me it was also about creating a supportive space. As a woman working in a male-dominated academic environment, creating and nurturing this space was also an important part of the process of looking after myself and others. It can also be understood as a feminist practice. Regular, sustaining and stimulating conversations and interactions with a number of like-minded female academics in my field, including Dr. Inge Daniels, at the University of Oxford and Dr. Brigitte Steger, University of Cambridge, created a space for intellectual and emotional growth. I felt supported and validated.

From Looking for a Role Model to Being a Role Model

I have also gained intellectual stimulation and validation from my graduate students. I have been lucky enough to be able to work with some incredibly talented masters and doctoral students. Most are international students or Japanese students with very international backgrounds. We have created a hybrid space where we have grown the field of Critical Studies in Education for Transformation.

Student who are affiliated to a particular research field, a small unit of academic activity, belong to what is referred to as a zemi (lab.) in Japanese. The *zemi* can be seen as a community of practice. My *zemi* is top heavy with doctoral students, many of whom are female. Although this is soon to change, for the past year to 18 months I have managed the running of the *zemi* alone. I have consciously tried to create a safe and caring space where students support each other in their academic work.

Something that I am quite proud of, is that the *zemi* has become a space where students feel able to combine their studies with pregnancies and child raising. We will have two new babies in our *zemi* this summer. In an environment where many women feel they have to choose between academia and a family life, it is highly meaningful that my students imagine the possibility of combining both.

Seeing my growth over the past six years, I realized, rather belatedly, that I may become a role model for women and some men around me. This is quite a humbling thought. I have raised two kids and still made it to professor level. I have talked about how it is possible to combine—get work-life balance around—family and academic work. If I am creating a small space where painful 'either/or decisions' around career or family do not have to be made, then I think there is some added value in my professorship as a woman professor.

Life Beyond the Academy

The women at Cambridge that Bostock interviewed all commented on the importance of life outside the academy. They also noted the difficulties of balancing the demands of university life and that of life outside the university. Of course, I am forced to agree with these sentiments. When I was a junior academic, my children were a break that stopped me seriously overworking. Nine until five was my time for work, but beyond this was their time. My husband worked the long, grueling hours of a Japanese company employee and so could rarely offer support other than at weekends.

I carefully managed my time and made clear when I was hired at Osaka University that staying late as an ordinary, everyday practice was not something I could do as I had to be there for my children in the evening. I was pleasantly surprised that this was not an issue. By the time I became a full professor, my husband had been posted overseas, my daughter was at university in the UK, and my son at high school in the USA. Since becoming a professor, my family time has been enjoyed largely over Skype, apart from the long holidays when we are able to get together. With my family overseas, there was initially no brake on working excessively. I found myself staying later and later in my office I felt more stressed and less productive at this point in my career. I decided I needed to create some other avenue beyond family and the academy.

In addition to joining a gym, I started taking vocal lessons and singing opera. This is my new break that stops me seriously overworking. This creates a community outside and beyond the university. This investment in life and learning outside the academy feeds directly back into it. I feel my academic output alone attests to this.

Conclusion

As a British woman who became a professor in a leading Japanese research university, the process outlined here of constructing myself as a professor undoubtedly has some novel aspects as I have sought to create a space of my own in this highly male-dominated environment that has few foreigners in positions of leadership. Yet, counter intuitively, this context has also been an empowering one for me personally, and a space where I have been able to innovate and grow as an academic leader. Despite the gradual encroachment of neoliberal management practices into Japanese national universities (Kitamura 2014), deeply embedded values, such as harmony, reciprocity, benevolence, and respect for those senior to you, have been protective factors that have helped me grow as a senior academic, even in the face of gender norms and institutional practices that place female academics at a disadvantage.

While my own story is rooted in the physical space of a Japanese national university, it has also relied on sustaining relationships and collegiality that crosses borders. Finding a way to write socially, thanks to the relationship with Rowena Murray, raised my productivity level and enhanced the joy of writing. My relatively high research output has helped me inhabit comfortably this professorship. Networking with other female leaders has been enabling and creative. As mentioned, I only belatedly realized the extent to which I have also been supported by my graduate students, other internationally minded academics trying to carve out a path for themselves in the rather conservative space of a national Japanese university. Finally, creating a life outside the academy has helped me carry better some of the weight of being in a senior leadership position. Family time and working with others passionate about music, especially opera, have made this journey smoother and happier.

References

Blackmore, J. (1999). *Troubling women: Feminism, leadership and educational change* (Feminist Educational Thinking). Buckingham: Open University Press.

Bostock, J. (2014). *The meaning of success: Insights from women at Cambridge.* Cambridge: University of Press.
Bourdieu, P. (1977). *Outline of a theory of practice* (Vol. 16). New York, NY: Cambridge University Press.
Bourdieu, P. (1990). *The logic of practice.* Stanford, CA: Stanford University Press.
Bourdieu, P. (1993). *The field of cultural production.* Cambridge, UK: Polity Press.
Connell, R. W. (2005). *Masculinities* (2nd ed.). Berkeley: University of California Press.
Gender Equality Bureau Cabinet Office. 2019. *Kihon de-ta* [Basic data]. http://www.gender.go.jp/research/index.html.
Howard, J. (2000). Social psychology of identities. *Annual Review of Sociology, 26,* 367–393.
Japan Times. (2018, August 2). Tokyo Medical University discriminated against female applicants lowering entrance exam scores. *Japan Times.* https://www.japantimes.co.jp/news/2018/08/02/national/tokyo-medical-university-discriminated-female-applicants-lowering-entrance-exam-scores-sources/#.XMbDMvZuI2w.
Jo, H. (2013). *Habitus transformation: Immigrant mother's cultural translation of educational strategies* (Korea Asia Pacific Education, Language Minorities and Migration (ELMM) Network Working Paper Series 7). http://repository.upenn.edu/elmm/7.
Kitamura, Y. (2014). The influence of neo-liberalism on Japan's educational reforms. In D. Turner & Y. Huseyin (Eds.), *Neo-liberal educational reforms: A critical analysis.* Abington, OX: Routledge.
MEXT. (2018). *Gakkô kihon chôsa - Heisei 30 nendo kekka gaiyô* (Basic school survey - Summary of the report for 2018). http://www.mext.go.jp/b_menu/toukei/chousa01/kihon/kekka/k_detail/1407849.htm.
Murray, R., & Yamamoto, B. (2019). Writing retreats for Japanese second-language graduate students: Beyond the language deficit model. *Journal of Academic Language and Learning, 13*(1), A1–A14.
OECD. (2015). *Education at a glance 2015.* Paris: OECD Publishing.
OECD. (2019). *OECD Better policies for better lives: Gender equality.* http://www.oecd.org/gender/data/gender-gap-in-education.htm.
Osaka University. (2019). *Centre for Gender Equality Promotion: Data, surveys and statistics.* http://www.danjo.osaka-u.ac.jp/data/#a1.
Ueno, C. (2004). *Nationalism and Gender.* Melbourne: Trans Pacific Press.
University of Tokyo. (2019). *Enrollment.* https://www.u-tokyo.ac.jp/en/about/enrollment.html.

Yamamoto, B. A. (2017a). Being a woman academic leader in Japan: Intellectual leadership and culture difference. In F. Su & M. Wood (Eds.), *Cosmopolitan perspectives on academic leadership in higher education* (pp. 123–133). London: Bloomsbury Academic.

Yamamoto, B. A. (2017b). Diversifying admissions through top-down entrance examination reform in Japanese elite universities: What is happening on the ground? In A. Mountford-Zimdars & N. Harrison (Eds.), *Access to higher education: Theoretical perspectives and contemporary challenges* (pp. 216–231). London: Routledge.

9

Mis-Making an Academic Career: Power, Discipline, Structures, and Practices

Devorah Kalekin-Fishman

Even today, when the glass ceiling seems to be receding, the hurdles seem less intimidating, and there are indeed women leaders in academia, how to 'make' it can still be a puzzle. The official sets of procedures laid out in universities describe what is accepted as the legitimate pattern of career advancement. But even in these institutions dedicated to expanding knowledge through disciplined study, discovering what kind of knowledge supplies the means for realizing the promise of a climb to professorial heights can be a challenge. There is an unregulated diffusion of control that colors everyday life in the academe, and provides an ironic tint to the Foucauldian mantra of 'knowledge is power.'

In this chapter, I frame my failure to reach the highest level on the professional ladder as an indication of the interweaving of the socioeconomic realities of the university, the omnipresence of power and the subjective adoption of roles and rules from inappropriate

D. Kalekin-Fishman (✉)
University of Haifa, Haifa, Israel
e-mail: dkalekin@edu.haifa.ac.il

repertoires. The story is a theoretically grounded (Anderson 2006) auto-ethnographic account of past mis-readings and mis-applications of rules, and the mis-taken identification of steps in the progressive control of scientific knowledge with the advancement of an academic career. There are five sections.

First ("Auto-Ethnography as a Sociological Tool"), I explain what I mean by a theoretically grounded auto-ethnography. In the section "Power, Structuration and Organizational Learning", I discuss the approach to the topic in terms of Foucault's description of sweeping social forces cumulating through monitored and unmonitored series of local activities and Giddens' structuration theory with a glance at a theory of organizational learning. In the section "Practices as Mis-Confrontations with Power and Discipline", I point out how my practices led me into mis-confrontations with the flows of power and their impact on disciplines that were the grounding of a new university. Section "The University as a Capitalist Organization" relates to the possibility that as a tool of capitalism, the contemporary university constrains agency in a new way, while the section "Concluding Remarks (Power, Discipline, Structures, and Practices)" sums up the argument in terms of power, discipline, structures, and practices.

Auto-Ethnography as a Sociological Tool

The idea that life stories are of sociological concern has given rise to increasing interest in auto-ethnography (Adams et al. 2015; Ellis et al. 2011; Hagoel and Kalekin-Fishman 2016). In adopting this method, sociologists assume a transgressive stance. For one thing, the researcher takes on the double role of subject-observer and object-observed. She bears witness to life events without the defense of investigative armor or even of a mask. Joining forces with tellers of tales, auto-ethnographers propose the downfall of the bulwark between the private and the public. We disclose the messy talk of reality alongside the selective discourse of justification. By documenting events that have shaped our own lives, we present ourselves as subjects of authentic accounts colored by reflective scrutiny. As is to be expected, however, auto-ethnography is not a monolithic methodology. Among some researchers, auto-ethnography is honed as an instrument for evoking emotions. Bordering on literature, their writing deliberately attacks the rationality which is often seen as the basis for acclaiming sociology as a science (Ellis 2004; Ellis and Bochner 2000). According to Anderson (2006), auto-ethnography can and should be anchored in sociological analysis, given three conditions. The auto-ethnographer must have 'complete member status' in the social context that she is describing; she must be seen to be reflexive, and she must be visible throughout the document.

In this auto-ethnographic account of how I 'didn't make it' at the university, I use the first person singular to describe how I established my membership status and, visible throughout, I analyze my experiences relying on theorizations of power, structuration, and organizational learning.

Power, Structuration, and Organizational Learning

> We must cease once and for all to describe the effects of power in negative terms: it 'excludes', it 'represses', it 'censors', it 'abstracts', it 'masks', it 'conceals'. **In fact, power produces; it produces reality; it produces domains of objects and rituals of truth. The individual and the knowledge that may be gained of him [*and her!*] belong to this production.** (Foucault in Rabinow 1991, p. 194)

By insisting that power can have a positive as well as a negative impact in human relations, Foucault contributed a new twist to the movement of critique which, since Comte, has characterized the entire enterprise of sociology (cf. Kalekin-Fishman 2016). In his analyses, power has a dispersed origin and circulates freely in relations among groups and among institutions. There are in its movement, however, three strategic moments: variation, selection, and retention. There is *variation* in the objects, the subjects, the purposes, and all told, in the technologies of power. Over time, some technologies and practices rather than others are *selected*, legitimated, and adopted in discourse and practice. Of the selected clusters, some are *retained* and integrated into broader and more stable emergent strategies in relational ensembles, such as class or race or state, or, on local levels, of organization. But because of the incessant flow of power, these, too, are constantly differentiated and modified (Foucault 1988). Thus, in its operation, power individualizes.

Foucault demonstrates in all his writings that a 'micro-physics' of cumulative actions in everyday life propels the circulation of power as both the impulse of sweeping social trends and the source of individuality. His investigations of mental illness, of incarceration, and of sexuality (Foucault 1965, 1975, 1978) in different historical periods hinge on evidence that in the living reality there are ongoing decisions about how to define the 'other' and how to relate to them, what to demand, and how insistently, but also, for the 'other,' about what to hear, if and how to request help, how to submit to orders. Subjects are constituted through what is for the most part unconscious accommodation or adaptation of the body and its desires to the demands of power in context. Through the manipulation of language and practice, the ceaseless implementation of power produces human agency via a curious circuit, simultaneously constraining spontaneity and producing the energy that infuses the prevalent regime of truth. Because the Foucauldian subject is confronted by choices, he/she may, at any given moment, take part in the flow of power and/or mobilize a consciousness of resistance (Morris and Patton 1979, p. 52). Thus, Foucault does hint at the possibility, albeit often fleeting and not necessarily conscious, of a duality of agency and structure.

But his approach is anathema to Giddens for whom (conscious) agency and (stable) structure are the pillars of social reality. In his perception, personal agency is an existential given that is predominant in producing and reproducing social structure, which is 'both the medium and outcome of the reproduction of [individuals'] practices.' A necessary feature of this conception is that 'all social agents are knowledgeable about the social systems which they constitute and reproduce in their action' (Giddens 1979, p. 5). Through their participation in social action that advances processes of structuration, agents play a part in rearranging configurations of constraints and enablements and in ensuring that the repertoire of available positionings is constantly enriched. Thus, for Giddens (1964, 1976, 1979), dynamic expressions of agency, self and persona, are crucial to the accomplishment of structuration. The process relies on routine encounters in which members implement practices that they have chosen from available sociocultural repertoires.

Organizations provide a testing ground for the consciously processed intermingling of agency and structure as well as for uncovering the nature of flows of power. In practice, they provide an arena of discursive encounters designed for the reproduction of established moral codes as well as for revisions of traditional models. Thus, life in organizations is experienced as structures maintained by acts of communication that realize the implications of consensual rhetorical traditions. Yet they are likely, at the same time, to introduce novelty by absorbing matched components in diverse ways. This phenomenological description of the mutual formation and reformation of structure and agency enables Giddens to allow for a broad range of practices both in the implementation of choice, from complete acceptance to radical resistance on the part of agents, and, in structures, from rigid stability to flaccidity. The consciousness of structure does not, however, eliminate questions about an underlying flow of power. As complex systems, organizational change surfaces through relational processes such as 'connectivity, interconnectedness, emergence, and feedback' among elements within the organization and between the organization and the environment on all levels (Mitleton-Kelly 2003). To capture the relational processes that make for organizational change, some approaches point to human learning as the motor of organizational life and to learning by organizations as the source of modification and transformation.

Nonaka and Toyama (2003), for example, indicate a way of overcoming differences between the theorizations of Foucault and Giddens; they propose a model of individual and organizational learning that explicates processes that Mitleton attributes to system elements. In their model, acquiring new knowledge is a metaphor for the capitalist imperative of maximizing profit. They suggest that all organizations participate in a process of creating knowledge which is used and kept as a basis for furthering the development of new knowledge.

Clearly in the ongoing process, all the elements in an organization take part, as do the many groups in the environment with which the organization has contact. To track how knowledge is created in the experiences of individuals-in-relation and in the experiences of the organization as a whole, the researchers posit a spiral of Socialization—Externalization–Combination–Internalization (Nonaka and Toyama 2003, p. 5). By performing organizational routines in contact with others (*socialization*), members of the organization acquire tacit knowledge. They go on to make their knowledge explicit (*externalization*) in speech acts that fit their position and their 'story line' (Langenhove and Harré 1999, p. 113). In successive dialoguing, the newly explicated knowledge is combined with explicit knowledge acquired earlier, edited, and disseminated throughout the organization (*combination*). Once disseminated, the explicated knowledge is internalized in action and in practice (*internalization*); it is reflected on and embedded in new bodies of tacit knowledge. Thus, each cycle ends in the performance of new or revised routines and these in turn mark the beginning of a new spiraling cycle.

While individuals are learning and operating on the basis of the knowledge that is produced and reproduced in daily operations, the organization as a whole is creating and elaborating its working knowledge in its interchanges with the environment. The context, which Nonaka and Toyama denote as 'ba,' is a mélange of spaces which are at once existential, physical, and virtual (Nonaka and Toyama 2003, pp. 7–8). That is to say that while individuals are creating knowledge for use in internal routines, the organization as a whole is creating knowledge through its ongoing contacts with all the groups and organizations in its environs, a dynamic shifting context with many unpredictable participants.[1] The spiraling process of Socialization–Externalization–Combination–Internalization (SECI) is, therefore, no less than a model of profit as knowledge acquisition, which, under capitalism, is carried out in all organizations.

---

[1] The researchers explain that in this sense the environment and the relationships generated with each organization are best denoted by a special term to describe the relentless dynamic. They adopt the comprehensive term 'ba' from the Japanese philosopher, Kitaro Nishida (Nonaka and Toyama 2003 cf. too the discussion of multi-dimensional feedback in Mitleton-Kelly 2003).

From the ideas presented above, it is possible to describe my failure to reach the summit of an academic career as a structured malfunction of learning. The malfunction includes a general mis-reading of organizational reality and of the sources of power, as well as mis-taken choices from the available discursive repertoires. Alternatively, it can be seen as submission to uncontrollable flows of power and exclusion from the hidden subjectivities at play of variability, selection, and retention in fashioning (successively accepted) regimes of truth.

Practices as Mis-Confrontations with Power and Discipline

As part and parcel of the disciplinary society, and its intellectual emblem, universities are organizations structured via a complex layering of power and a special relationship to knowledge. Like all organizations in capitalist regimes, they are constantly given to learning. In addition, however, they are both the authoritative representatives of disciplined learning and research, and the arbiters of its meanings. The disciplines that make up the university are sources of power over the students, over the staff both administrative and academic, and in fact over the entire public sphere. Resistance is stigmatized as ignorance, vulgarity, or obstinate error.

In experiential terms, the university operates according to the logic of bureaucratic government. Since its central task is to demonstrate accomplishments in extending human knowledge, the organization exercises formal and informal surveillance over the implementation of agency by individuals. Participants in the university organization—students, administrators, and members of the academic staff—are obliged to follow 'known' rules of behavior and to legitimate them in practices and in discourse. The immanent goal is to reproduce structure as a means of furthering the creation of knowledge across a panoply of disciplines.

In the following, I will examine how each of these points played a part in my missing out on an appointment as professor. Clearly, I was completely unschooled in the choices that were available and repeatedly mis-read structures.

Mis-understanding the importance of politics: As a novice, I had no understanding of political considerations that are central to choosing academic administrators, in deciding on how to do graduate theses, and even on self-positionings on national and international events that are not overtly related to the academe.

It took me far too long to discover the complicated political motivations of those who appointed administrators and of those who accepted the positions, and even longer to locate the gaps between the positions and the performances. I interpreted administrative appointments as recognition of professional excellence. Endowed in this way, department heads were, to my mind, masterfully in charge of furthering the interests of the faculty which in turn I mis-read as identical with the interests of producing knowledge. For myself, I interpreted every interchange with the head of the department or with the dean of the faculty as highly meaningful, but let slide their potential as political opportunities to advance their appreciation of my professionalism.

The integration of political maneuvering was patent even in situations where considerations for disciplinary knowledge would seem to be uppermost. An example of how an astute friend chose a doctoral advisor is ample evidence. Although she shared the widespread view that as a researcher, the then dean of her faculty lacked academic stature, she asked the dean to act as her doctoral adviser. When she was carrying out the research, she was careful to consult more respected professors, but the name of her adviser was a long-term political boon. She had wisely positioned herself among the faculty's decision makers, key to the advancement of a university career.

The popular opinion that the 'civilian' orientations of academics are always consistent with 'known' left-wing political stands is far from the reality that takes shape within the university. I found, however, that taking sides in macro-political issues was (and is) in fact a crucial discursive site in the university. Implicit understandings about appropriate political attitudes seem to be attached to every discipline and to the academics that study it. Members of the faculty who differ from what is perceived as the majority opinion of those associated with their discipline are summarily badgered. Across all the disciplines, moreover, there is political posturing in defense of academic freedom, denoted as free speech and freedom of association. Clarifications are often offered in support of the positivist ideal, namely that academics only elaborate political opinions in accordance with the outcomes of their research.

Without compromise, however, the practices of the university combine into an emphatic pursuit of conventional politics, strengthening the status quo tagged 'middle of the road' in the public sphere. The academic year is dotted with displays of identification with holidays that are defined by the state, with ceremonies that define what constitutes the sacred civil religion of the 'man and woman in the street,' with self-censorship regarding ongoing political situations. While the possibility of discrimination according to political opinions is vigorously denied, there are from time to time cases of redundancy that can only be explained on the basis of non-consensual political stands. From the onset of my association with the university, my penchant for nonpartisan but radically flavored critique was antithetical to the stance sought in a government-funded institution of higher education.

Mis-understanding intra-disciplinary conflicts: A series of inept choices led to my failure to fit in with a desirable discipline.

Imbued with the enthusiasm of a person 'reborn' as a sociologist (Berger and Luckmann 1972), I sought topics, methods, theories, and conjunctions that would hopefully lead me to novel discoveries about the social. In my mind, relations with my home university were details that had to be dealt with but did not present a significant challenge. So, for my dissertation, I chose to study music as a force for socialization in early childhood education. The qualitative study of how music was introduced into kindergartens in Germany and in Israel taught me that for the most part music (which I defined as intentional rhythms and intentional pitch) was a means for exerting control over children's bodies and over their behavior rather than a means to promote their creativity (Kalekin-Fishman 1980). I explored plural methodologies and interpreted the data in a constructivist framework with the aid of critical sociological theories. Encouraged by the interest my work evoked in peers at the European university at which I was enrolled, I felt that I was burrowing in approaches of some value. When I was asked to report on my research to a sociologists' colloquium in my home university, I was pleased to be presenting a research project that was relatively novel. To my chagrin, the chair of the session made it clear that my work was unworthy of interest. It turned out that my research was anathema to both the empiricist majority and the neo-Marxist minority in the Faculty of the Social Sciences. The empiricists wanted to see 'objective' data collected by means of validated questionnaires. The neo-Marxists did not see any value in studying the lives of children without highlighting the processes that create gaps between social classes and are evidence of discrimination. The data I had collected on the uses of music in early education had implications for understanding repression but the connections were too abstruse. I had neglected phenomena that were most significant in the eyes of my sociologist colleagues and their reaction was inevitable—rejection.

Looking back, I remember a conversation with a younger colleague who was admitted to the department at about the same time as I. He told me about his decision to do graduate research in a sociological field central to the work of a researcher from abroad who was spending his sabbatical in the university at the time. The new assistant professor had a two-pronged plan: how to do the graduate thesis efficiently and how to manage the chronology of professional advancement. I was astounded and put off by what I saw as his cold instrumentality. He did indeed become a full professor.

Rejected by one department, my case for becoming a member of the academe was not totally lost. I had a partial appointment in the School of Education, and luckily, I thought, I was invited to take on a full-time position in teacher education. I was assigned two relatively important courses. But I discovered that my skills, even combined with industry, were not enough to ensure academic status. There were two unexpected obstacles: disciplinary discourse and a derogation of teaching.

Although there were several departments in the School of Education, the discipline in which almost all the members of the staff had been trained was psychology. Child psychology, clinical psychology, school psychology, and more recently, psychology and technology—all based on a solid body of theory and a gigantic and often useful empirical literature—were, and still are, the foundations of the prevailing approaches to the study of education. The terminology, the methods, and the questions that were important to me as a sociologist were almost like a foreign language and the solutions implied were bizarre in the framework of the prevailing disciplinary ethos. Among my colleagues, psychologists trained to look at sociality as the **outcome** of individuals' intentions, neither the themes nor the goals of sociological rhetoric could be perceived as foundational.

Apart from my identification with the 'peculiar' discipline of sociology, I soon discovered that not all educational skills are valued equally. The courses I was teaching were key courses for the students who planned to teach and my reputation as a teacher was solid. The common wisdom in the faculty, however, was that it is impossible to be a teacher and a researcher at the same time (cf. Newman 2014/1852). Even though I succeeded in having several articles published in refereed journals and also contributed chapters to three edited books in the field of education, I was notified that I could not be considered an academic. The consolation, presumably, was that it was fine for me to go on teaching.

Missing out on organizational learning: At least some of the pitfalls might have been avoided had I understood the importance of socialization (in the terminology of the Nonako and Tomayo model) in the organization. Throughout my initiation into life at the university, I shunned opportunities to enter into a relationship of socialization with a mentor.

Although I did not appreciate his help at the time, the head of the department did have my interests at heart when he assigned me as research and teaching assistant to a new member of the department. She was a woman who had a doctorate in education from a highly respected American university and had a good reputation for having done important research. This was a task to be added on to my concern with completing my own doctorate and doing some demanding teaching. Contact with her was providing me with an introduction to the behaviors *selected* and *retained* in the organization, as well as an acquaintance with the store of tacit knowledge acquired through experience. The work was not overwhelming but I mis-read the few hours that I had to spend on the tasks she requested as an unnecessary burden and resigned.

The argument that she would be a good mentor did not make sense to me and I followed my heart. In my resistance to having a mentor, there were two strands: my early education and my position in everyday life. Having grown up in the USA, I was the product of an educational system that glorified the lone intellectual. I was inspired by the myth of having people 'beat a path to my door' if I could only get an idea for 'building a better mousetrap.' In none of the folklore we were exposed to in and out of school—from Johnny Appleseed to Alexander Graham Bell, and Edison, for example—was there mention of a mentor. The lesson was that if a person has a good idea and works hard, his [sic] contribution or invention will be embraced enthusiastically. And I mistakenly absorbed that message uncritically.

Then, there was the obstacle of age and life experience. Since I started out as a junior academic in my forties, the very idea of latching on to a mentor roughly of the same age as I appeared unnatural, demeaning, and humbling. I was incapable of freeing myself from my relative security as a pro-active agent. I was a woman responsible for a household, with constant demands to make decisions for children, and a teacher who could get along with classes of 35–40 students of any age. Accepting a mentor meant that I had to re-read myself as not yet competent academically—which I was—but that was an idea I simply could not entertain.

Had I interpreted the relationship differently, I would have been in a position to acquire tacit knowledge essential to a smooth rise to the top of the ladder. In the practical world of the university, by leaving that researcher 'in the lurch' after the start of the school year, I not only lost out on organizational socialization. I also made an enemy of a person who might otherwise have been at worst indifferent to my strange discourse as a sociologist and my status as a teacher. Several years later, as dean of the faculty, she actively opposed my promotion.

Mis-reading power without a face: While the circulation of power is multi-dimensional, often, like stereotyping, it has no face.

At critical temporal nodes, decisions as to my future status at the university were taken in the presumably most objective way possible, in discussions where participants' names were not disclosed. Judgments were handed down from 'on high' and the anonymity lent them both excessive authority in the institution and protection from appeals I could have formulated if I had known who said what, that is, from what

9 Mis-Making an Academic Career: Power, Discipline, Structures ...

disciplinary and administrative status/point of view the assessments were formulated. What I should have explored were opportunities for undermining the ways in which criticisms raised in committee discourses had inserted me and my work into a niche of ostensibly benign difference, constraining me to an irretrievably damaged state of consciousness (Oatley 2012).

Anonymity in refereeing my written work was also difficult to cope with.

On the face of it, anonymity in refereeing is an advantage. Those assessing articles for publication do not have to see themselves as limited by personal affinities. They can relate to the work they are reviewing in the manner idealized as respectable positive science. Moreover, anonymity establishes similarity and situated equality between the referee and the material to be assessed. The author of the work reviewed has choices and here, too, I managed to mis-read the situation.

Immediately after completing my doctorate, I made enormous efforts to translate some of the findings into journal articles. Anonymous reviewers made cutting remarks without compunction when asking for improvements. When I discovered that behind the cloak of anonymity it is possible to exercise repressive power without reprisals, my first reaction was self-flagellation. While I had no way of knowing who was attacking my work, I was overcome with shame. I interpreted the referees' notes as unbending confirmation of my inferiority as a researcher and condemned those early articles to the wastepaper basket instead of undertaking to revise and resubmit as requested. Thus, I defended myself against another round of criticism and of opportunities to learn.

Misplacing norms: In her blog, the anthropologist, Carole McGranahan (2017) quotes three different academic interviewees on the importance of saying no.

> *I wish I had known how to say 'No' at important turning points.*
> *I wish someone had told me when to say "no," how to say "no," and why to say "no."*
> *I wish I knew earlier that saying* NO, *no matter how scary, is a muscle that gets stronger.*

Not only did I make poor choices, I also refrained from making choices that challenge power. After all, institutional rules have lacunae that even the weak, novice researcher-lecturer can use adeptly to her advantage. A critical junction is the point of the school year, during the third quarter, when heads of departments make plans for courses to be taught in the subsequent year. For people who understand the rules, that is when there are opportunities for saying 'no.' Saying 'no' is an important indicator of clarity of purpose and individuality. A novice who knows when to say 'no' is taking control of her career and passing a covert test on whether she has a clear vision of her goals. Furthermore, prestige accrues to a person who knows how to insist on teaching only the courses that are important and meaningful to her, preferably those that are important to the organization as well. In sum, it is good to choose to teach courses defined as 'seminars,' with prerequisites, and limited enrollment. Thus, the person destined for professorship does well to insist on teaching electives designed for advanced students in the institution while refusing to teach required courses.

Here, too, I mis-read the potential for agency and the dynamic flexibility of structures. When I was asked to accept responsibilities at work, I applied rules that govern the intimacies of family life and friendship. My instinct was to identify with the 'needs,' so to speak, of the faculty. So I 'did' introductory lecture courses to well over a hundred students with minimal assistance. I took responsibility for administering the coordination of didactic practica, a service to the students and to the schools in the district with no academic aura. I took the lead in introducing organizational innovations. Although I had no official title, I substituted for the head of the department when he was abroad. It never occurred to me that as a junior academic it would have been more impressive to say 'no' and come across as securely 'selfish' professorial material.

Academic capital—deficits and surplus: Having moved from a small town in the north of the country, I was a newcomer to the city. It seemed appropriate to be working at a university that was also new. But there was a big difference in the meaning of being 'new' as a migrant to the city and being 'new' as an organization.

9 Mis-Making an Academic Career: Power, Discipline, Structures …

For me, becoming part of the urban scene was severance from a known and loved world. Gone were the familiar backdrops to everyday life: the lawn and the olive tree, the mountains behind the house and the mountains that were a few miles to the east, the smell of bonfires from a nearby hill, the steel blue skies, and the dry winds that attacked us every morning at 11:00. Gone were the shops, the people, the schools, we had known. Over twenty years of life experience was to be re-appropriated in a new milieu in a context diversely unfamiliar.

While the local university was 'new,' it shared the authority of the oldest and the most respected university in the country, the Hebrew University of Jerusalem. Founded in 1918, the Hebrew University was established by academic ideologists of higher learning who immigrated to the Middle East from the civilized centers of the European continent. For a time, the new university was a knowledgeable branch of the venerated institution. When it was chartered as an independent institution of higher education, it was already equipped with the rules and regulations, with the clusters of practices and with the academic discourse that the veteran university had selected and retained. Defining reality—the domains of objects and the rituals of truth—was not an issue. To some, it might appear that the fledgling organization was encrusted with customs and procedures that had to be reviewed and revised. To the members of the staff, administrative as well as academic, the copies of traditional practices and discourse were resources that constituted proof of academic soundness.

Those positioned as academics and as administrators were, moreover, reputed locally to be the educational elite of the town. Until the founding of the university, they had been associated with the best secondary school in the city, many as teachers and others as enthusiastic alumni. Having been born to families who had immigrated from what were perceived to be privileged countries of origin, nurtured on exaltation of the heroism of establishing a new state, and grown up in particular sections of the (now) university town, members of the academic staff not only shared a similar socioeconomic status and memories of a cultured background, but also partisaned similar ideals. Thus, codes of civic beliefs and the standards of behavior rooted in a complex of traditional cultural understandings inadvertently constituted the moral infrastructure of the departments in formation. I was someone not partner to the lifestyle and the traditional biases of the key groups and so could not expect to have my framing of everyday life recognized.

True, moving to the city where the university is located was fulfilling an ambition of many years. But my credentials, attendance at a selective secondary school, and a magna cum laude bachelor's degree from a college in New York City were far from compensation for my lack of skill in the discursive practices of the already solidary boys' and girls' networks that peopled the university.

Colleagues who were also novices at the university found ways to overcome the sociocultural estrangement. They cultivated personal relations, created opportunities for informal ties, found ways of connecting with the families of veteran professors, the proverbial academic 'peers,' who were the decision makers of key committees. But I did not realize the importance of the informal infrastructure. The misalignments were exacerbated by my complicated everyday life, on the one hand, and paradoxically by my personal resources, on the other.

The conditions of my residence in the city were not helping me become 'just like' the desirable group. I could not afford a lifestyle as an ivory tower academic. I lived in 'another' area of the town, was the mother of a large family for whose support both my spouse and I had to work. The history of my family of origin did not fit in with the values and principles that were taken for granted in the 'club,' and in no sense did my qualifications accord with the mythological nobility of the pioneers whose exploits were considered key to understanding the unique traits of Israeli society. Moreover, by contrast with those who had 'made it' by carrying out graduate studies in American universities, my doctorate, albeit mentored by an internationally revered sociologist and rated outstanding, was denoted less prestigious at the time because it was awarded by a European university.

On the other hand, I sported a set of unconventional, and apparently provocative, 'accomplishments,' a surplus of cultural capital. I became interested academically in education after having acquired broad experience as a teacher in a variety of settings. My experience served as a secure practical basis for understanding the complexities of education and for understanding the neat differences between what could and should be changed and what was best preserved. Furthermore, by contrast with those who had to work at English as a second language in order to facilitate their careers, I had an intimidating native speaker acquaintance with it which made it vexingly easy for me to take part in encounters with people from abroad.

Realizing, however, that I was something of an outsider, I thought that in the long run, I would be able to find a way of working through the difficulties. I filtered my perceptions of an alien reality through a lens focused romantically on 'science.' In my view, it was possible to ignore the context of organizational politics and carry on a life in the service of knowledge creation by doing whatever job was tossed to me. Blindly, I presumed that I could rely on my compliance and consideration for department needs, to gain points toward fulfilling the formal demands for promotion. After all, after a few years, my record in fulfilling the criteria for promotion (publications, contributions to faculty programs, quality of lecturing and mentoring; participation in professional associations, and service to the community) met the written requirements.

What I discovered was that promotion on the track to the level of full professor did depend on formal criteria, but only to a certain extent. From the point of view of the candidate what was required was a rational plan for managing an appointment at the new university as a *career* which could be advanced only if one paid attention to the implicit as well as the explicit rules for manipulating human relations. Or, in the formulation of Nonaka and Toyama (2003), gaining a feel for how the university was part of a 'ba' creating knowledge about social living through the constant interchange of understandings with the towns in the region, with the politicians and the families, with the firms and the workers, with the ties with academic and lay institutions throughout the world.

The University as a Capitalist Organization

After itemizing my mis-readings of rules and roles and my mis-taken practices, it would be a comfort to think that the fault lay with the general failing of the contemporary university—avoiding its original mission—that of furthering the acquisition of knowledge for its own sake. The contemporary literature of critique insists that the all-encompassing sweep of economism, patterns of behavior that imitate the capitalist economy, undermines authentically dedicated efforts to preserve or recreate, if need be, universities as institutions dedicated to producing truly disinterested knowledge within the academic disciplines. Action in the academe that is influenced by the general culture, guided by consideration for the economic environs, or directed toward the attainment of political goals is frequently denounced (inter alia: McGettigan 2013; Naidoo et al. 2011; Neary and Winn 2009; Palfreyman and Tapper 2014; Winn 2015). To the minds of critics, the university as an institution has betrayed its destiny as an organization of enablements, dedicated to the discovery and the creation of unbiased scientific knowledge. Universities are now, they say, establishments that emulate the ills of a social system saturated by principles of bureaucratic calculation and callous competition (Giroux 2014; McLaren 2005).

As a matter of fact, however, the history of how universities as we know them today were established in Europe is far from being a tale of impartial devotion to learning (*Encyclopaedia Britannica* 1911; Feret 1911; de Ridder-Symoens 1992). Documentation of the first universities confirms that they were usually set up because of developments in the economy. The increase in trade in Bologna and its environs at the turn of the first millennium, for example, led to a demand for legal expertise. Thus, the first university in Europe, the University of Bologna (founded in 1088) was a corporation chartered by the political leadership of the city to educate and train experts in law. Similarly, the University of Salerno capitalized on the medical lore collected for economic purposes in the Abbey of Montecassino and became the most important school of medicine in Europe from the tenth to the thirteenth centuries. The University of Paris was exceptional in cultivating philosophical speculation for its own sake because it was conceived as a center for training theologians. Faculties of Arts were set up in all the universities, but their purpose was to equip students with skills prerequisite to advanced professional study in law, medicine, or theology. Economic relevance was underlined by the fact that positions of authority in the new institutions were filled by leaders of the wealthiest guilds in every relevant area. Moreover, the academic structure of the universities emulated that of the guilds with masters overseeing students' gradual acquisition of vocational expertise.

For the students, problems of finances and politics were integral to the choices and challenges of everyday life. Since each university was recognized for its expertise in training for a specific vocation, students from different parts of Europe flocked to the institutions that promised the best vocational preparation in whatever field was of interest to them. But this did not prevent conflict. In Bologna, for example, the mature students who enrolled to study law were frequently embroiled, often physically, with the local landlords, who refused to rent them accommodations. In Paris, where the university administrators were clerics who decided issues according to canonic law, there were clashes between students and masters, on the one hand, and the local population on the other because students were held to the rule of ecclesiastical law while the townsfolk were held to the laws of the city. Clashes with merchants also broke out because of the cost of living and because the students' unruly behavior aroused residents' ire.

This lightning survey of the nature of universities in the early Middle Ages shows that the ideal of the university as an institution dedicated wholly to the production of knowledge and to providing an education that is both critical and intellectually stimulating can be cited as a philosophical ideal, not as a characterization of any particular institution. Only after the Revolution of 1789 is the ideal stated as a specific goal and the decision of the French constitutional assembly that there should be a degree of instruction beyond basic skills (level 1) and instruction for vocational expertise (level 2). The third level was to be designed to disseminate branches of learning that are not accessible to all.

Among historians, the declaration of the French constitutional assembly is heralded as the opening volley in the romantic view of higher education that developed in the nineteenth century (cf. Newman 2014/1852). Here, the university is defined as the locale for spreading intellectualism, 'branches of instruction' beyond the understanding of 'all men,' knowledge for its own sake. The literature of the nineteenth century emphasized the ideal of the university as a setting for gaining knowledge for its own sake. Yet in its forms it steadily took on the style of life that is embodied in modern metropolitan life. As Simmel aptly described it:

> The technique of metropolitan life is unimaginable without the most punctual integration of all activities and mutual relations into a stable and impersonal time schedule.... A model of metropolitan existence. As many writers have pointed out, the university can increasingly be identified as an excrescence of the metropolis. (Simmel, in Wolff, p. 413)

In principle, therefore, there is no reason to bemoan the loss of what are identified as truly academic pursuits in the rapidly expanding corporate university. Driven by a neoliberal bias toward the free market, often avowing an administrative dedication, even addiction, to efficiency and to profit, contemporary universities harmonize with the forms of commerce and the means of production that have taken over the economies of most states in different parts of the globe. These processes are no different from those that governed universities when they were established as guilds of learners who were seeking profitable careers.

Concluding Remarks (Power, Discipline, Structures, and Practices)

As auto-ethnographer, I have been visible throughout this chapter, summarizing my reflections on a career mis-made in an organizational context in which I have 'complete member status' (Anderson 2006). While I have emphasized mis-readings and distorted applications of rules as failings of my own, it is clear throughout that my choices were mis-taken in light of the socioeconomic realities of the university as an organization and the interconnectedness of elements that implement power in support of disciplined structuring and restructuring regimes of truth in the internal reality of the organization.

The conceptions of Foucault are clearly to be found in the life of the university. While the circulation of power can be discerned in the complexities of administration, and in the disciplinary frameworks that diversify the rules, it is far from consistent.

9 Mis-Making an Academic Career: Power, Discipline, Structures ...

Like all organizations, the university mirrors the dynamic flows of power that are characteristic of society as a whole. Within it, there are at least two levels of power plays: One is the microphysics of human relationships—patterns of behavior carried over from domains of living outside the institution that are shared in different degrees among the individuals that make up the personnel of the university. Another is in the realm of knowledge production, where the meso-physics of power is manifested in two ways: in the endless calculation of performance as defined formally in regulations that have been culled from the variety of possibilities, selected and retained in writing; and in the frameworks of the disciplines where themes that are being explored in the forms of disciplinary discourse are constantly being divided anew to provide more nuanced criteria for rituals of truth and for legitimate repression within the halls of the discipline.

Subjectively individual academics are engaged in making conscious choices in the sense that Giddens describes structuration. Each member of the organization is obliged to find the positioning that makes possible the construction of an academic career. In her practices, every member of the academic staff is obliged to assume that as an agent she is capable of confronting existing structures and reinforcing those that serve career ends. Picking her way among the paths she must be sensitive to which rules are indeed obligatory and which are easily ignored at every level of contact: administrative, disciplinary, informal sociation; to what roles are appropriate to advancement and which foretell defeat, what norms that are grasped as universal are valid in the university, how ideologies of science interact with the complex connectivities of elements in the system. And while learning, the individual has to develop a capacity to follow how the university is functioning in its 'ba' and how it is advancing in its self-learning.

In sum, my formal advancement at the university was stymied because I did not acquire a working knowledge of all of the above. In practical sociological terms, this meant that I was the target of power plays of different kinds, none of which I recognized in time. In each configuration of group relations, I managed to position myself outside what was perceived to be the traditional discourse of the organization. More importantly, I located myself outside the ongoing conversations of groups deeply involved in redescribing and reproducing and reworking the comfortable university structures. I shunted myself out of the minimum power that every participant in the institution at every level holds—the power to affect the shape of traditions and the power of presence in the discourse that inevitably structures the future.

There is a distinct difference between gaining command of a tradition and a discourse in a university discipline and learning the keys to building a career in a university, even within this very discipline.

As Simmel perceives, there is a maelstrom of information, of impressions, and of social experiences that configure the experiences that impinge on the person in academic life. The carefully organized, transparent criteria for success provide what seems to be a scale of progress that can be relied on as key to structuring a career. They are modeled on the qualities of the metropolis, the emblem of modernity. It is not easy to accept the obvious consequences. Deviations from the explicitly primed rules are in keeping with the invasion of 'metropolitanism' into the most pressing aspirations of every individual. Inevitably,

> [w]e find superiority and subordination, competition, division of labor, formation of parties, representation, inner solidarity coupled with exclusiveness toward the outside and *innumerable similar features* in the state, in a religious community, in a band of conspirators, in an economic association, in an art school, in the family (Simmel in Wolff, p. 22);

… and in the university.

Bibliography

Adams, T. E., Holman Jones, S., & Ellis, C. (2015). *Autoethnography: Understanding qualitative research*. New York: Oxford University Press.

Anderson, I. (2006). Analytical autoethnography. *Journal of Contemporary Ethnography, 35*(4), 373–395. https://doi.org/10.1177/0891241605280449.

Berger, P., & Luckmann, T. (1972). *The social construction of reality*. London: Penguin.

de Ridder-Symoens, H. (Ed.). (1992). *A history of the university in Europe, vol. i: Universities in the middle ages*. Cambridge, UK: Cambridge University Press.

Ellis, C. (2004). *The ethnographic I: A methodological novel about autoethnography*. Walnut Creek, CA and Lanham, MD: Rowman Altamira Press.
Ellis, C., & Bochner, A. P. (2000). Autoethnography, personal narrative, reflexivity. In N. K. Denzin & Y. S. Lincoln (Eds.), *Handbook of qualitative research* (2nd ed., pp. 733–768). Thousand Oaks, CA: Sage.
Ellis, C., Adams, T. E., & Bochner, A. P. (2011, January). Autoethnography: An overview. *Forum of Qualitative Research, 12*(1), Art. 10.
Feret, P. (1911). University of Paris. In *The Catholic encyclopedia*. New York: Robert Appleton Company. Retrieved October 4, 2018 from New Advent: http://www.newadvent.org/cathen/11495a.htm.
Foucault, M. (1975). *Discipline and punish: The birth of the prison* (A. Sheridan, Trans.). New York: Random House.
Foucault, M. (1978/1976). *The history of sexuality, vol. 1: An introduction*. London: Allen Lane.
Foucault, M. (1965/1961). *Madness and civilization: A history of insanity in the age of reason* (R. Howard, Trans.). New York: Random House.
Foucault, M. (1988). *Technologies of the self*. Amherst, MA: University of Massachusetts Press.
Giddens, A. (1964). *The constitution of society: An outline of the theory of structuration*. Oakland, CA: University of California Press.
Giddens, A. (1976). *New rules of sociological method: A positive critique of interpretative sociologies*. New York: Basic Books.
Giddens, A. (1979). *Central problems in social theory: Action, structure and contradiction in social analysis*. London: Macmillan.
Giroux, H. (2014). *Neoliberalism's war on higher education*. Chicago, IL: Haymarket Books and Toronto, ON: Between the Lines Books. I
Hagoel, L., & Kalekin-Fishman, D. (2016). *From the margins to new ground*. Rotterdam: Sense Publishers.
History of the University. (1911). *Encyclopaedia britannica* (11th ed.). London.
Kalekin-Fishman, D. (1980). *Time, sound, and control: Aspects of socialization in the kindergarten*. Dissertation submitted in partial fulfillment of the requirements for the degree of Dr. Soc. Rer. (Dr. of Social Science), University of Konstanz, Konstanz, W. Germany.
Kalekin-Fishman, D. (2016). *Practicing social science: Sociologists and their craft*. London: Routledge.
Langenhove, L., & Harré, R. (1999). Positioning and the writing of science. In R. Harré & L. van Langenhove (Eds.), *Positioning theory: Moral contexts of intentional action* (pp. 102–115). Oxford: Blackwell.

McGettigan, A. (2013). *The great university gamble: Money markets and the future of higher education*. London: Pluto Press.
McGranahan, C. (2017). *What I wish I knew before becoming a professor*. https://anthrodendum.org/2017/11/27/what-I-wish-I-knew-before-becoming-a-professor.
McLaren, P. (2005). *Capitalists and conquerors: A critical pedagogy against empire*. Lanham, MD: Rowman and Littlefield.
Mitleton-Kelly, E. (2003). *Complex systems and evolutionary perspectives on organisations: The application of complexity theory to organisations*. Amsterdam: Pergamon.
Morris, M., & Patton, P. (Eds.). (1979). *Michel Foucault: Power, truth and strategy*. Sydney: Feral.
Naidoo, R., Shankar, A., & Veer, E. (2011). The consumerist turn in higher education: Policy aspirations and outcomes. *Journal of Marketing Management, 27*(11–12), 1142–1162.
Neary, M., & Winn, J. (2009). The student as producer: Reinventing the student experience in higher education. In L. Bell, M. Neary, & H. Stevenson (Eds.), *The future of higher education: Policy, pedagogy and the student experience* (pp. 126–138). London: Continuum.
Newman, J. H. (2014/1852). Knowledge as its own reward: Discourse V. In *The idea of a university*. Kindle Edition.
Nonaka, I., & Toyama, R. (2003). The knowledge-creating theory revisited: Knowledge creation as a synthesizing process. *Knowledge Management Research and Practice, 1*, 2–10.
Oatley, K. (2012). Narrative modes of consciousness and selfhood. In P. D. Zelazo, M. Moscovich, & E. Thompson (Eds.), *The Cambridge handbook of consciousness*. Cambridge, UK: Cambridge University Press. Chapter 14. https://doi.org/10.1017/CBO9780511816789.015.
Palfreyman, D., & Tapper, T. (2014). *Reshaping the university: The rise of the regulated market in higher education*. Oxford: Oxford University Press Van.
Rabinow, P. (Ed.). (1991). *The Foucault reader: An introduction to Foucault's thought*. London: Penguin.
Simmel, G. (1950a). The field of sociology. In K. Wolff (Ed.), *The sociology of Georg Simmel* (pp. 3–39). New York: The Free Press.
Simmel, G. (1950b). The metropolis and mental life. In K. Wolff (Ed.), *The sociology of Georg Simmel* (pp. 409–423). New York: The Free Press.
Winn, J. (2015). *Academic labour and the capitalist university: A critique of higher education*. Thesis submitted in partial fulfillment of the requirements of the University of Lincoln for the degree of Doctor of Philosophy.

10

A Personal Journey of a Long and Winding Road to Professorial Status: An Alternative Pathway and the Challenges, Trials and Tribulations

Moira Lafferty

Introduction

When given the opportunity to contribute to this much-needed volume, I was intrigued by the concept of talking about "making it" as a woman professor. Immediately I began to ask myself "Have I made it?" and more importantly, "What does it mean, not to me, but more widely in the academic community to women in academia and beyond?"

In taking you on a journey from my entry into academia, through to my current position as one of the Deputy Heads in the School of Psychology and Professor of Applied Sport Psychology at the University of Chester, I hope to show that many roads can lead to Rome.

At the same time, I want to be open and honest about my own thoughts and feelings. The challenges, rewards and self-doubts that have been part of that journey and still remain. Importantly, I want to also reflect on how I feel a title has not personally defined me but

M. Lafferty (✉)
University of Chester, Chester, UK
e-mail: m.lafferty@chester.ac.uk

© The Author(s) 2019
R. Murray and D. Mifsud (eds.), *The Positioning and Making of Female Professors*, Palgrave Studies in Gender and Education,
https://doi.org/10.1007/978-3-030-26187-0_10

has allowed me to help other women strive to achieve what some may consider the lofty heights of a Chair.

In starting this narrative, I begin not at the outset of my journey in academia but what some may consider the pinnacle, when one is awarded a Chair. To me the position of Chair is another point in the journey, possibly a frightening one, and from which I have to personally develop. Most importantly, one of the challenges is how I can use the position and my knowledge of career development to help others. Along with describing my journey, I also, through my reflections, leave you with some take home messages about what I feel we need to do.

An Ending or Start of a New Journey

On a cold, damp and typically British November evening in 2018 I gave my inaugural lecture. 18 months had passed since the awarding of a Chair and title. The hours prior to this event, and in honesty during the weeks and days before, I was plagued with self-doubt and worry. Would I be good enough? Who would want to hear what I had to say given my professorial title as you will see was awarded not on research alone but on contributions across numerous criteria that included my applied work, teaching and national engagement with the British Psychological Society. More importantly, would anyone come? Would I be presenting to a few people, my words echoing in the lecture room? Nothing in my mind would have been worse than presenting to a handful of people who looked bored and were there because protocol and ceremony dictated their attendance.

At the same time as battling these inner demons, I also reflected on whether everyone felt like this. Having listened to numerous inaugural lectures it always seemed that my male colleagues commanded the stage, spoke with authority never doubting their rhetoric, and I apologise to all if this is not the case. Interestingly, of the far fewer inaugural lectures of female colleagues there was a different tone and atmosphere. No less a celebration, but more of an acknowledgement about the collaboration in their journey and the role of significant others. I made a decision, speak about my journey, be proud, acknowledge all those but never the less not shy away from how my involvement on many levels had shaped both my field and the journey of others.

Fast forward to a full lecture room, an engaging audience, and post-lecture one of my colleagues, a young female lecturer tweeting:

> The #inspirational @ProfMoiraL giving her professorial inaugural lecture on "Leaving the jersey in a better place. From dancing ponies to odd shaped balls." @uochester what a #career & what a woman. Very well deserved @UoCPsych …

A humbling tribute, of all the positive comments and congratulations that night this one resonated with me. Why? Possibly because this was a young female colleague who through 50 minutes of listening to my journey might now believe that what looked impossible could become possible. The title not reserved for only those on a research path, at least at Chester but you could achieve through differing ways. It also made me realise that my "odd journey" and story was important, not just to me, but to others. So critically, where did this journey start and what lessons have I learnt that can help others?

My Entry into Academia

As with many young people in the late 1980s who achieved good O level grades, and who entered the 6th form, there was a certain expectation that you would transition from school to Higher Education. Like many, I found myself on that treadmill. The 6th form years, when not playing sport were defined by open days, UCAS forms and personal statements, and key discussions about choosing the right course. This, combined with a huge amount of self-doubt, left me at times floundering, at other times wondering where I was going, and how I could make sense and join the dots of my own love of learning and quest for knowledge.

In a small sixth form, thinking back, there perhaps was the first divide. My male counterparts knew their course—medicine, law and engineering—they seemed to have a life map in place, I certainly did not. For a sport playing, sport-oriented young female, this in and of itself created tensions. I knew what I wanted to do but there seemed to be no appealing career pathway. The obvious one, become a PE teacher, it was a role I could have done, a path I could have walked but I was interested in intellectual arguments, intrigued by people and how they interacted with their world and the problems they faced. I had chosen an eclectic mix of A levels: physics, geography and English literature. I was at that point not a hard-core scientist or social scientist I was a hybrid taking subjects that allowed me to explore the areas of interest to me, challenged me but also allowed me to combine my love of the scientific with the expressive, elusive and intellectually challenging world of people's views.

Hindsight and reflection are two incredibly powerful attributes. Looking back now, I wonder how much of my lack of direction was down not just to my own insecurities but also not being exposed to "role models". In saying this, I do not belittle any of those teachers I came into contact with, many shaped me. Not least my PE teacher, who saw a spark and encouraged that, nurtured me and throughout my career has always been the go-to person. But, was I ever shown what could be achieved and the different paths open and available for women that wanted to excel in academia? I know now they were out there, striving as we do now, but their stories did not reach me, or importantly their knowledge and experiences did not guide me at that moment.

Reflecting on my early years and the pre-transition into Higher Education, I am struck with the thought we need to do more to get our stories out there. More importantly, if we want to help more women achieve in academia and become professors, we must do more to enlighten the younger female generation. Take our stories back, not just into higher education but into schools, colleges and show young aspiring females that you can achieve and it is okay to follow different paths and that "Many paths do lead to Rome".

Take Home Message One

Getting out there, sharing stories and inspiring our young females at a young age are the starting point of developing and shaping academia.

The Academic Experience

A levels completed, I found myself on a course that combined both my love of sport and, something I was good at, with my curiosity about human behaviour and the numerous factors that impacted on that. But to this day, whilst having no regrets I was still on that treadmill, career pathways mainly defined as going on into PGCE training, no clear guidance on how I could move out of this and progress or, at this stage even become an academic. With no clear careers advice and after a hiatus year as student union president, I embarked on an MSc in Sports Science, major sport psychology at Liverpool John Moores University.

This was my first experience of total immersion in a culture that aligned both my sporting and psychological interest. I began to evolve, both as a person and as an academic. Following the successful completion of the MSc, I embarked on a graduate teaching assistantship with Ph.D. funding at Liverpool John Moores. Interestingly, when I think back, one conversation remains clear in my mind. A friend's parent asked me why I was doing a Ph.D.? For once, I didn't have to think of an appropriate answer, I knew the answer, "I did a degree because that's what everyone did, I did an MSc because the family did, the PhD that is about me and what I want to do, I want to challenge myself and find my limits".

During this time, I found my limits many times, pushed past them and learnt that we are limited in part because of our own fears and insecurities and the false ceilings put on us by others. We can push the boundaries if we try, and in many ways, my career was shaped at this moment in time.

Immersed in a culture of Ph.D. students, where the number of females exceeded males at least when I began, I gained my first sense of belonging and of not belonging. Whilst there was undoubtedly a higher number of female Ph.D. students, the majority of academic staff were male. This brought home to me that if I was to thrive and succeed in academia and sport psychology I would more likely than not work in a male-dominated culture and have to find and define myself in that context.

My Ph.D. was a very practical one, focusing on using physical activity to develop interventions for children with Down's syndrome. There are many high and low lights of this time, but I do remember sitting in our Ph.D. room with a fellow male student who said "I've written and submitted two papers this week". I reflected why had I not done the same, it wasn't that I couldn't or didn't write but actually submitting my research was a whole different matter. Somewhere in a box, there remains to this day several floppy disks containing those early writings, never submitted. Looking back, the obvious factor was confidence, but at the same time I also now know that what I needed was advice. Not merely on how to publish, but advice and support that would help me grow and develop. I didn't need the competition of who wrote more, but a supportive writing environment with feedback provided in a way that nurtured me academically and developed self-confidence. Is this a male/female difference or my own self-doubt and demons, possibly a bit of both but my own experience has shaped my supervision philosophy to this day for my Ph.D. students.

Take Home Message Two

For more women to become professors, we must create the right supportive culture at the earliest points in their career. Look at supervision, recognise needs and build environments that allow development.

A Job and Position in Academia

In 1997, I secured a lectureship in the Department of Physical Education at the University of Chester, which became the Department of Sport and Exercise Science. I spent 15 years in the Department, progressing up the ladder to senior lecturer, wrote programs and held numerous roles, developing sport psychology and the teaching of it. During this time, I became increasingly interested in the "teaching of sport psychology", the pedagogical elements of learning and the differing ways we could impart knowledge, ignite academic curiosity and most importantly, help those studying. I was awarded grants to conduct pedagogic research, gave keynotes at teaching and learning conferences and wrote teaching and learning strategies. At the same time, I was fortunate enough to be able to work as an applied sport psychologist with numerous national and international teams and athletes, National Governing Bodies and shape and develop the integration of sport psychology support in the sporting world. I sat on numerous committees external to the University that enhanced and developed my "applied practice CV". I also became involved with the British Psychological Society and secured the position of Chief Supervisor for the UK for sport psychology. I had numerous markers of esteem, what I did not have was research esteem. In part, on reflection this was due to a lack of confidence, in other ways down to the fact that working as an applied sport psychologist brought embargos on what could be published. I was excelling in numerous areas, but I had also reached a ceiling. My expertise across and in numerous areas seldom recognised, rarely rewarded, as research publication was seen as the "status symbol".

Reflecting on this point in my career, I was in many ways satisfied, doing what I loved but, also frustrated as my pockets of excellence were not considered that. I was doing all, professionally developing, contributing to the National agenda in my area, but in academia going nowhere. Personal development planning or reviews depending on terminology became an increasing source of frustration, applied work, pedagogical research and external activity ticked off, but never really acknowledged. More importantly, no advice as to how I could join the dots between these areas and how I could use these to further my career.

Take Home Message Three

There needs to be further training for those conducting Personal Development Reviews that acknowledges academic and professional practice diversity and importantly recognises individual differences and embraces professional diversity.

A Change of Scenery—Stepping into the Unknown

In 2013, after 15 years in the Department of Sport and Exercise Science I was given the opportunity to move into the Department of Psychology. This opportunity excited, worried, but also intrigued me. Could I prove myself in a different environment, would immersion within psychology further enhance me as an individual and professional and would that impact on my external work and positions and my pedagogical practice?

Like many, this career-changing decision was not taken lightly. There were sleepless nights, long lists of pros and cons, numerous conversations with my mentor, friends and family. I knew I was stagnating where I was. Yes, I was happy with my professional and applied life, my CV building in those areas. My teaching and pedagogical research still progressing but as I alluded to, there was no joined up sense of self. I moved and at the same time I had one of those life-changing conversations.

A colleague from within the Department of Psychology rang me and said come for a chat. That simple chat, with someone that I knew by sight, had exchanged limited small talk with, but who seemingly knew of my work in the wider academic community led to me applying for a position as Deputy Head. For once, I threw caution to the wind, wrote my application on a red-eye back from a teaching and learning exchange at Alverno College in the USA and submitted it. I was of the opinion nothing to lose and all to gain with a little self-doubt as to how this would be perceived by my soon to be new colleagues.

Whilst none of us like interviews and the process of "selling yourself" to colleagues, I was able for once to talk openly and freely about what some would consider my wealth of experience in numerous aspects of academic development and management. Nobody was more surprised than I was when I was offered the position. To this day, the recognition that I had something to offer at a management level and could help contribute and shape not only the Department but the journey of others has driven me forward in all that I do. A light bulb moment those disparate pockets of all I had done suddenly became joined together and I began to see the roadblocks on my career lifted.

The early days in the Department presented a steep personal learning curve, especially given this new role. Moving from a male-dominated Sport Science culture to a female-dominated Psychology one made me acutely aware of the differences in management style, needs of colleagues and the differences that you never see in how other Departments operate when looking from the outside in. Whilst learning, I was also suddenly thriving, I was being challenged, but in a positive way. My knowledge and experience suddenly had importance and more importantly, I was beginning to help others on their academic journey, I had something to give back. Reflecting now, why did this happen? Was it this new environment? A differing support structure that brought a new-found sense of belonging? Or more importantly, had I somewhere in this move found the confidence to be myself and take a moment to acknowledge all that I had done in my career that could be of use in helping others?

Take Home Message Four

Supporting our female colleagues is both formal possibly via roles and also importantly informal, and creating a collegiate and developmental environment is critical. We must create those networks of support for female colleagues.

Conversations Change Position

With a new-found sense of self, I began to question "what next and what could I achieve?" and that led me to an impromptu meeting with my Head of Department. Prior to this, I had read the call for Professorial Applications and interestingly, at Chester, Chairs were being awarded not for research and grant income alone but included: enterprise and professional activity, academic leadership, and teaching and learning. In essence, you could apply across any of the four core areas of activity. You had to identify one as your primary area of esteem and excellence and show esteem in two of the three others.

Suddenly, those disparate areas of my academic life had congruence and could possibly be joined together in the future, or so I thought, and this meeting was for me a testing of the water and to ask the question what do I have to do. Out of curiosity and in preparation for this impromptu personal development meeting, I mapped my experience and expertise against the non-research areas. Yes I was research active, but my research alone would never allow me to climb further. The outcome of that meeting was yes in the future, it could happen but, go and see the Vice Chancellor and ask his opinion. Off I trotted, fairly confident until faced with having to say "I've come to talk to you about in the future against Chester criteria applying for a Chair". I mumbled, stuttered the words hoping I would neither be seen as a fool for thinking I could reach these heights or, be told you're good at what you do and you have reached your limit.

I found myself wondering how I could feel like this, I held National markers of esteem, worked with countless teams and athletes and National Governing Bodies, had grants for pedagogical research, was held in regard by my Department and Faculty; yet when it came to asking questions about myself and my career development, I crumbled, doubted and double doubted myself. Was it actually saying out loud what I wanted? Was it talking to others? Seeking the views of those we hold in esteem? Was it because I was female and putting myself forward was not something I was either used to or good at?

The outcome of this conversation shocked me, "..apply now. Write the application and bring it back in a week and we will look at it together..". I can never thank enough my Head of Department or the Vice Chancellor for their support and unwavering belief, but it does make me think looking back that there are lessons in my trials and tribulations at this point.

Take Home Message Five

Having a national or even international network of female professors who are willing to mentor and help others is something that is critical. A sounding board and place for women to talk and share their feelings and aspirations away from the confines of their home institution will afford safe developmental space.

The Application and Weeks of Worry

I duly sat down with the application criteria, my CV, my evidence map and opened Word and stared at the blank document. How to write this? What to say? I knew the theory of what I should be doing, the concept being one of selling your academic self, your expertise and status but, this was far more challenging than writing the opening paragraph to a paper. I sat there, typing and deleting in equal measures. I could not this time overcome the writing block by turning to theoretical concepts, or present my arguments through the critical analysis of research, in this instance the opening, middle and end had to be about me. I shut the computer down and this process went on for several nights, often long into the night.

Eventually, with the deadline of the application review meeting looming and self-reflection in danger of turning into self defeating rumination I took a step back. I wrote a list of what was worrying me about writing about myself, my experiences and expertise. I wish now I had kept that list as I am sure it would resonate with others. But critically, I still remember looking at that list and realising along with the obvious what if I fail at this and am I really good enough, many of the worries were external factors linked to the fear of being judged, and what others would think. In my applied practice, I talk to athletes about the need to find and be their authentic self, to control the controllables, to maximise their performance, to focus only on themselves. It was time I applied that to myself, "*Medice, cura te ipsum*".

How did I do that? The first point was to remind myself in no uncertain terms that I had support; my Head of Department and the Vice Chancellor were not hanging me out to dry. They had belief. Secondly, the worry about others' views, I had probably, like most people, made a conscious decision early on in this process that what I was doing was on a need to know basis.

Nobody, save my inner circle knew and as the application process was shrouded in the academic process and secrecy no one would know. Thirdly, I wrote a note to myself with a term I often use in applied practice, "Don't think, just do". Used to remind athletes that performance at key moments can be disrupted through over analysis, I stuck this next to the computer. Each time I doubted, I looked at it to remind myself to write and not think. Finally, I devised a formula; for each category, state the criteria, map to it, evidence it and then write a statement about the impact at the University, Higher Education and/or national/international level. This approach overcame the initial writer's block, a draft was completed and I had something on paper.

Strangely, reading this initial draft I began to gain confidence. My experiences and expertise across my primary category area of enterprise and professional activity, and secondary areas of academic leadership and teaching and learning filled several sides of A4. I realised in applying my rather formulaic approach that I had finally joined the dots in my unconventional academic life. My pedagogical research and work, teaching and academic management combined with my applied work as a sport psychologist and national positions shaping the development of sport psychology were not isolated activities. They evidenced an academic whose career had not been confined or contained by working only within their University but had significant impact externally and that externality had been brought back to my home institution in numerous ways. I had achieved more than many of my colleagues but, I had done so in relative silence, my contributions more widely not acknowledged in the same way as research publications. How many other women in academia are making contributions that are not rewarded, acknowledged or celebrated as they fall outside of research publication? Interestingly, with the move towards Universities having to do more to show impact at a local, regional and societal level is this when women will come to the fore?

With confidence, I turned my attention to the actual application. Two pages, how hard could two pages be? In my case, it was extremely hard when the second page asked for three referees and three reviewers all of professorial standing. My new-found confidence in all I had achieved suddenly started to crumble. I now had to approach six professors that knew me and could attest to me being worthy of the awarding of a Chair. I wrote a list of all the professors I knew in my field, quite a long list but interestingly only one female professor. I went through the list quickly crossing off names of those I didn't know well enough to ask. Those whose career trajectory was so different that I didn't see a match to my alternative application, those who I could never ring and ask not because I didn't know them, more I was worried about their reaction. The demons of self-doubt and self-worth were beginning to gather pace in my mind again.

A long list became a short list and it dawned on me that one of my strongest areas was my applied practice/contribution. Why could I not have someone in esteem that could attest to that? I went and asked the question, given this was an application that could be considered "alternative" was there no scope to allow this. For once, being proactive in and for my own cause led to this being allowed. In reflecting on this point in my professorial journey, is this another example of why we don't have enough female professors? Finding support for the application, having the confidence to ask esteemed colleagues who are more likely than not to be male for support, I don't know the answer but it is an area worthy of consideration.

With the application completed, I submitted it and spent the next three months forgetting, not forgetting and trying to forget about it. As many will know the process of appointment is one of several committees and stages, scrutiny and debate behind closed doors. Eventually, one June day after a day full of meetings I returned to the Department to be told the Vice Chancellor was trying to contact me. This in and of itself was not unusual, the ensuing phone call was, I was greeted with the words "Hello Professor Lafferty". At that moment what did I feel? It's hard to put into words, it was a similar feeling to when told I had successfully defended my Ph.D. at viva, a relative numbness, a sense of satisfaction but also a part of me wanting to say "are you sure?" Is this the usual response? I don't know, but even at that juncture this was the informal result. Ratification by Council still was needed. Over the following couple of hours, thinking over my secret knowledge of the outcome, I began to realise what I had achieved and that the journey along with its trials and tribulations had brought rewards never dreamed of.

Take Home Message Six

The application process can be the biggest challenge and we must do more to provide avenues of support. We must also work for institutional change at national and international level so that those who excel in areas beyond research have the chance for this to be acknowledged.

From Title to Roles, Responsibilities and Challenges

Whilst awarded my Chair in 2016, it was 2018 before I gave my inaugural lecture. In part, this was due to system and process and a queue for which I was thankful. Strangely some may say, I also managed to find excuses for dates offered—I was away from the University on applied practice/business, the summer months unacceptable as those in the sporting world would not be able to attend and as ever the self-doubt of myself. With avenues of excuses and get out clauses exhausted, a date was set. What no one ever shares with you is the amount of time one 50 minute lecture takes. Firstly the title, then an abstract written in layman's terms, then in the case of Chester dinner menus, dinner guest lists, invites. As I alluded to in the beginning, I wanted to speak about the journey, to finally join the dots of my academic endeavours and remain true to myself. The title: "Leaving the jersey in a better place – From dancing ponies to odd shaped balls. A journey of teaching, applying and developing sport psychology". Possibly one of the longest, but one that encapsulated all that I had done.

In the three years since 2016, I have supported several female colleagues within and external to the University in their application for professorial title. I have also shared my journey and career route with others through talks and discussions. Showing that you can achieve professorial status through and by alternative career journeys and embracing aspects of academia that have relevance at an individual level. The route is no less arduous, still requires time and dedication and the development of a portfolio of national and international recognition and esteem markers but the landscape is changing.

My role as I continue in academia is threefold. Firstly, to continue my own professional journey and development, to strive to better myself, learn and embrace the challenges of working in a changing academic landscape. Secondly, to use all that I have achieved to help and support other women as they progress their careers and finally, to ensure that we create a culture of supporting diversity in career development for women, to ensure that they can thrive, strive and achieve career progression.

11

How to Fall into a Career Trap (Without Even Realising)

Inger Mewburn

I had my second existential career crisis in 2005. The earlier, Great Career Crisis of 1999 resulted in a transition from architectural practice to architecture academic. The second was triggered by the realisation that I was never going to secure a full-time role in an architecture school. I'd formed this opinion after five unsuccessful job interviews which made me realise the glass ceiling was real. For one of the jobs, my ten years of experience working in architecture offices was deemed inferior to man's two years of experience and ongoing relationship with a powerful male mentor. I succeeded at interview for another job, only to be ruled out of the race by a (male) Dean because 'there are already two women in the department and they keep fighting with each other'. The same Dean was immediately forced to hire me on a casual basis when the man they appointed to the role admitted he couldn't teach

I. Mewburn (✉)
The Australian National University, Canberra, Australia
e-mail: Inger.Mewburn@anu.edu.au

the technology subjects he was given. I charged them double the rate to pick up the classes and then left at the end of semester, vowing never to be some man's deputy again.

I was done with architecture in the academy, but I felt good about it. The blatant sexism was a salutary lesson in the machinations of the patriarchy and forced me to re-assess my options. I thought deeply about what was important to me and what sort of work environment and rewards would be satisfying. I've never been motivated enough by money (sadly) and I liked hanging around in academia, so the choice was obvious. I horrified my research supervisor by declaring I wanted an administrative job in the university (before such jobs were labelled 'alt-ac' and thereby gained some status in academic eyes). My master's supervisor recommended I apply for a maternity replacement role when a good friend of hers was going on leave. The role was in educational support but was labelled as an academic job. My supervisor thought it would be a good fit.

She turned out to be right; research education was a good fit. They hired me, even though I was manifestly under-qualified for the role. I took a design approach to classroom activities for Ph.D. students, thinking about the needs and the experience first and content second. It seemed to work. I started a blog in 2011, with the idea I would translate my classroom materials online. I estimated this would take about six months, but The Thesis Whisperer is still going strong, some eight years later. I had more to say than I thought.

Blogging bought me some measure of internet celebrity, a strange kind of fame which means you remain largely anonymous but enjoy significant benefits. One benefit was a job offer from a more prestigious university in another state. 'We're interested in what you're doing there', they said 'let's talk'. My new job had a fancy title ('director') and a pay upgrade. For the first time in my life, I got my own office with my name on the door. Success? Maybe. I found myself in a highly feminised and (surprise!) underfunded and devalued side of the university business: 'Learning and teaching support'.

Any person in what is called a learning and teaching support role will tell you that it's a difficult position to find yourself. Universities in Australia have become more diverse in the last forty years or so. Up to

11 How to Fall into a Career Trap (Without Even Realising)

50% of the undergraduate cohort are international fee-paying students, most of who are not fluent in English for academic purposes (EAP). And it's not just these students who need help with writing and speaking academic English: broadening access (a good thing) means local students come to university with varying levels of ability too. Teaching and learning centres are often positioned by other academics in the hierarchy as a rehabilitation centre, which only those who have some kind of deficit need to attend. Universities need you, but don't *want* to need you. We like to think of ourselves as professionals who coach others to reach their full potential; but in reality, we are viewed as intensive care nurses ministering to the academically unwell. Respect? It can be in short supply. Funding is often precarious and given grudgingly. Those of us who work these spaces must develop sharp survival instincts as the next restructure might well be the last. One of the most difficult things about being in an academic role in a teaching and learning centre is that we are close to problems and see solutions, but have little to no power to enact necessary changes because we are positioned as other and 'extra', not as essential.

Staying in an academic role, let alone getting a promotion is difficult because you become literally 'un-disciplined' in a teaching and learning centre. I managed a transition between senior lecturer to associate professor and it was something like a double backwards pike off the high diving board, with the aim of landing on your toes. People don't understand the complexity of the multi-disciplinary, highly diverse classroom settings that academics like me deal with on a daily basis. Every kind of evidence that I presented needed to be translated so that I looked like a 'real' academic. My research is directed at practitioners, so a panel full of social scientists had trouble even seeing it as research because it was 'under theorised'. My approach was to fight numbers with numbers—graphs of satisfaction, net promotor scores, even a social network analysis to prove that community promotes Ph.D. completions—were tools I had to bring to bear to justify my existence, as much as a higher salary. If you are not data driven, or have a manager who is, you may very well find yourself restructured out rather than promoted up.

As much as I love the work—it's deeply satisfying to help pull someone out of a hole and set their feet back on the path to academic success—teaching and learning support is a career trap, and one that I see far more women than men fall into. In fact, there seems to be more and more women aspiring to these roles, perhaps because they see senior women there and not in other spaces. How to fix these systemic problems? I'm not sure, but I urge readers to beware the dangers of becoming 'undisciplined' and existential crises!

12

Conclusion: The Process of *Becoming* a Woman Professor and *Unbecoming* Gender Equality: A Female Drama of Resistance

Denise Mifsud

Women Professors' Career Trajectories and Narrative Methodology

I present an analysis of the data in the case studies in order to highlight the themes that contributed to the positioning and making of the participant women professors, to tell how they overcame obstacles in their journey of *becoming*. These specific narratives demonstrate that women professors are relegated to a gender inequity positioning due to misconfrontations with power and discipline; distinct markers of discrimination; mothering; and being products of specific social and organizational contexts. Notwithstanding, they succeed in their endeavour to professorship via toughness; resistance to 'expected' roles; disregarding gender as a contributing issue; in addition to positive experiences intertwined with empowering events. These are the main themes

D. Mifsud (✉)
Euro-Mediterranean Centre for Educational Research,
University of Malta, Msida, Malta

that emerged after I carried out an 'analysis of narratives' (Polkinghorne 1995) of the participants' individual case studies.

The 'positioning of the self in relation to the other' (Watson 2012, p. 460) emerges in narratives as 'we narratively construct the other and through this construction we establish claims for our own identities' (ibid. 2012, p. 471). In my approach to narrative analysis, the perspectives of 'both narrator and analyst' (Riessman 2001) come into view as I attempt to switch from the role of researcher and adopt the stance of what Smith and Sparkes (2008, p. 20) label as the 'storyteller', where the analysis is the story or the story is the analysis. I do not consider myself just as a 'story analyst' (ibid. 2008, p. 20), where 'analytical procedures' are employed to examine features of the data. It is from the identification of themes in the individual analyses of narratives that I moved from 'story analyst' to 'storyteller' stance and carried out a 'narrative analysis' (Polkinghorne 1995) that provided the site for the production of 'another narrative' (Watson 2012, p. 460) that unfolded as I crafted another narrative from the individual case study narratives.

Bamberg (2003) conceives of positioning in two distinct ways: the 'being positioned' orientation in which the subject has little determination of agency and the 'positioning oneself' orientation where discursive repertoires are constructed rather than already given. These constitute two very different 'agent-world relationships' (p. 135). Utilizing this theory of positioning analysis, I explore how the women professors position themselves in relation to discourses by which they are positioned. According to Hendry (2007), 'Our narratives ... are the tales through which we constitute our identities. We are our narratives ... Who we are is embedded in our stories' (p. 495). Therefore, narrative has a trifold function in this chapter, serving as both the phenomenon being studied and the methodological approach adopted, in addition to being the mode of data representation. Acknowledging my multiple roles as narrator, observer, interpreter, analyst, playwright, and researcher, I make use of fictionalizing devices (in this case, particular moments from the contributors' narratives) in order to craft a semi-fictionalized narrative dramatization that unfolds during a writing retreat. I refer to the narrative dramatization as being 'semi-fictionalized' in the sense that the actual themes presented emerge from the analysis of the individual career trajectories in the preceding chapters. However, the writing retreat is fictionalized as the physical encounter never actually took place, while the characters were also made up according to the characteristics that emerged from the various narratives as I, Denise, did the interpretation and analysis. In fact, I refer to them as 'Voices' (hereafter referred to numerically as V1, V2, etc.) in order to preserve anonymity, but also as this is how they came across to me and thus inspired me to come up with the idea of a writing retreat as a backdrop for the analysis. This discussion unfolded entirely in my imagination and is hereby being presented to you as readers in order to celebrate these female voices of success and resistance.

This writing retreat is attended by some of the women professors, in addition to Michel Foucault, the French postmodernist/post-structuralist philosopher (dead and buried since 1984), who has been invited by me, Denise, in order to aid me interpret the themes unfolding during the ensuing discussion among the women professors through his theories of discipline, power relations, discourse, subjectification, and governmentality. This enables the incorporation of researcher interpretation and theory without breaking the flow of the narrative.

The Women Professors' Retreat: 'Revealing Our Experiences in Academia'

The idea for this edited book was discussed with my co-editor during my first writing retreat. Likewise, the final stage in the coming together of this manuscript/writing project unfolds during a writing retreat where all the contributors are working on the final revisions of their chapter, following the feedback provided by my colleague and myself as co-editors.

All the women professors are seated around the enormous conference table at 'The Writers' Secluded Spot', a particularly quaint hotel in the middle of a sparsely inhabited island, surrounded by stretches of the Mediterranean shimmering blue sea. They are all seated with a laptop in front of them, either staring pensively at the screen or typing away at the keyboard. Two seats at the far end of the table are vacant, with one open laptop that is on screensaver mode. I was finishing up my final chapter but had to leave the retreat briefly in order to collect Foucault from the ferry terminal at the harbour. When we arrive, all the professors are still working feverishly at their laptops, due to the looming manuscript submission deadline, so I offer Foucault a coffee and we take a stool by the side bar in order for me to be able to brief him about our writing project without disturbing the others until time for the next coffee break arrives.

> **Denise**: I would like to thank you profusely for accepting my invitation to join us on this particular writing retreat. It's such a coincidence that you happened to be giving a keynote speech at the *Philosophy and Feminism Conference* being held at the University of Gender Equity on this idyllic island. I, in particular, am a keen follower of your theories and philosophical thought. At book proposal stage, my co-editor and myself contacted several women professors from higher education institutions worldwide, inviting them to contribute by submitting an abstract. The 'must-haves' for each chapter were being explicit about a chosen theoretical framework; focusing on the book's theme of 'making it'; situating the narrative within a particular cultural context; and most important of all, being innovative and unconventional.
>
> **Foucault**: That sounds interesting ... I cannot wait to read the chapters about their unique career trajectories. I'm particularly struck by the innovation and unconventionality aspect of the edited volume. In my case, each book transforms what I was thinking when I was finishing the previous book. I am an experimenter and not a theorist ... I'm an experimenter in the sense that I write in order to change myself and in order not to think the same thing as before ... When I begin a book, not only do I not know what I'll be thinking at the end, but it's not very clear to me what method I will employ.
>
> **Denise**: That sounds very similar to our approach to this book. These women professors wrote about their career trajectories employing distinct methodologies and theoretical frameworks, with each narrative making a unique contribution. More women professors than those gathered here today had originally volunteered to contribute to our book, but pulled out along the way, for various reasons, both personal

and professional. These women professors were bold enough to write about their own experiences, quite a challenging task, in my opinion.
((Do I mention the fear factor? I detected particular silences within the narratives, as well as self-censoring among these courageous voices. Was it a fear of repercussions, a fear of being silenced by those same institutions that gave them voice via the professoriate? A number of contributors did pull out of this project… I don't want Foucault to hear about this retracting, although I wonder whether he'd attribute this withdrawal to the discursive practices of higher education institutions…))[1]

Foucault: Well, autoethnography can at times be tricky. Every time I have tried to do a piece of theoretical work it has been on the basis of elements of my own experience: always in connection with processes I saw unfolding around me. It was always because I thought I identified cracks, silent tremors, and dysfunctions in things I saw, institutions I was dealing with, or my relations with others, that I set out to do a piece of work, and each time was partly a fragment of autobiography.

Denise: In setting out to do autoethnographic work, these women professors focus on how they made it, while revealing the 'chilly climate' they experienced through stereotyping and discrimination practices in the process. They are not pointing their finger at any particular institution, but at higher education as a perpetrator of gender inequity, treating women as the institutional 'other'.

Foucault: Things have to change. Reforms do not come about in empty space, independently of those who make them … A critique does not consist in saying that things aren't good the way they are. It consists in seeing on what type of assumptions, of familiar notions, of established, unexamined ways of thinking the accepted practices are based.

Denise: Our manuscript can be regarded as a form of critique, therefore! The male-female ratio at undergraduate level is not mirrored at professorship level as our percentages remain so low …

Foucault: Your book will unveil the success stories … Criticism consists in uncovering that thought and trying to change it: showing that things are not as obvious as people believe, making it so that what is taken for granted is no longer taken for granted. To do criticism is to make harder those acts which are now too easy.

---

[1] Exchanges within double brackets in italics are thought bubbles that are not voiced out loud by the character concerned.

Denise: These women's narratives definitely challenge representational space in higher education leadership. Let me introduce you to them very briefly before they have their coffee break. *V1* purports herself as a by-product of her particular social context in the wake of the restoration of democracy. Despite experiencing her career trajectory in a predominantly female faculty, it is thanks to her 'toughness' that she got promoted. *V2* suffered due to the university's attitude towards a mother professor. She however succeeded in weaving the maternal narrative into her academic work, thus showing that maternal/pregnant bodies are not the 'other', but part of the 'norm'. We then have *V3*, who followed a different route to professorship, away from the usual focus on research and academic scholarship. Re-branding herself as the 'blended' professional, she initially felt the need to 'credentialize' her work, questioning its compatibility with normally held views of academic activity, due to her scholarship output in learning and teaching. *V4* resolved to become a professor by her fiftieth birthday at a very young age, when still an undergraduate. This was indeed achieved via an unconventional route through pursuit of her resilient, desirable outcomes. *V5* is the only one who did not manage to make it to professor because of what she defines as a series of 'inept' choices and politically incorrect decisions misaligned with her institutional discursive practices.

Foucault: A very remarkable gathering of academics, indeed ... I suppose they have very diverse experiences, given their unique trajectories within specific cultural contexts.

Denise: Yes, indeed ... We were very lucky to attract such authors and secure their contribution to our manuscript. It's time for a coffee break. Let's join them as they are all keen to discuss their career trajectories—this is the first time we're meeting physically as a group.

[We get off our stools and approach the others who are surrounding the side table that is lined with mouth-watering, calorie-laden cakes. Well, one does need all the energy one can get to finalize such a manuscript ...]

Denise: *[standing in line for a coffee]* You were all so focused on your writing that you didn't even realize I had left the room!

[Foucault blends in very easily with the rest of the Voices. V1 offers him a chocolate muffin that he accepts with pleasure.]

Foucault: *Merci beaucoup pour votre accueil chaleureux.* I've heard very positive things about you all. This is the first time I'm in the sole company of women professors who have done excellent work in scholarship, research, and teaching. I can't wait to read your narratives!

Denise: *[addressing the Voices]* Well, I don't think we can allow you to wait that long—the publication process will take another three to four months, at least. What do you say about having a longer coffee break, in order for you all to tell Foucault about your routes to professorship? *[All the others nod in agreement]*

Denise: Perhaps we can then have a longer writing session before dinner.

V1: We female professors are extremely adaptable, we had to develop this trait in order to qualify for professorship status. We feel that there is an unequal flow of power in terms of gender equity. Being women, we have to go that extra mile to obtain what is rightfully ours…

V4: We have to fight for our rights. If we had been men applying for professorial promotion, it would have been a completely different story…

Foucault: I fully understand your point, though I can't understand why higher education institutions allow gender inequity to unfold, in the first instance. The recent alliance between poststructuralism and contemporary feminism has been marked by an especially lively engagement with my work.

Denise: *[addressing Foucault]* Well, you do make few references to women or to the issue of gender in your writings. However, I'm surprised by the fact that your treatment of the relations between power, the body and sexuality has stimulated extensive feminist interest.

Foucault: *Oui, oui, c'est vrai*. My analysis of the relations between power, the body and sexuality overlap with the feminist project of exploring the micropolitics of personal life and exposing the mechanics of patriarchal power at the most intimate levels of women's experience. Besides, my theories have provided feminist thinkers with conceptual tools for the analysis of the social construction of gender and sexuality, as well as to analyse contemporary forms of social control over women's bodies and minds.

V3: It is not always easy for us to try to make sense of our career trajectories, let alone for the potential readers of our stories. Reflecting upon the various trials and tribulations, followed by actually writing them down and now even discussing them serves as a means of celebrating our successes and problematizing the obstacles for other female academics.

Foucault: Problematization constitutes the development of a given into a question, this transformation of a group of obstacles and difficulties into problems to which the diverse solutions will attempt to produce a response. As female professors, you can demonstrate that things are not as obvious as people believe, making it so that what is taken for granted is no longer taken for granted.

V1: I do speak out openly about the need for gender equality as I lived through the Portuguese revolution that restored democracy, urged 'speaking out' and 'normalized' pluralism. Resistance to women's subordination unfolded through work and education. Notwithstanding, women's rights were granted by law but questioned every day by practice.

Denise: V1, you are definitely a product of your social context. Your route to professorship commenced prior to being employed in higher education. V4, the same can be said for your childhood experiences, perhaps.

V4: Of course. It was a particular interview in rural north-west England that made me decide that any research I carried out had to make a direct difference in the participants' lives and aid them to reach out.

Foucault: Your experiences are an example of what I term '*savoir*', that is constructed knowledge about oneself, showing an interest in how it is possible for subjects to understand themselves in relation to others, and how they consequently use that knowledge constructed within relations and practices to transform themselves. Knowledge is not made for understanding; it is made for cutting. *Cutting*, in the form of resistance, criticism, struggle ... performs this work through the appearance of particular, local, regional knowledge, a differential knowledge incapable of unanimity and which owes its force only to the harshness with which it is opposed by everything around it.

Denise: Well laid-out, indeed. This 'cutting', therefore, works to produce individuals as knowing subjects in particular ways, and in response to particular power/knowledge practices.

V5: If only I had managed to comprehend the mutually generative relationship between knowledge and power! I would have managed to obtain the professorial title ... My career trajectory can be regarded as a perfect example of mis-reading, mis-applying and mis-identifying university practices, thus resulting in clashing mis-confrontations.

Denise: *((But why is V5 attributing this to her own actions and perceptions? I think that these were in turn nurtured by the gendered institutional cultures of the university that made her both object and subject, that treated female academics as institutional 'others'))*

12 Conclusion: The Process of *Becoming* a Woman Professor ...

V5: In retrospect, I can rationalize my 'failure' in terms of a series of inept choices. For example, I disregarded political manoeuvring, made the 'inappropriate' choice of PhD thesis topic, opposed having a mentor, was offended by anonymous refereeing, and never said 'no'. The university only served as a restraining force for my career progression.

Foucault: *Ma chere* V5, I'm so sorry to hear that. I'm afraid that you failed to grasp the discourses linked to your higher education institution, instead, attempting to subvert their normalizing and regularizing discursive practices. Discourses are practices that systematically form the objects of which they speak. In fact, it is in discourse that power and knowledge are joined together.

V5: *[addressing me]* Denise, do pay attention to the discourses your particular university constitutes and is constituted by. I have learnt at my own expense that discourses authorize what can and cannot be said; they produce relations of power and communities of consent and dissent, with discursive boundaries constantly being redrawn around what constitutes the desirable and the undesirable ...

Denise: Thank you for sharing this with us. V3, I also believe that your career was affected by the shifting focus of the higher education institutions where you were previously employed ...

V3: That happened after the birth of my first child, when I got a job at a university college, due to my not being ready for a job in the traditional, research-intensive sector. After my focus on 'becoming a good teacher' and putting research on the back burner, the college secured its university title, subsequently pressuring me to obtain disciplinary research funding. However, along my career, I turned this teaching focus to my advantage, by concentrating on scholarship for learning and teaching.

Foucault: That's an interesting turn, as you did turn yourself into a subject, by being active in the process of self-formation. For the subject is constituted through practices of subjection, or ... through practices of liberation, of freedom ...

V3: I am also proud of being the first researcher in the UK, supported by a particular research council, to be eligible for maternity leave.

V2: Well, listen to this. After my first pregnancy, a senior male colleague had the audacity to question my absence during that period, in order to express his jealousy of the maternity leave policy, that he considered as 'paid' vacation!

V1: I had initially thought of warding off motherhood after PhD completion, but then resolved that having a baby couldn't be postponed. I also naively offered to compensate for my three months of maternity leave by doubling my course load on my return ...

Denise: Well, your experiences confirm the initial doubts I started having over my decision not to have any children in order to follow an intensive academic career ... But you did learn from your first pregnancy and behaved differently the second and third time round ...

V1: Of course we did! But men are still regarded as the measure of all things, with female academics made to feel inadequate and disempowered when they become pregnant!

Denise: It seems that at times *((rather than saying 'at all times'))*, the values of the academy clash with personal familial responsibilities. Why do women in academia have to sacrifice personal life for a professorial life?

Foucault: The presence of a gendered organizational culture in higher education calls for my notion of 'docility'. A body is docile that may be subjected, used, transformed and improved, in order to illustrate how discipline produces subjected and practised bodies, 'docile' bodies.

Denise: Getting pregnant and being a mother professor may still be regarded as deviant behaviour in certain universities. But there are women among us who have also suffered discrimination through a series of undermining strategies from senior male colleagues. There are many women professors out there who are not mothers ...

V4: I can tell you about a colleague of mine whose confidence was shattered almost beyond repair ... Both her work and her field were downgraded, with complaints to HR and senior management falling on deaf ears. She thus turned to writing as a way of retreating from this abusive context in order to survive.

Foucault: The way you women professors deal with such a situation calls for my theory of power relations, *mes relations de pouvoir* ... You managed to subvert the flow of power in relation to the perpetrators of discriminatory practices! Power is exercised from innumerable points, in the interplay of nonegalitarian and mobile relations ... relations of power are not in superstructural positions, with merely a role of prohibition or accompaniment; they have a directly productive role, wherever they come into play.

12 Conclusion: The Process of *Becoming* a Woman Professor ...

V4: I can confirm this. It is only thanks to writing for publication workshops, and subsequent writing retreats, that I managed to master writing for peer review. This was another milestone towards achieving my professorship, as well as an appointment in a permanent research position.

V3: I have managed to obtain the much-coveted academic title and role, despite my unconventional route to the professoriate. My career is a direct embodiment of what can be termed as 'academic fluidity'.

Foucault: It seems to me that power must be understood as the multiplicity of force relations immanent in the sphere in which they operate and which constitute their own organization. Moreover, power's condition of possibility must not be sought in the primary existence of a central point—it is the moving substrate of force relations which, by virtue of their inequality, constantly engender states of power, but the latter are always local and unstable.

V4: Well, I've always exercised decisiveness and ambition, while sticking to my research narrative, networking outside my institution, and joining informal, all-female support groups.

Foucault: I have been engaged in an attempt to move the conception of power away from the 'repressive hypothesis' model towards a framework extolling its productive nature. Your narratives of 'making it' are testimony to this. The term 'power' designates relationships between partners. While the human subject is placed in relations of production and of signification, he is equally placed in power relations that are very complex. Relations of power are not something bad in themselves. I don't believe there can be a society without relations of power.

Denise: You also state that where there is power, there is resistance. In this case, female professors exercised resistance to 'expected' roles associated with gender.

V5: Being a good academic citizen does not mean picking up all the work within your own department that no-one else wants to do. This may be expected of women scholars, as is assumed that childless female academics have plenty of 'extra' time! Saying 'yes' to everything does not expedite the promotion process.

V3: At a certain point in my career, I felt pulled in so many directions in terms of expectations to achieve promotion. I decided it was time to re-write myself and look at other jobs in my bid to combat institutional archetypes. I now consider myself as a 'blended' professional.

V2: We exercised our resistance in diverse ways. My first pregnancy was a learning curve for me, an eye-opener in terms of setting work/home boundaries. I developed focusing strategies on publishing and grant applications in order to utilize my maternity leave for its original purpose of nurturing my new-born babies. I demonstrated that maternity leave is not paid vacation, definitely not. I strongly resisted academia ousting my maternal narrative, especially by the time the third baby was on my way.

Foucault: Where there is power, there is resistance, and yet, or rather consequently, this resistance is never in a position of exteriority in relation to power. The existence of power relationships depends on a multiplicity of points of resistance: these play the role of adversary, target, support, or handle in power relations. These points of resistance are present everywhere in the power network. There is a plurality of resistances, each of them a special case: resistances that are possible, necessary, improbable; others that are spontaneous, savage, solitary, concerted, rampant, or violent; still others that are quick to compromise, interested, or sacrificial.

V1: Resistance is only one of the multiple strategies—being tough is equally effective. It was my reputation for being tough that got my colleagues to vote for me on the University Council, where the majority of the elected were men. Even humour can be used as a form of feminist resistance.

V3: Modern university makes a binary divide between academic and non-academic, aka professional, roles. Circumstance has pushed me into the latter group, so I tried to step into the academic turf through scholarship in teaching and learning. After being rejected as Centre leader at the same Centre I used to administer, I applied for the same job at a university that recognized my work as a route to the professoriate. This university recognizes five routes to the professoriate!

Foucault: This has been a very enlightening discussion, indeed. I have noticed an underlying preoccupation with the 'art of government', through your subtle inquiries about how to govern oneself, how to be governed, how to govern others, by whom the people will accept being governed, how to become the best possible governor. I understand 'government' as 'the conduct of conduct', encompassing forms of activity to affect the conduct of others, as well as the relation between self and self.

12 Conclusion: The Process of *Becoming* a Woman Professor ...

Denise: I am really pleased by the way this discussion has unfolded as it has given me an insight into how to write the concluding chapter of our manuscript.
Foucault: What I've written is never prescriptive either for me or for others—at most it's instrumental and tentative.
Denise: *[addressing the women professors at the table]* Your unique career trajectories are awe-inspiring ... they have strengthened my resolve to go against all odds to re-enter academia and aspire to be a professor. I was struck by your specific struggles against forms of subjection by higher education institutions to combat normalizing identity categories, as well as your use of counter-domination to alter power relationships, thus expanding possibilities for action.
[Denise looks at her watch, in the hope of conveying the message that it's time for everyone to get back to business...]
You have given me the required impetus to carry on writing and publishing ... In a way, I am already writing myself into an academic career from the margins.
V3: Always remember my experiences of academic fluidity that still got me the professoriate.
V2: Denise, live by my mantra: *Take up space. Raise your voice. Your work matters.*
V1: I know that you are tough, and you also know how to be humorous when the need arises. Mistrust and confront power while advocating against gender maldistribution and misrecognition.
V5: Denise, try not to misread, mis-identify or mis-apply the factors that will gain you the professor title. Be politically smart and savvy.
V4: Develop resilience. You are the one to decide on the outcomes that are desirable and undesirable for you. I was mislabelled as a 'Jack-of-all-trades-but-master-of-none' but used this to my advantage in my nomination.
Denise: Working with you all on this writing project has been a very enriching experience for me on various levels: personal, professional, and academic. I know that I will always have the full support of this exclusive women professors' network. Our publication will make a difference and encourage female academics to work towards getting a Chair. *[looking at her watch]* Now it's time to get back to our chapters as we still have plenty of work to do and I assured Eleanor that our manuscript will be submitted by the originally proposed deadline ....

References

Bamberg, M. (2003). Positioning with Davie Hogan: Stories, tellings, and identities. In C. Daiute (Ed.), *Narrative analysis: Studying the development of individuals in society* (pp. 135–157). London: Sage.

Hendry, P. M. (2007). The future of narrative. *Qualitative Inquiry, 13*(4), 487–498.

Mifsud, D. (2016). Data representation with a dramatic difference: Negotiating the methodological tensions and contradictions in qualitative inquiry. Confessions of a budding playwright…. *International Journal of Qualitative Studies in Education, 29*(7), 863–881.

Mifsud, D. (2017). *Foucault and school leadership research: Bridging theory and method.* London: Bloomsbury Academic.

Polkinghorne, D. E. (1995). Narrative configuration in qualitative analysis. In J. A. Hatch (Ed.), *Life history and narrative* (pp. 5–23). London: Falmer Press.

Riessman, C. K. (2001). Analysis of personal narratives. In J. F. Gubrium & J. A. Holstein (Eds.), *Handbook of interviewing* (pp. 695–707). London, UK: Sage.

Smith, B., & Sparkes, A. C. (2008). Contrasting perspectives on narrating selves and identities: An invitation to dialogue. *Qualitative Research, 8*(1), 5–35.

Watson, C. (2012). Analysing narratives: The narrative construction of identity. In S. Delamont (Ed.), *Handbook of qualitative research in education* (pp. 460–473). Cheltenham, UK: Edward Elgar.

Index

A

Academia 2–5, 7, 8, 10, 11, 13–15, 17–19, 34, 36, 37, 43, 44, 66–68, 76–79, 81, 83–87, 94, 143, 147, 161, 172, 177, 201, 202, 204, 205, 207, 212, 214, 215, 218, 230, 232, 233
Academic capital 190
Academic community 64, 125–127, 201, 208
Academic development 15, 114, 117, 120–123, 125, 126, 128, 208
Academic fluidity 18, 126–129, 231, 233
Academic hierarchy 3
Academic identity 12, 125–127
Academic mothers 7, 75, 77, 85
Academic writing 86, 92, 95, 97, 105–107, 121
Affirmative action 160

Agency 7, 18, 76, 97, 98, 109, 110, 121, 178, 180, 181, 183, 190, 222
Anxiety 52, 59, 91, 99, 103, 106
Applications 11, 14, 15, 58, 77, 90, 93, 116, 117, 125, 196, 208–214, 232
Applied practice 207, 211–214
Archetype 119, 120, 231
Authenticity 169
Autoethnography 16, 66, 225

B

Barriers 4, 5, 7, 8, 10, 17, 90, 94, 160
Blended professional 119, 120, 122, 125
Break down 98
Burnout 84

C

Career 2–8, 11, 14–19, 36–41, 44, 50, 54, 55, 60, 61, 63–67, 69, 79, 81, 86, 87, 89–92, 94, 95, 97–101, 104, 106–110, 113, 114, 116, 118, 122, 126–129, 134, 138, 142–144, 147, 156, 160, 161, 164, 171, 173, 177, 178, 183, 184, 190, 193, 196–198, 202, 204–210, 212–215, 217, 220, 229–231, 233

Career pathways 164, 204, 205

Career progression 5–7, 10, 14, 18, 19, 60, 94, 97, 98, 102, 103, 107, 109, 110, 215, 229

Career trajectories 14, 223, 224, 226, 227, 233

Challenges 8, 13, 19, 30, 40, 54, 58, 61, 76, 91, 95, 100, 102, 119, 121, 143, 145–149, 159, 164, 166, 171, 177, 185, 190, 195, 201, 202, 205, 214, 215, 226

Change 1, 2, 4, 12, 18, 30, 33, 41, 51, 57, 58, 64, 66, 78, 86, 91, 94, 102, 103, 105, 108, 109, 114–117, 119, 120, 123–129, 135, 136, 145, 149, 172, 181, 214, 219, 224, 225

Changing landscape 19

Chilly climate 4, 8, 225

Collegial 37, 63, 91, 95, 157

Combination 6, 15, 42, 182

Community 30, 37, 38, 61, 80, 121, 122, 125, 134–137, 144, 145, 149, 172, 173, 193, 198, 219

Confidence 4, 57, 62, 90, 94, 95, 100, 103, 106, 116–118, 146, 160, 206, 207, 209, 212, 213, 230

Culture 4, 5, 7, 9, 11–13, 15, 16, 30, 40, 68, 77, 86, 94, 105, 108, 125, 162, 168, 170, 194, 205, 206, 209, 215, 228, 230

D

Data representation 19, 222

Democracy 28, 30, 32, 33, 38, 226, 228

Discipline(s) 2, 6, 18, 40, 41, 59, 100, 102, 114, 116, 118, 120–122, 125–129, 138, 139, 143, 178, 183–187, 194, 197, 198, 221, 223, 230

Discourse 7, 12, 19, 33, 34, 40, 178, 180, 183, 186, 188, 189, 191, 197, 198, 222, 223, 229

Discrimination 11, 12, 29, 32–35, 37, 44, 90–92, 94, 97, 103, 105, 108, 110, 158, 164, 185, 186, 221, 225, 230

Disempowerment 40

Diverse 2, 9, 13–15, 19, 42, 44, 115, 118, 136, 142, 157, 181, 218, 219, 226, 228, 232

Domestication of the female academic 9

Domestic violence 34

Dominated 18, 19, 160, 171, 174, 205, 209

E

Early career researcher 66, 116

Education 29, 30, 32, 36, 38, 107, 125, 157, 162, 163, 166, 185–188, 192, 195, 218, 228
Embodiment 16, 157, 231
Empowered mothering 76
Empowerment 13, 146
Evidence 9, 56, 57, 78, 91, 106, 126, 140, 145, 146, 149, 150, 180, 184, 186, 211, 212, 219
Excellence 1, 14, 44, 124, 143, 184, 207, 209
Exclusion 8, 10, 33, 35, 68, 158, 183
Expectations 2, 5, 7, 12, 14, 61, 67, 119, 120, 123, 128, 159, 203, 231
Externalization 182

F
Fear 8, 32, 78, 91, 100, 137, 148, 150, 205, 211, 225
Female 2, 6, 7, 10, 12, 13, 15–17, 19, 29, 33, 37, 39, 42, 43, 49, 51, 52, 58, 60, 142, 147, 156, 157, 159–162, 164, 166, 168, 172, 174, 202–206, 209, 210, 213, 214, 223, 226–228, 231
Female academics 1, 3, 4, 9, 12, 14, 16, 19, 61, 161, 171, 172, 174, 227, 228, 230, 231, 233
Female bodies in academia 167
Feminist resistance 34, 232
Feminist theory 78
Fictionalizing devices 222
Flows of power 178, 181, 183, 197
Foreign faculty 157
Foucault, Michel 168, 178–181, 196, 223–233
Freedom of speech 32

G
Gender 3–7, 9–13, 17, 19, 29, 30, 34, 36–38, 40, 43, 56, 58, 67, 90, 91, 94, 105, 127, 158–160, 162–164, 170, 221, 225, 227, 228, 231, 233
Gender bias 11, 90, 157
Gendered culture 12, 41
Gender gap 2–4, 158
Gender imbalance 17
Gender justice 44
Gender norms 174
Glass ceiling index (GCI) 36
Global narrative 14
Goals 11, 18, 55, 64, 97, 100, 105, 106, 116, 134, 138, 145, 163, 183, 187, 190, 194, 195
Governmentality 223
Group support 99

H
Harassment 90, 93, 166
Heads of educational development group (HEDG) 123
Hegemonic masculinity 2, 9
Hierarchy 2, 150, 158, 166, 219
Higher education 1–5, 8, 9, 13, 14, 17, 19, 29, 36, 40, 113–118, 120, 123, 124, 126, 145, 157, 158, 185, 191, 195, 204, 212, 224, 225, 227–230, 233
Higher education leadership 8–11, 226
Higher education statistics agency (HESA) 89
Human agency 18, 136, 180
Humour 8, 33, 34, 41, 232

I

Inaugural lecture 202, 203, 214
Inequality 1, 5, 17, 19, 30, 136, 159, 231
Inter-disciplinarity/Interdisciplinary 34, 102, 141, 143, 147
Internalization 168, 182
Internationalization 157, 162, 163
Invisible 7, 150

J

Japan 3, 14, 15, 155–161, 163, 167, 170, 171
Japanese 3, 15, 18, 155, 157, 159–162, 164–168, 170, 172–174, 182

K

Knowledge 5, 8–11, 14, 19, 44, 56, 68, 99, 107–109, 115, 118–122, 125, 127, 136, 139, 143, 177–179, 181–184, 187, 188, 193–195, 197, 202–204, 206, 209, 213, 228, 229

L

Leader 9–13, 19, 100, 114, 122–124, 127, 156, 160, 167, 168, 171, 174, 177, 195, 232
Leaderist turn 10
Leadership 3–6, 9–12, 14, 18, 39, 103, 104, 114, 119, 122, 124, 126, 128, 136, 156, 159, 162, 165–168, 171, 174, 194, 209, 212

Leaky pipeline 6
Life stories 178
Lived experience 16, 145

M

Male 2, 3, 6–10, 12, 13, 18, 19, 29, 54–56, 60, 61, 68, 75, 77, 84, 91, 140, 156, 160, 162–164, 167, 168, 170, 171, 174, 202, 203, 205, 206, 209, 213, 217, 229, 230
Masculine norm 66, 168
Masks of motherhood 76, 77
Maternity leave 17, 28, 39, 52, 53, 64, 75, 76, 80–82, 85, 115, 229, 230, 232
Matrifocal narratives 77, 79
Mental health 38, 148, 150
Mentoring/Mentorship 61, 62, 86, 156, 193
Micro-physics 180, 197
Mothering 39, 76, 221

N

Narrative methodology 221
Navigate burnout 79
Neoliberal higher education 1
Networking 14, 64, 94, 99, 100, 171, 174, 231
Non-linear 157
Nurturing 6, 60, 171, 232

O

Oppression 4, 32–35, 39–41
Organizational learning 178, 179, 181, 187

Outcomes 18, 108, 118, 120, 123–125, 134, 136, 138, 143–147, 151, 160, 180, 185, 187, 210, 213, 226, 233
Outside 10, 17, 32, 35, 43, 44, 62, 65, 80, 100, 118, 122, 134, 140, 164, 167, 173, 174, 197, 198, 209, 212, 231

P

Parenting in academia 84
Partnership 127, 128, 146–149
Patriarchal motherhood 76
Persona 181
Planning maternity leave 84
Policy 5, 30, 75, 137, 138, 144–146, 149, 150, 159, 229
Politics 28, 31, 38, 40, 185, 193, 195
Portfolios 119, 122
Positioning 6, 8, 11, 17, 100, 157, 164, 181, 197, 221, 222
Power 2, 4, 5, 9, 12, 18, 19, 30, 40, 43, 44, 81, 97, 105, 134, 156, 159, 160, 162, 167, 177–181, 183, 188–190, 196–198, 219, 221, 223, 227–233
Practice 1, 6, 8, 18, 30, 33, 34, 44, 49, 65, 86, 90, 94, 99, 102, 109, 117, 118, 120–122, 124–127, 136, 159, 163, 167, 170–174, 178–183, 185, 191–193, 197, 207, 208, 217, 225, 226, 228–230
Pregnancy in academia 39, 66, 77, 78
Prestige 2, 50, 59, 127, 190

Process 6, 8, 12, 14–16, 19, 38–40, 42, 44, 58, 60, 62, 64, 68, 78, 81, 96, 98, 99, 104, 114, 118, 124, 126, 136, 144, 156, 157, 165–171, 174, 180–182, 186, 196, 208, 211–214, 225, 227, 229, 231
Professional services 114, 119, 120, 127, 129
Professor 3, 6, 7, 11–19, 36, 37, 39, 40, 49, 54, 55, 58, 59, 68, 69, 76, 79, 81, 84, 85, 87, 89, 90, 92, 98, 105, 107–110, 113, 114, 125, 127, 134, 139–141, 143, 144, 147, 149, 151, 155–157, 160–162, 164–174, 183, 184, 186, 192, 193, 201, 204, 206, 210, 213, 219, 221–228, 230, 231, 233
Progression 5, 6, 10, 14, 37, 97, 107, 109
Publications 13, 15, 57–59, 66, 79, 85, 87, 89, 91, 95, 97, 99, 103, 105, 121, 124, 147, 155, 156, 165, 189, 193, 207, 212, 227, 231, 233

R

Regime of truth 180
Relations of power 229–231
Representation 3, 5, 8, 9, 11, 44, 158, 198
Resilience 18, 97, 133–138, 144, 146, 149, 151, 233
Retention 179, 183
Revolution 27, 28, 30–32, 34, 35, 37, 115, 195, 228

Rhetoric 34, 44, 145, 146, 160, 187, 202
Rural 80, 142, 144–146, 148–150, 228

S
Scholarly writing 121
Scholarship research 116, 122
Selection 6, 179, 183
Self 5, 11, 127–129, 181, 208, 209, 222, 232
Self-care 107
Self-efficacy 97, 105, 106
Self-reflection 157, 211
Self-worth 90, 95, 102, 103, 213
Sexism 13, 41, 43, 54, 90, 218
Sexist 8, 44
Sexist gaffs 159
She figures 3, 36
Socialization 182, 185, 187, 188
Social justice 12, 146, 150, 167, 170
Social rights 28
Social system 180, 194
Social writing 18, 96–98, 108, 109, 171
Social writing theory 97
Southern Europe 32
Staff and Educational Development Association 122
Stress 84, 87, 106, 140
Structuration 178–181, 197
Structured writing retreat (SWR) 95–97, 102, 105–107, 171
Structures 4, 5, 8, 10, 18, 37, 41, 68, 102, 123, 124, 144, 161, 169, 178, 180, 181, 183, 190, 195, 197, 198, 209

Subjectification 223
Supervision 14, 93, 116, 206
Support networks 6
Systems thinking 139

T
Teaching scholarship 118
Thriving 209
Time 6, 11, 13, 17, 31–35, 37–40, 43, 44, 50, 51, 55, 60–62, 64, 66, 68, 69, 79–85, 90–94, 98–105, 107, 109, 113–115, 117, 120, 121, 126, 127, 135, 136, 139–141, 144, 145, 147, 148, 151, 159–161, 164, 166–168, 171, 173, 174, 179, 181, 185–187, 191, 192, 196, 197, 201–203, 205–208, 211, 212, 214, 218, 224–226, 230–233
Toughness 33, 41, 42, 221, 226
Training for Retreat Facilitators 108
Transdisciplinary 147
Transgenerational transmission 32

U
Undermining 91–94, 97, 108, 148, 189, 230

V
Variation 109, 114, 123, 161, 179
Virtual writing retreats and groups 97
Voting rights 29

W

Well-being 11, 87
Window of opportunity 164
Work 2, 4–8, 10–12, 18, 19, 28,
  30, 33, 37, 40, 41, 43, 50–58,
  60, 61, 63–67, 75, 76, 78,
  80–87, 90–95, 99, 100, 102,
  103, 108, 113, 114, 116, 117,
  119–129, 140–147, 150, 156,
  157, 161, 162, 164–166, 169,
  171–173, 185–190, 192, 193,
  202, 205, 207, 208, 212, 214,
  218, 219, 225–228, 230–233
Work-life balance 57, 103, 173
Writer's group 97, 99, 100, 107
Writing retreat 95, 101–103, 105,
  106, 108, 109, 144, 171,
  222–224, 231

Printed in the United States
By Bookmasters